IN THE MIRROR, A MONSTER

MARTEN WEBER

Published in the UK and Europe by
Dog Horn Publishing
45 Monk Ings
Birstall
Batley
WF17 9HU
United Kingdom
doghornpublishing.com

Edited by
Adam Lowe
with
Leanne Haynes

Cover credits:
STILLOUT PHOTOGRAPHY
stillout.net

Cover concept by Gary Benner of Peep Hole Photographers
www.facebook.com/garylbenner

Photography by David Lari
facebook.com/davidlari
and Brandon Schauf
facebook.com/anopenwindow

Staging by Gil Croy
gilcroy.com

Technical direction and website work by Nicole Olver
NeaMatt.com.

STILLOUT is an LGBT Photography club in Charlotte, North Carolina, welcoming all LGBT and affirming members of the Charlotte metro community. STILLOUT is a programme of the LGBT Community Centre of Charlotte, enriching lives and the LGBT community through photographic arts.

UK & European Distribution: Central Books
99 Wallis Road, London, E9 5LN, United Kingdom
orders@centralbooks.com
Phone:+44 (0) 845 458 9911
Fax: +44 (0) 845 458 9912

'There is something higher and nobler
and purer than love—there is friendship.'
—W. Somerset Maugham

PART I

Will you lollop with me, Mr Dedalus—will you dawdle? Will you take me on your lap and show me the world, drilling your cock into me with the grace of a wrecking ball? No—you never did. Always the gentleman. I always wished you were more ... aggressive. But not in *your* circles, not with *your* tailor.

What whisky bottle? I am not drinking—I am not! I don't even like whisky—can't stomach it; not any more. This is an aberration, I swear, this is just to celebrate that all is over. We are new people now, all of us, and we have gone through fire!

Ah, Mr Dedalus, you can't even hear me, can you, you coward! Six feet under and already decaying, your mouth smiles no longer. Mark my words, Mr Dedalus, he said, Scotland is in the hands of the queers now! Queers in wheelchairs, picketing your funeral! Your black coffin, your pallbearers in satin! What chests! What thighs! Queers in all the highest places: her finance, her press, up and down Princes Street. And they are the signs of a nation's decay. Wherever they gather they eat up the nation's vital strength; they suck cock in dark alleys and die like flies. Only I have survived, but I will not rise again, if I say so mesen!

—What? said the woman passing the house in this ungodly hour. Daft bugger sitting by the window, she's thinking. In his chair, fat old sod, naught else to do but spy!

This is the transparent society. If I don't spies on you from my window, I spies on you on Facebook. I can see where you are going with that truncheon.

—Hi there!

But I need only close the window to be alone again. Privacy enshrouds me. I am the temple inviolate. I am the body sacred. I am a fat git who can't walk. Sorry, dear, about the yelling—it is only for my benefit: I want to know that I am still alive sometimes. It's daft. But it's me—as I said, naught else to do but to celebrate now, that all is over and different. I am a changed woman!

Shite and onions! Was it Jews he meant—and why now Scotland, over the rainbow at three in the morning out the window: you can see the world walk by! I owe three quid to

4

the man at the corner shop. Must remember! Look, there is Mrs Erskine with her walker. Now where's the dog, Mr Dedalus, you seen the fucking dog? There he is, shitting by the church gate. It's called a lichgate, which I always thought was a lynch-gate, on account of the lynchings the Puritans were prone to.

Lynch a Jew and a queer by the lynch-gate, walk the aisle to the altar with your axe held high!

She's going to pick up the poo—there she goes, with her plastic bag. Javier collected funny sayings about dog shit from all over Europe, like the pooper-scooper, and something German with a sack and gack—the gack being the poop. Then we found a website with motorcycle slogans for Asia, nonsense English they stick on scooters: 'The Life is for your Scenery!' and 'Ride Fever to Insertion!'

May the tea be with you, and your life be excremental. How often can you really fetch yourself off in a day, when does your cock start hurtin'? Daft buggers as can't feel their dong any more. No surgery in the world can restore it. Tha'll never shag again, lad! But then, I never were much of a top, to be sure, Mrs Erskine. Always a bit of a queen, even afore. Always on me back!

Lunch with a Jew and wank a queer by the lunch-gate, walk the ice to the fridge with your eyes held high! Taratatamtam, taratatatam. I should have been a fucking opera singer! And if not Lucia di Lammermoor with her mad aria (that would have been for me, truly), then at least something trashy like Lloyd-Webber's, something working-class melodic. I would have made a fab Phantom I would, honest. No need for a mask even! I'd row my boat in the sewer and—I sang on the boat, you remember, on the sun deck, do you remember, and Rafael made you sing in the cabin, Mr Dedalus. Were I jealous then? You bet I were! But I didn't have the guts! Those as haven't got the jimp ... And you were such a gentleman! Oh yes, Mr Dedalus, from New York, he were highly spoke of, so highly, like a fucking Trump he were with his money—and his boys!

I am that, I am a philosopher-fornicator, a philosofornicator, that is my job, said Mr Dedalus, and so say I, arse bandit on wheels! That woman were in front of me at Tesco's and hit her child, naughty boy, grabbing again for the tenth time that bar, or something. He couldn't keep his hands to himself, so the mother smacks him—get yir face panned—something Scottish she shouts, can't get the lingo right, and suddenly there is this German matron yelling,

—Madam, don't hit ze child, stop at vonce!

So the slag says,

—Wha'?

And the German tourist goes,

—In Germany ve don't hit our childrens!

Whereuponst the woman bleated,

—Ya don't, do ya not? Well ayn Scotland we donna birn our Jews!

Lunch with a Jew and dunk a queer by the launchgate—funny, launchgates do exists, don't they, in Cape *Carnival*—walk the fries in the itsy part, Samuel Becks was a beer to me! I'd like to propose a toast to Cape Carnivorous and the moon-faring, moon-fairy nation of America. A nation full of moon-fairies, captain Dedalus! Tha'll get to heaven yet, if tha keepst sucking with a vengeance.

And Mary asks with a vengeance—a sheer *vennergence*, a vennerennergance is it? How much darling beer can you drink if you are already dead-drunk on whisky, and it is time to go to bed? Sod it!

Talking to meself again, am I, and I am not even dispressed, disserpressed—not this time. Only one can't. One needs to drown another day in sorrow, another day of *miscapitulations* and *verbosiations*!

Got rid of them Slovak lads, adorable as they were, and then one revelleration—rebelleration—after another. One can't just leave one's bloody post by the window! One's got one's responsereribilities. I think we have clearly establisherated the factum that I is pigglety pogglety pagglety blind puggled like a cream-pie distillery. But it's not like afore—this is different, I am celebrationing! My head's full of porn and my cock's explomodating—expumidating—exfoliating? No, it's not that—it's in one piece, but no thanks to him up there sleeping peacefully.

God bless me husband. He never clocked any of it, until it were well too late.

6

In them days, on the big boat, under the hot sun, you read to me, remember? You read to me on the sun deck. And I don't remember a thing. No'a ting! Nowt, nada.

There stultepifies the world; it congeals, maniacally, around incompetence and the allure of the simplistically stupidoic! Not that I know anything about clitorature—I am but a butcher's son from Leeds, with my feet in a mangle and my hand on the moose—the computer moose! Moose in the hoose! Da Scottish hoose! *Oh! the auld hoose, the auld hoose, what tho' the rooms were wee, oh, kind hearts were dwelling there,* and massive cocks!

Without computers? Without the Internet? Well—I suppose I'd be a worthless cripple, watching television; be a zombie with a remote in my hand, like the very rest of them, Mr Dedalus. Just like the soddin' rest of them.

Why do you only come at night—in the deadly, cold, night; the wet, secretive night when I hide from Tim and the boys and ... myself? Why is I only eloquented in the wee hours? Why am I such a dunce by daylight?

I am an eloquentious vampire: only the night and plenty of whisky brings out the poet in me. Is it because of how I look?—I is well a monster. Is it 'cos I have so many—what is the word?—internalized issues? Is it because I have haemorrhoids?

What am I saying! I am the philosofornicator in this household. Tim doesn't know soddin' shit about philosofornication and neither do you, you sag-hag-fag-tag—Craig! I remember Craig, he should have been round to fix the awning. He's—oh, I'll call him first thing in the morning, make a note. Call Craig in the morning.

The fucking bastard's never here when you need him. Craig fix my awning! Keep me from yawning! I would like to go spawning, put the river, I would, into the loch.

Did you know 'loch' means hole in German? So Scotland is full of holes. Gaping holes!

That Syrian guy said to me on the ship,

—Do you ever feel your arse is turning into a gigantic gaping hole? An enormous pulsating anal vulva?

—Not presently.

—No, I mean when you get fucked!

—Me, darling, I don't feel ANYTHING when I get fucked!

Anything at all!

I were grateful for the thought though, that he still thought I were gettin' some at my age. God bless.

Goodbye now. Give my regards to Stephen Fry! I am sure he'll do a documentary about Scottish gaping holes one of these days. And cocks. Cocks with labels on them: hot and cold—there were two, Mr Dedalus, weren't there, in the book you read to me, one of them, on our cruise, two cocks: mine and Rafael's. It were very queer that, very queer. And it were a lifetime ago.

Getting up, putting the bottle back, not being bothered by stench and not washing up now, on my way to bed. Just one last glass. One itsy-bitsy last drink for the night—naught else to do. The house is asleep. I can't go up now with the lift; I'd wake everybody. Better stay here and have another. We've shipped them back off to Slovakia, and now the *hoose* it at peace again with itself.

Watching porn, I often get bored and make lists of things you catch in the background. The type of electric socket, the shape of a stove. Shagging on a samovar—had to look that one up, from *Russian Soldiers 3*. Eastern European porn is fantastic for that— they've got sets like me nan's kitchen.

I found an antique bench in one that would fetch a packet here, and they just fucked on it, completely ignorant of its worth at a good English boot sale! One Hungarian porn film has by accident a world-famous soccer player sitting at a table, in a café, while two boys cruise each other in the foreground.

One has Thonet furniture in a posh living room, and a view over Budapest so unique—balustrades and all, and wrought iron stanchions—you can identify the exact flat of a former government minister's ex-wife (pornstar herself, I read it on a blog, it must be true, it's *on da innernet*). Another one has a robbery in progress in the background: a bank, a pharmacy?

Funny things you see on porn TV while you are not watching the cocks.

There is one where they run on the beach, and a dog is barking off to the right—barking because there is a man fighting with a woman, holding her down. It looks like part of the scene, but Mr Dedalus said it was not.

We know Chi Chi LaRue, and he told us the story too, over dinner in Malibu, with the blond boy from Illinois who said he'd do anything, absolutely anything for money—so you lost all interest in him.

My personal favourite is the video in New York of the Czech porn star with the massive cock, and he walks on that aircraft carrier (one of these filler scenes), and in the background you see a well-known general and a White House consultant, faces anybody recognized at the time. And this, general, I imagine him saying, is Pavel, from Czech Republic, here to get his monster cock sucked by American privates.

Why are they called 'privates?' Because of their privates?

—Nice to meet you Pavel. Oh, you wanna be careful with that gun!

There she is again, Mrs Erskine—wouldn't wanna be in *'er skin*— and her dog, shitting all over the church lawn at four in the morning. If the vicar caught you, it'd be no loafy Jesus for you on Sunday. Cute mutt. She's ninety! And there—ka-zzzoing that's the last of the Macallan gone.

I am by nature not a Macallan man, Paul used to say, and I never knew what he meant. I am by nature not a whisky man. I was born to sip champaign!

We should smash glasses like the Greeks smashed plates! What a stupid custom!

And as the wind blows and the cold mows and the cock crows, I am slowly sobering up. Why, regardless of how much I drink, do I always get sober just afore sunrise? It must be my internal sobriety clock.

I wanted to tell you a story, Mr Dedalus, about two Slovaks who weren't gay, but I've drunken away the wee hours again, gave it all to the laird of Macallan. What a night! Shite and onions! I can't see the Joe Miller, can you? The seventh sleepless night in a row. Medicate me, medicate me! More whisky! More crisps! More gaping holes! Long live the Scottish Anal Movement!

You say it's time to call it a night, but can I sleep, Mr Dedalus?

How could I sleep, all those summer weeks, with that question on my mind? Every night I spent brooding—pondering and

9

pissing. Ponderously pissing the night away.

It were a nightmare. A summer of nightmares, and an autumn of despair, and thanks to Macallan it won't be a winter of discontent.

But I promised Tim I'd stop drinking now—except, of course, that was afore he dropped his fucking bombshell. But forgive and forget, and on with me life. Dropped it right into my lap. My barren Yorkshire loins, and onto my full bladder, bursting, spraying the piss all over the shag-pile. Yes, Mr Dedalus, the same shag-pile, still; the one you bought and sent to me; the one worth more than the whole house (I think, only I've never told a soul).

I were a lad once, with nice muscles—all natural—and a fair smile, and you gave me presents.

You've got it easy. You just lie there and fester and foul, but I, I have to live. At the age of fifty-seven, I have still not drawn any conclusions. I know naught about life, about living! Once I thought life is to be lived, to be experienced, to be *undertaken*, that we are here to grow and to learn. But it's all rubbish. Nobody learns nowt. People stop learning in their teens and then for the rest of their miserable lives they just sit there regurgitaterating and absorbationing rubbish, and there ain't no evolution of the mind either, only devolution, like the Scottish fucking Parliament, wasting taxpayer's money on a colossal *devolutionary* scale in the name of self-determination. Self-determination my arse!

People as votes don't want self-determination; they don't want freedom, they want boxing in and being told what to do! At fifty-eight (soon), a drunkard and serial porn-watcher; mother of eight, nine, ten lodgers at a time—I have their problems to deal with, too, you see—a cleaner of boarding houses and wiper of stairs; a discarder of cum-stained tissues from the rooms of our oh-so-manly visitors in oh-so-many months, with oh-so-many scars to heal and puberties to overcome; I stand afore thee no' a wee bi' wiser—on the contrary. Bottoms up! (I would, if I could move mine.) Bottoms up, nonetheless—to thine health, ye daft bugger.

And then I had this on my hands, these boys from Slovakia. Going on June when they first arrived—what a couple of lookers!

Aye, it were a shock to us all: revelations, revelations. A

10

summer of revelations, a great summerly unravelling. One of them—the more muscly one—I spent a night watching over him, holding him, comforting him. Just one of them—the other one had run off again.

We been *awroonrihooses* looking, and then we found him, guess where?

They came as a couple and left as a couple and in between turned Edinburgh on its fucking *heid*.

What's a lass from Leeds to do? Just play mother. Shall I be mother? How many cups o' tea ye think I poured over dashed hopes and regrets—wretched regrets?

I will tell you it all—tomorrow, when I am sober. But first I have to go pee. Go pee—laugh out loud, as they say onna innernet. *Go to pee!* I'm roaring for a slosh is what I am. Wheels on fire!

Ta, listen to this duh-rrivel:

They were there in the room in that awful morning, in that light so green and outlandish, long before the sun would come to douse the city in golden rays of warmth and kindness—but there is more kindness still in the night, where it has always lingered between the small hours and the cruel dawn. They sat far away from each other, the heavy-set man almost bald by the door, keeping watch over his charge; stopping, swaying even with uncertainty; the young man with his legs draped over a sofa chair, a tea cup in hand, too hot to drink, too comforting to put down, too welcome a distraction from the pains of the day; what a painful day it had been. The armrests torn, desperately in need of repair—but it will last another season, another change of the guard. The boy behind the door, against the panorama window, looking peevishly embarrassed, frightened even, shaking with fear still, but at last the tears have stopped coming. He is quiet now, and somewhat calmer.

—You and your fucking tea, Jamie says when he's been dumped again and sits on that very chair, usually at four in the morning, after having woken the bald man.

But this young man isn't Jamie, and it's not four in the morning—not quite, but getting on—half hour to go. His name is Claudio, although that isn't his real name, but Claudio will do.

11

So much confusion. Do you like my strained prose? I wrote that some nights ago, afore the bombshell, when I could still think straight, until I found the bottle of Bourbon Jamie had hidden behind the skirting board.

One does tend to find things when one isn't looking. And I am always not looking.

I am stable, Jamie says. I am the one stable star around all else revolves in this house, this world, for him. I am the fat blob in the centre, the axis, the centre of gravity, gravity, gravitity. No matter how drunk I am, I am always here, always cheerful-cum-suicidal, always ready to roll.

If I were an Australian backyard, I'd be the barbie and the shrimp and the grill-master-chief-meat-turner-over all rolled in one affable squishy exterior.

Did you know they now do liposuction on paraplegics for half the price? It's well worth it, if you want to be fair and square. Bit too late for me, but twenty years ago, I'd have had everything done; and I mean everything. Aye, I'd have been Kylie on steroids. Don't you say nowt about that lass—I love her to bits.

This here is Edinburgh, Scotland, on a cold October night—and nights start early here. It ain't the Caribbean, that's for sure, even in the balmy summer. I haven't started drinking today—not yet, so we can talk easy. I won't be doing the farm accent so much, and I won't invent any fancy words what don't exist, which I only do anyway to annoy Tim. I'll try to be coherent too, which I hardly ever am. I'll try not to waffle and I'll try to stick to the story like cum to a hairy belly—I'll be me unadulatterated, cheerful self. When I can. In between, I'll do do *Dancing Queen* and shit mesen' like the yokel I am. Tim—the kinky sod—bought me nappies once—aaaactually. Daft. I'd rather throw meself off the bridge than roll about in adult nappies.

I have made so many attempts now at telling this story, I have lost track. I told it first to Simon in instalments over the phone, and then to Tim, who only witnessed part of it, on account of his busy schedule at the school, and I told it to a window pane when a scud of rain assaulted it, and to an overgrown gravestone in Perth, but

12

what's the point? There was no point.

I tried writing it down, but I don't have the skill or the patience. I were never good with words. Nor with people, come to think of it. Nor with anything, really.

I got as far as the paragraph above, only made it as far as 'the heavy-set man almost bald by the door, keeping watch over his charge; the young man with his legs draped over a sofa chair, a tea cup in hand, too hot to drink,' that's where my resolve broke down.

Heavy-set is too friendly a word for a fat white blob in a wheelchair, and why did I write 'almost bald' when I haven't got a single hair left on my shaved head? Because I want to be 'almost' where I am already 'completely?' We are polite to ourselves, ever so—so we can live with ourselves? It's a bonnie concept, self-delusion. It makes you go places.

If I can't be honest about it, I should not attempt the tale. And then I put 'young man with legs draped,' it's all wrong again. Women in operas, them's draped over sofa chairs, not studly young Slovaks with firm abs and thick thighs. His posture was that of a hurt animal, the dying swan maybe; certainly there weren't no draping. Making that comely lad sound like a piece of cloth.

Anyroad, if I ever want to tell this story coherently, it only remains to be brutally honest, unpoetic, unadorned—like my life, pretty much, which should have been so much more glamorous.

I could have been on the cover of fucking Cosmopolitan, not reading it in the back of a lorry up from London! There's a taste of shite in my mouth—that's how unpoetic I will get.

I will get back at you, Mr Dedalus, for reading books to me I didnae understand. Why didn't you just shag me in your cabin, like you did the other boys? Why didn't you just *force* me—force your love and your money down my fucking throat? Why the fuck did you give me a choice?

It's like you asked me to marry you, only those were the seventies, and gay marriage hadn't verily been invented yet. Not the way they talk about it now. Not politically.

We've been running this place nigh on thirty year now, me boyfriend Tim and I—husband, I should say, we've done the registration thingy, although he doesn't believe in it—which also means I've been living in bonnie Scotland for as many years. How time flies.

You don't need to *believe*, I told him you only need to sign. Took me ages to convince him.

He's a school teacher you see, out and gay, and loud and proud, no problem there, but when it came to marrying me, in the end, he clenched up—figuratively speaking. I'll never know why; we have almighty rows about role models that never lead anywhere. Turns out you need to make a political statement, just to get a bit of bum fun these days.

Maybe I am just too simple for him—I am a simple person. For me things are black and white like a Chinese cat. Tha's either queer or tha's not; end of story. But that, as Mr Attenborough would say, is exactly the point of our story. And how we make the world a better place, and not end up with a dysfunctional democracy like the Americans, where everybody shouts 'we want more rights!' trying to drown out the other voices. Selfish democracy. People only think in their own terms; only judge by their own standards. Instead of being open and tolerant. Should come to our place, our B&B. That's where tolerance lives. We is ever so *toleratious*.

Now then, where's me baffies? My feet look like they are cold. Lost a slipper last week by the lift, and it dropped through a gap under the boards—can't get to it. So there's me new ones, with a little dragon on the side. Them's like Chinese *emberrhoidery*. And only £1.99! That's globali-fucking-sation for you! Probably stitched by wee bairns in a dingy coal cellar.

Tim and I are as different as you can be as a couple, and if I were to give a reason why we are together, I would have to make one up; which isn't difficult for a man who's fibbed his way through life the way I have.

Me husband is smart, eloquent, tall, always friendly with everyone, courteous, frugal, inventive, resourceful, and he's got a head full of white hair. He never gets angry. He is the most considerate and honest man you can imagine; he has taken care of me, selflessly, for thirty-some years. He's never once complained, never said a mean word.

I am ... the opposite, in every which way. I hate meself half the time, and the other I am banging my head against the wainscotting—unable to reach the proverbial wall, really. He is always reasonable and collected; I am the queen with the tantrums, ungrateful, sullen—his bold bauchle, who used to be famous for a year in her youth; the hag with the hissing fits she feels entitled to. I have been dealt a difficult hand, and I feel I deserve a break; and a little extra love. Tim would turn that on its head, immediately. He would say, if it were he in this chair, that even though he'd been dealt a difficult hand, he'd not feel he deserved any special treatment.

He is generous, alive, loving and caring to the point of fastidiousness—he asks me sometimes how much I love him *today,* and *now.* I always answer as much as you love me, honey, but it's not what he wants to hear—he's a school teacher, he wants to quantify things. You can't quantify a thirty-year relationship of two men who have nothing in common—nothing but a B&B, a handful of memories, and a shitload of self-pity.

But, not to worry. Life persists even in impossible environments. I am like lichen in the Hebrides. Life's tough, and so am I, aye. That's the spirit.

The canny thing about a B&B is that everything comes from somewhere, like in a Victorian manor house, whose men have gone out to India and Africa and America, over generations have left silver, paintings, dogs, wives, staff—running a small hotel is a bit like that; one is always in possession of *things from abroad*: young men, the underwear they leave—it were CK for many years, but now they are as likely to leave any other brand sponsored in porn studios—the plonk and ciggies they brings, and the books they discard, the condom wrappers between bed frame and mattress, the travel plug abandoned in the socket, but most of all they themselves—there is nothing more interesting in life than dealing with foreigners, exploring them, learning them, absorbing them, studying.

So then, I've got me tea, me woolly blanket, me lumbar support pillow ... here's the story then, you've been waiting for, Mr Dedalus. You just sit over there on the sofa and look gorgeous, figuratively speaking. Wouldn't want a real corpse posing—now that would be daft. Just don't interrupt too much, will ya. I'll loose me threads and drop me stitches.

Six months ago they arrived, Claudio and his friend Lukáš from Slovakia, six whole months ago—and that's our name Lucas, or Luke, but with a 'k' and with an accent and a thingy on the 's' that makes it a 'sh' really. He taught me to pronounce it—sounds very Russian and all. The 'a' is long, like his gorgeous eye-lashes. Claudio were of course much easier.

One tall and dark and mysterious and ever so dishy, in a perfectly Eastern European kind of way, the other stocky and blond and muscly, could pass for the boy next door, only with an all-year gym membership. I say stocky, but that's merely in comparison to his mate.

They were both tall, with narrow waists, like a man should be if he looks after himself and stays off the éclairs. But those as got the wrong genes will never look like that, even with so many hours bench-pressing. It is a matter of breeding, as you would say, Mr Dedalus. Tha'll be salivatin' in your grave by now, old lecher.

Mary said, when she saw them, they was like out of a movie. Yeah, a porn movie said I!

Anyroad, they were the nicest couple we'd ever had staying with us, but . . . then it got complicated.

I am a simple person, I didn't—still don't—clock half the things that went on between them; I don't read books and I don't watch talk shows—I know naught about life and how it *should* be, and I certainly did not think on . . . That's why it surprised me so much, why I never saw it coming. Tim is much better at reading people, being a teacher and all. Tim is better at everything, period, even macramé—but even so, he were taken aback too.

They arrived in the week we made our last visit to the mosque. Tim as headmaster were part of an outreach programme talking to Muslims about values in modern British society, about finding common ground, and burying the hatchet—and keeping an eye on their radical young lads, one likes to surmise, in more ways than one.

At some point towards the end, they were told we were actually a gay couple, Tim and Tim, the faggots from Manor Place.

16

They wouldn't attack a man in a wheelchair, it was thought, and Tim's position as a headmaster gave him gravity—gravity?

A woman pelted me with food from the buffet after we had had the most amiable conversation. They learned we were gay, and irrational fear—Tim said—overcame them; although to me it seemed so much more like hatred, pure and simple.

The Muslim council then sent a letter to the city council that Tim and I should be removed from the outreach programme, whose intent, wrote the esteemed (and steaming) Imam, surely had been to bring down the walls, a purpose hardly achieved by sending sexual deviants nobody could respect.

We wanted, the Imam said, respect from each other, so why send people 'nobody would respect; people with no morality under either religion.' There was no point, he wrote—I quote— talking about tolerance and understanding to people who didn't believe in god. Unquote. Knock on head . . . anybody home? Seems all the little grey cells have gone out to Mecca on the hajj.

We had to call the police after this, twice, because balaclava'd lads threw fire bombs through our windows. The attacks stopped just when Claudio and Lukáš arrived—our guardian angels. I don't know why they stopped. The police never showed up. Well, they did: they sent a gay officer who assured us that the police respect the needs of gay citizens—then spent the whole night in our living room, telling us how horrible it was being out and gay as a policeman, and have everybody look at you like you had AIDS and leprosy at the same time.

—They even made it clear I would never be promoted. I would take a special place, a very special one, to appease the faggots— special, but never normal. The Commissioner herself said it like that: 'you haven't got a chance in hell for any serious career in the force, so you might as well get used to your role as permanent homo liaison.' Not in so many words, but I'll always be a copper on the beat. The gay beat.

A bit like the Indian officer in Hanover street—gay too, but deep in the mahogany closet.

Jamie had him over once for a shag. He told us he'd be 'Asian liaison' forever. Beware of specialities. As soon as you have one, you are stuck with it, aye! Only the truly bland and brainless, the adaptable arse-faced rise to the very top.

Well, maybe things will change one day even in Britain—they have changed in our B&B, in our *auld hoose*: the Slovaks brought so much change, to all our lives. I wonder what became of the gay copper? I did like his attempt at a moustache.

I were never much of anything, certainly no connoisseur of human emotions. I have a tendency to misinterpret everything that happens—it's more than a tendency really, it's an intentional quirk. I'd throw my hands up in the air and say 'it's wha' I do!'—if my joints wouldn't hurt so badly. No more throwing of hands, no more sudden movements. I want to misread things in order to make them fit neatly and not turn into obstacles—obstacles put me off. I am an obstacle-fiend, a hater of obstructions, a despiser of hurdles, from high steps to holes in the road; obstacles are offensive!

I want human relationships to work smoothly and plainly—plain sailing, on tranquil waters, easy to navigate the seas of the heart. I always give in, I always mediate, I always search for the most peaceful outcome. And now, here is the truth: nothing have I misread more than the relationship between the two Slovaks.

Never have I been more embarrassed; never more clueless how to proceed, more lost for remedy. How to heal? To reunite? There were only pain—hard, self-inflicted pain, or rather fated pain, the inescapable agony of senseless events. The very thing that makes people religious in the first place—but the Slovaks weren't of the church-going type either, so they suffered.

They were a riddle, the two of them, glorious, muscular enigmas from day one, and I was out on a limb and then clueless and guessing, then pushy and nosey, and then utterly devastated. They were a riddle—a handsome, touching, fascinating riddle. The hottest boys you could want, such a perfect couple them two. They made Jamie ache and babble, they did, and that's something! Jamie don't ache easily—no Sir! And he certainly don't babble.

Why did I not see it coming? Why did I not lift the veil sooner? Why did I end up on the heath, wondering what had happened? We tried everything: cajole them, seduce them, beguile them; threaten them, lure them, command them: Tim talked to them his school talk, and I talked to them my matron talk. We talked and asked, and prodded and queried, and we still got it all wrong.

So this is the story of life, Mr Dedalus, and of that summer, and of our cunning, and our cries for help. What went wrong that summer that left me so blind? And what did we do right, so that in the end, it all came out all right—came out faster and harder than I wanted it to, and another pile of shit with it? Oh bugger, Mr Dedalus, are you even listening?

My life started out such a simple proposition. I took a cruise with a rich man when I were nineteen—as a kept boy, yes. Do you remember, Mr Dedalus, on the sun deck, when we looked at all the rich South American ladies and their toy boys? Do you remember Rafael, with the wispy beard, and what you made him do? Oh dear, did I blush! The lady wants blushing, served me right.

Do you remember what you made him do to me, you naughty old gaffer? Now you're not so naughty any more, are ya, in the cold wet earth? I always wondered why you hadn't been cremated—cremation surely would have been more your style. I went to the funeral—nobody knew me; nobody knew who I was, of course. Just a man in a wheelchair.

Do you remember the sun deck, the lounge chairs in green and yellow? Do you remember the shrimp cocktails?—they were all the rage. Do you remember how you read to me in the hot sun, that book you thought would be more about travelling in ancient Greece?

I don't remember even the title, and not what it were about, except that you read it with that beautiful sonorous voice—people were looking at you—and that it had a Stephen Dedalus in it, and *summat* about Jews taking over; it were a lifetime ago—yes it were, MY lifetime. It were 1972, we read our first *Cosmopolitan*, and I still had that lovely accent then you tried to break me of—oh, tha drilled me like a soddin' poodle!

Afore that daft cruise, were there anything? A mother, a father, drudgery, beatings, a vegetable garden and dead seagulls each winter, lying on the asphalt. And school—abomination, school with a sadistic woman. I told Mr Dedalus about her, and he had her sacked—too late for me, much too late. It were a lifetime ago:

19

my lifetime.

After the cruise, after America, after I left you, after I went to sleep, after the accident, I worked in television—programming, local stuff.

In those days you didn't put your profile on Rent-a-hunk.com and sleep with everyone in Blackpool; those were different times.

I could have stayed with the man, I could have, he were right generous and all, and so in love with me, but in the end, I couldn't handle all the shaggin' for cash, or even for trinkets—rewards for services rendered on my back.

Money's not sexy; it's cold and smelly, and at the end of the day—or night—you hate yourself for it. At least I did.

Well and then ... things happened, when my old man found out, after the village got talking, after that ... anyroad, that were that. A life lived, a dream dreamt, a boy banged, a seed spent—I do go on a bit if you will let me, so you have to stop me. I got that from my mother god bless her. That and me ravishing looks, and my child-bearing hips. It's the chair as makes my hips wider and wider. In a good frock, I can do without the hoops. That's my wardrobe sorted.

Now off to programming: this was your life. The TV slut and factotum. I remember a series about seals with a man with a lisp so bad we couldn't understand him, so they made me do the voice-over on the cheap. And then they complained about the regional accent, and that were the end of my career, somehow. It's curious, isn't it? It had nothing to do with me, with my abilities, it weren't even my job, and these days, if you don't have a bit of countryside colour, they think you weird. But in them days, it were all plummy accents and clear *enunciektoring*.

So after that, it were always 'Tim as did the bad voice-over,' and 'Tim dinnae speak proper English,' and somehow I was stuck in my job till the end then, and everybody else was promoted or moved or had some semblance of variance, some chance at joy, some indication, however general of a career path, whereas I had my chair and psoriasis on the knees.

I made a right hash of things after you—remember, Mr Dedalus, when in the nineties people started saying that spending your life in the same company were bad, and you had to move about a lot and 'sell yourself?' How ironic, weren't it? How very ironic! Go out and sell thaself.

On that note, here's some more *reflectorimming*: I can pinpoint everything that went wrong in me life, every single pivotal moment at which I should have made other choices, the missteps that could have lead me down a much different—and a better— path. Better? Are you sure? Aye, I am sure, but I can't prove a thing.

The first one is clear: I should have stayed with you, Mr Dedalus, I should have stayed with money and influence and safety and protection and Latin American heiresses and their toy boys, not been daft and prissy, played on the centre court 'stead of gone back to muck and nettles. The necklace she wore, do you remember? I were nineteen, sat next to you at the captain's table, and across from me a lady with a soddin' diadem! Haven't they gone out of fashion! I had a quiff that year—how ridiculous I looked. It were the year they turned out a man from Disneyland for wearing a gay T-shirt, or made him wear it inside-out. Nowadays they give pensions to gay spouses. It were a lifetime ago—not just a lifetime; it were a different world! How did we ever make it thus far?

So why did I leave Mr Dedalus? He were a man who in the late 1960s gave 100 dollar tips to waiters and porters, that sort of money. We had dinner with Donald Trump for crying out loud, and a month later in New York, we met Andrew Holleran.

We went to parties on Fire Island, and lunched with the Kennedys. There is a picture of Mr Dedalus, Gore Vidal, senator Kennedy and my cute self, looking bloody well out of place, hanging in some American museum of presidential history-something. I were surfing the crest, the very crème de la crème, and I didn't even have to suck cock for it! It were my annus mirabilis—and it were my *anus* mirabilis that got me there!

We chartered a private plane just to go shopping in Paris; we had dinner with Lagerfeld, groping and wearing corduroys! We had boys in the hotel suite, seven or eight—I don't know where they came from; certainly not from the Internet. Nobody knew what a computer was back then, or a condom! We rented a small hotel in Switzerland—not a room, the whole hotel, just because

21

he wanted to be alone with me for a while. He called a man, who called a man who brought round a crate of champagne that cost eighteen thousand pound!

And I left him. Left him there with the bane of solitude and money, 'cos I reckoned it were wrong to sell myself, 'cos I thought it were *a bit* degrading; in my Victorian delusion I thought that I could do better, and have a life, and self-esteem. Do better how? When? Why? Self-esteem? Don't make me laugh!

He rented a ski slope for a whole day, had it blocked, so he could teach me to ski. And I said sorry, can't be bothered, my booty is not for sale—how daft were I?

His money offended me! Why does money offend one at nineteen? Why does one have these ideals at an age when one doesn't need them? And then abandons them just when one should have them, to ward off the devils and shield against old age? Why is everything in life the wrong way round? So bloody well upside down and widdershins? Why are we stupid and passionate and idealistic only while we are beautiful and virginal, and utterly useless in bed?

The second thing I should have done different is this: I should have never agreed to stay with Tim. He doesn't love me. He pitied me then; he stayed with me because he thought me an assignment, a challenge, summat odd and inconvenient he forced himself to do, to prove to himself that he could love a soddin' paraplegic. Maybe he learned to love me later; maybe he loves me now—I think he does, I think he learned to love me, maybe, later, but what kind of bargain is it to exchange pity for self-pity? Wouldn't it have been so much better to get love for it, rather than pity? But love I tossed away, 'cos I thought it were shamefully bought, and money—what an awful stench it had when I were nineteen. I had money with Mr Dedalus—yes, you, you old git: looking at me, laughing; smirking, surely, at my daftness—I had money and a body to die for; and ideals; and now I've got naught.

What I've got is this wheelchair—condign punishment for my sins—and a bed and breakfast in Scotland.

Oh! the auld hoose, the auld hoose! Wild rose and the jessamine, still hang upon the wall, hoo mony cherished memories do they sweet flow'rs reca'.

We've had this B&B for going on thirty years now. It used to be that really it were a B&B, but then we became more and more drawn towards the dark side.

Tim said we ought to set an example and be out and proud—so it became a gay boarding house, and since gay boys don't have breakfast—partying all night and not rising afore noon, as it were—we dropped a B. Only that weren't right either—because people said we had more than one B for boy, and it really did stand for B&B—boys and boys or boys in bed. But if that were the case, it should have been named B&B&B&B&B&B&B&B—for we'd got lots of boys in lots of beds here, especially since Jamie moved in. He's going through them like underwear. What am I saying? He don't change his knickers that often!

Oh, the auld Laird, the auld Laird! (that's me!) *Sae canty, kind and crouse! Hoo mony did he welcome there, his ain wee dear auld hoose. And the laddy, too, sae genty, tere shelter'd Scotland's heir, An' clipt a lock wi' his ain han' frae his long yellow hair* (that's Jamie! But I don't have a lock of his hair. And it's not long—it's short now, quite fashionable, sexy, definitely, as is the rest of him! Fair lad our Jamie.)

Hoo mony we welcomed over the years, indeed, *hoo mony,* in the dear *auld hoose!* After the language schools opened, we've only ever been getting guests who come to study English here—imagine, teaching them English, here, in the north, daft plan! But it worked, apparently; so over the years we've been through all of Europe and farther afield—without leaving the house.

Aye, we're a regular European Commission here, we are. We've had Italians (plenty!), Spaniards (always love triangles), Germans, Dutch and Danes (so polite, so kinky in bed), Swedes and Swiss, one Finn, who pretended he liked girls till the day he were briefly arrested for sucking dick in Inverleith Park.

In the past few years it's been Eastern Europeans often, Poles, Croats, Slovaks, Slov ... what's the other one? I can never tell these countries apart. Romanians too, and we've had an older man from Greece with his wife staying here—don't know where exactly communication broke down, until I found out he were shagging the local lads while she was sitting her English classes, learning how to spell 'bisexuality.' He also did some research about triremes, and had lunch with people from St Andrew's House and the university. I didn't take to him though, funny, even though he were always nice to me.

Oh we've had plenty of those—people who come here to *find* themselves. Had a German bank manager here with his colleague, to brush up their English at the school. The two never went back; took their last bonus and live near Perth now, run a B&B same as us; we've become friends of sorts.

We had an Australian who deserted his rowing team to find a lover in Dundee. We've had a Croat and an Algerian come and fall in love, and now put up tents and run the Fringe festival catering.

We've had pure debauch too: a gay couple from Duisburg who picked up girls in straight clubs who wanted to watch them; and a straight couple from Poland who picked up gay boys. We had a porn star stay with us for a month, and a porn producer from California.

We had half of Randy Blue on a weekend, and a man from Hong Kong who hired a different hustler each day. We've had a painter from Taiwan who was the toy-boy of a priest, and we've had two blond Mormons on the run from their own idiotic church.

We had a fat boy who tried to kill himself and a thin boy who tried to get his hands on steroids. We had two Bulgarians who beat each other, and a French boy who drank his own piss and fancied a hairy rentboy who went to anthroposophic meetings.

We had a spiritualist who believed he could achieve nirvana by stretching his anus wider and wider, and we had a Swiss man who preached fervently against anal sex, but gave blow jobs in public toilets.

We had a hockey coach who fancied one of his own players, and a father of three who was in love with his own son.

Aye, we had all sorts over the years, and it makes you wonder what the world is really like, if there is any sanity left, and what sanity is, if I could define it. All sorts went through my hands and slept in our beds, but most of all—and every year, all the time, in at least two of the rooms—we had gay men: young and middle-aged; on the prowl; confident and horny; shy and nerdy—we had all sorts; and many of them, I hope I can say that, were happy here, and found love. And if not love, then at least friends (if that is the right order); and if not friends, then at least a body or two to hold on to.

Aye, we are a roundabout of gay passion we are, matching boys from around the world in our little homestead. Come to Manor Place, and find happiness! A lover for every lodger! We are a beacon of tolerance and depravity!

People tend to fall in love in our house, and in love with Scotland—I must be the only person who really doesn't like it here. I do miss the south. Duh, only joking! Life blossoms in the harshest climes.

There were a scene, after the first big revelation, when Claudio sat over there on the chair, finally drinking his tea—I think I'd made it too hot again. His face had gone a bit pinkish, finally, after all that *sanguinaciousness*. It were a dark red when he cried; he's like one of those signal lamps out on the coast. His complexion is fair, blond, wan, always; but when he gets excited, it's like a rainbow of colours; like a fireworks of emotions, and his eyes glowering over you with longing, or fear, or hate—I could never tell.

He had come home at three in the morning, caught me on the stairs. Now I know, but then already I thought, bloody'ell, something's happened to the lad. Got into a fight I thought first, but there were no marks on him: no blood, no wound, and no shiner; and he only looked drunk and excited, not beaten up. I thought he'd been hit over the head—you know, another bashing—but then, it didn't fit; he hadn't ... and after all, they were so peace-loving, so soft, so kind, both of them. They'd know how to avoid a fight.

He sat there without speaking, drinking his tea, going through a whole box of tissues, and I can still see him. I will always see him: the handsome boy, like a marble statue of a dying—dead—Christ, down off the cross, in the arms of his lover. Only the lover were a nicked old chair, armrest almost polished white. We do need to get it upholstered. They were such a dark red when we got them, so long ago. Draped, yes, like a figure in an opera; like a dying swan, over the armrest, breathing; with blood under his skin, but clearly dead inside, for a night at least. That's how I will always remember him. I think of Claudio and his friend, and that's what I will remember: that night we spent together, I watching over him, he in the depth of despair. But that weren't the worst of it—so much happened after!

The house is truly grand—one of the reasons I moved here. No, not moved here—the reason I stayed on—apart from Tim, of course.

It's in New Town, a Georgian town house if that's what they really call them, on Manor Place. Across from the church, where the consulates are, so really close to the language school—although you are never far from anything in Edinburgh—even death.

I don't mean it's a violent city—but it's so depressing most of the year. It lives and sparkles and shines in summer, and then it dies and hibernates and everybody turns serious and hates their mother, or boyfriend, or Polish neighbour.

They are miserable people, the Scots—stubbornly nationalistic, with a nation-building cult that rivals the best fascists, all justified by hundred years of domination from down south—and like most in these latitudes only happy in the brief sun, when they can laugh at the Americans mispronouncing the city's name; and relish an Italian tourist; or make fun of the Germans.

At the end of the day, they are harmless, in general; barking dogs only, like the rest of us: whiners, but not killers. Although some of the characters you meet down in Leith in the wee hours of the night can give ye the shivers.

Tim's always had a thing for sailors and workmen, and with all them tattoos now being so popular, it's fetish galore for him. Personally, I hate them: they look fun on a nineteen year old bum, but rubbish once you are forty, aye? What are they all hoping for? That medicine will catch up and keep them young forever? Or do they all want to be dead afore Alzheimer's sets in?

I think so, sometimes, with the young people we have staying here. It's as if people didn't care any more how long they lived. And it's like AIDS never happened; but then I may be living in the past too much. Seen from the safety of my chair, and my house, and the protection of my lover, the world is a daft place.

We've had a lad up from Germany, somewhere Hanover—his English was already very good. Not a bad sort; he done a course in business English (that's what he signed up for), but then he got distracted by all the boys.

Edinburgh in summer is like a little Brussels—every nation of Europe is here, but of course younger, with firm skin and bright smiles; and cocks hard as cricket balls; and of course Spaniards aplenty; and handsome Italians, which wreak havoc on our northern souls.

We do—us northerners, I mean—*European* northerners, I mean—we do fall for the southern type. The dark, mysterious, sexy ones with the teaky skin and the white teeth. Edinburgh in summer is fag central: caber tossing highlanders, our embarrassed, spotty lads, meeting the boys of their dreams.

So this German—don't recall what were his name, something atypical—shagged his summer through the gay bars and the park—and at some point I meet him in the kitchen downstairs and he confides in me, after I warn him that so much sex with so many partners is still dangerous, and that AIDS . . .

—But don't worry, he interrupts me. And he were a smart lad; he'd been to university and all, studying engineering or summat Teutonic, or management—I can't remember, truly, only his eyes, I remember his eyes—and he says,

—Don't worry, Tim, he says, don't worry, I only *not* use a condom when they *really* look clean.

Nearly spilled me Ovaltine! Twenty-four, engineering, good German family, smart, not bad looking, and he does it bareback—but only with people who *look* clean. Hello?

Those as lived through the eighties and nineties—those as seen our friends die like flies all around us—we'd be gob-smacked, truly, by such stupidity, I told him. We had a decade of reason, and now (maybe because infection rates are falling, or with all the Internet porn—all them poor Eastern European lads with second-rate looks; those as can only do bareback if they want to make a living in filth), I says to him, we are back to shooting up people's bums. But—mind you—only when they *look* clean. Heavens!

There's plenty of daft buggers around, but a studied type with

27

a degree? Makes your bleedin' heart bleed.

At least with Claudio and Lukáš we didn't have those sorts of problems. But problems we did have, until the big revelations, the big denouement—denudement rather, for there weren't no clouds involved, but plenty of nudity.

He didn't like tea before he came to England, did Claudio, he said, only coffee. But here, he's taken a liking to breakfast tea with milk, and he's a snob—we've had to buy *Twinings* just for him. It is the better tea, but usually we don't afford it. Tim doesn't take tea, I can't taste the difference, and for the twenty-somethings we get as borders here, it's really not worth it, is it, buying the expensive ones—they can't tell the difference either, can they? Might as well get the cheap store brand—but not for Claudio.

I should have known then they was trouble. We've had all sorts over the years, but never ones fussy about tea.

We had an Italian once—oh what a queen! She did her own shopping did she, not to use the low-cost items in our refrigerator, which we keep stocked for all to use. We are not stingy, honest to god, but with a house full of growing lads what go through the fridge like bulldozers, who'd gobble up the fois gras like gristle without batting an eyelid, you need to economize.

We've had an American who was *glucatose* intolerant—glutose, something. We had to do separate shopping for him too, only he didn't chip in, and he didn't leave any tips in the pot either.

But, where were I going with this . . . aye, it's this year, we've got the most exiting house ever, since September last—very stable, no moving-ins and moving-outs since the summer—summer always gets to me, because of the summer schools, and we have people here for weeks only.

I prefer the rest of the year, when they stay for the whole term or even longer. That's what he have now. I'll start at the top. Time enough. I should have talked more to Claudio, should have tried harder. But then I feel like a mother on some days, a big matriarch, the comforting diva, I can tell you. Nothing but daft young lads with problems!

The house—yes, the *auld hoose.* You come in through the front

28

door, and right away you are in this enormous hall, with a staircase at the end.

To the left is the living room, which the lodgers can use at any time; my gracious drawing room, where my gentlemen lodgers assemble to talk, to drink, to socialize—and to copulate at odd hours. It's got a TV and a lovely fireplace with a comfy rug to prevent chafing when you're flat out on your back. The wainscoting is all scuffed and nicked and looks terribly old; it's also got cigarette burns and there's a mouse moved in I think, slinking about somewhere in the woodwork.

I need to see to that later—get some poison. What if it's a rat?—oh dear. I hate killing things! Tim will have to do it, or Craig. I wonder if it found the panel where Jamie hides the booze. I imagine a cute wee rodent burping, trying to find its hole—ha! A bit like Jamie's lovers when he's on the rug . . .

I am being mean. But what else is there? And I do love Jamie.

That's the living room. Next is the kitchen: big, with an old trestle table in the centre, a stove dating back to the days of yore, a sink with incrustations that have been there since afore the great war, and plenty of hooks, and cabinets, and shelf space, and a treasure chest we picked up at an auction, right under the window looking out into the yard—that's where the flowers go and the fruit bowl. One gas oven, one microwave, and a prehistoric dishwasher we have stopped using because of the noise. Two refrigerators—one communal, one private for Tim and me—also to keep the medicines. It's got a lock, but that's broken.

That's it downstairs, not much to look at, but we call it home, and it's cosy and friendly, and exciting—it's our marketplace, our town hall, our meeting point.

Then you come up the round stairs and to the right is Jamie's room—Jamie the impatient American, that is; the mettlesome blond from New Jersey, not any of the other Jamies we've had over the years.

We've had a *Jaime* too, from Alicante—we just made him a Jamie—and a James from Seattle. He were a Jamie too—a big one. And then we had a Jamie from Birmingham, who left us with a huge bill for repairs, and a broken-hearted Danish boy. It's such a popular name, and we try to always have the Jamies stay in that

29

room.

At least we tried, afore this Jamie, who's been here with us for four years—I thought he'd stay forever. Canny lad, but far too handsome for his own good. Only dates the best-looking, and then he's always disappointed. But he'll learn. Well—he has learned, I have to say. Still can't believe it.

Jamie, oh, Jamie. What heartaches you gave us! What worries, what night sweat—well, *you* sweat more, with your conquests, I suppose. We fretted and you sweated.

Jamie was—is—a sight, a wonderful sight, so sure of himself; and at first, you'd be thinking, nothing much there if you are looking for deep thought and the potential to be prime minister. He's got no ambition beyond his own looks; plans for naught further in future than the next night, the next trick. Was, I must say, and had, because he too has changed quite a bit. He'd been addicted to sex, to men, to being attractive—he were addicted to attracting men, one after the other. He were vanity incorporated, his scarf were permanently apricot! But he were gorgeous, and lovable too, in his own way; and smart when he wanted to— maybe not the sharpest knife in the box, but no dummy neither— with his feet on the ground more than anyone I've ever met.

He found them everywhere, his lovers: in the street, at work, in bars. Out on a leisurely afternoon in the Botanical Gardens, when he had tea and scones, he disappeared with a guy who just happened to look at him a second too long. He lived only for love, I think, for I never heard him talk about his job, his future—he read books, but even those he didn't share.

He never spoke about his lovers to us until after they were gone. They never existed except in his strong embrace, bucking under the force of his muscular body, the assault, the cock.

They only became humans to remember after they were gone: notches on the bedposts, parts of his sexual and our collective memory, people who stopped by our B&B to sleep with the handsome American.

They talk about him like that: the American hunk who lives at . . . He didn't share his lovers. Not for a quick chat in the kitchen, not for a night out in a pub, not for family lunch on Saturday. He never referred to them by their names (often I think he didn't know

30

them), but only as shadows—heaps of attractive flesh passing through his sheets, between his legs; leaving nothing more than a wad of cum somewhere; and parting with the assurance that they were worthy to sleep with the American god all the city knows.

You know, Manor Place, where *the American* lives, I imagine them gabbing. None of them wanted a relationship with him, I've come to think; they weren't there to be friends, to talk, to become anything other than memories.

They didn't have names.

They were always the blond one with the mole, the dark lad with the amazing bum, the German who was into fisting—remember him? We never did, but Jamie does.

They are etched into his memory like parts of a collection; like pictures, smells, feelings, in a giant scrapbook—but none of them were people.

Except, maybe, for Philip the banker, with the perfectly tailored suits and the enormous salary, and even larger bonus. The type the newspapers go on about—with a wife and child in a beautiful house. He came once a month to let Jamie fuck him, and left him a tip that allowed—for at least two years—Jamie to do square root of fuck-all for a living.

He weren't a hustler; he were just—is, still—the most handsome man in Edinburgh, that virile American with his generous loins.

One time he had Jehovah's Witnesses, two of them—fresh-faced, blond, red-cheeked, in fair shape—come almost daily, and I were well worried already he'd found Jesus. But he only invited them back, he said, because he fancied them; and little by little, he let them know what he was up to for real, and what he thought of their so-called god; and little by little, they fell for him, and converted to his *religion;* and he buggered the bejeezus right out of them.

—It's amazing, he said afterwards, the shit these people believe. Truly brainwashed. But I sure as hell cured them now.

Like many young men of his persuasion, Jamie counted the months, the weeks, the days even by the physical attributes of his lovers.

There was the month he were with Ryan—crooked Ryan, with

31

the strange mole on his buttock; and the week he spent with the Chinese model with the lisp; the week he went with the Austrian to Paris, when firemen stormed into the bedroom because the sodding building were on fire, just as he was finally getting used to the large prick; the time he converted the missionaries and the rainy Tuesday he fucked a famous actor in a public toilet, and the day he met a man called Jimmy, who had a tattoo on his balls (didn't it hurt unbearably?).

Weeks passed like this, and months, counted only by the number of adventures, the sizes of cocks, the skills in bed—and it rubbed off on us, all of us at the B&B.

We all started measuring time by the lovers who passed through Jamie's beautiful, brutal hands. It were about the time he dated the French lawyer, remember? I went into hospital for a check-up—when was that?—aye, it were just afore Jamie dumped the Brazilian.

Jamie has but one thing to say about life: that it changes too fast, that people he meets change so quickly, over night. You go to bed with a nice guy, smart and well-read, and you wake up with a lazy sod. And he complains that even his friends are changing, and he wished them to stay the same, and be more—reliable?

He said so often he would never settle down, never marry, because you never know what type of person you'll end up with. He said he liked me, because, in my wheelchair, I were always about, always here, always the same—didn't know whether I should be insulted or pleased.

And to think of it that way—he was right, but what can you do? People change. Opinions change, invariably—one's views about everything. Except, of course, if you are fundamentalist-religious, one of them newborn evangelicals, the mind-amputated Jesus-freaks—then you are stuck three-thousand years ago, in a world that keeps everyone in chains.

Surely Jamie doesn't want that. If anything, he ran from the Christian maniacs in America, who do everything to make sure their country continues to be a laughing stock. *God bless* indeed. No other country in the world except Iran and the Arabs are so mindlessly god-obsessed, so nonsensically conservative.

There's nothing good about conservative, Tim likes to say;

it's basically evil and stupid. It denies everybody their rights. Yet somehow—in our house, until that summer—Jamie was the only constant, until he too changed. He was the buoy in the sea around which the sail boats turn; he was the icon they come to admire, the temple where they pray, and he didn't change—doesn't change at all, in a way.

He seems to be the same age now as when we met him. He was the fixed point around which everything seemed to coagulate—life itself in our town, in our world, seemed to revolve around him: the beautiful foreigner who had no fault, whom one didn't choose to befriend or to bed. One was chosen; one was elected, elevated, to be with him for a night; and then one was discarded.

Is that how they must feel, his conquests? Do they know when they first talk to him that they are one in a long line of petitioners, that only some of them will have their desires fulfilled? No wonder Jamie complained about the world and people changing around him.

Is it then the normal people, the ugly ones that change—change, because all they do is flutter around lights like Jamie? Lights with perfect pecs and wonderfully cut abs; lights with hard thighs and admirable stamina, with a smile that can change the course of empires—one feels—or at least make you forget for a night.

Now look, though! Even that has changed in the space of a long summer. The summer that changed all, even Jamie.

When they left, they never took with them the imprint of a human being. It was never 'oh he's a really nice guy,' or 'he studied this and that, did you know?' When they left Jamie, they took away a bundle of sensations like these: his naked figure leaning against the window (his cock in their mouths), the sun rising behind him. Their hands on his flesh, the line of hair from his navel, the smell of his arse; the force with which he drove his cock into them; the tenderness (they speak of that; I have heard it with my own ears) of his embrace after a long night of passion; even his breath is sweet when you wake with him in the morning.

His lovers are the luckiest people in the world: they acquire these icons of beauty, these lockets of perfection, so that in ten years, when they have settled down with a lover from Glasgow

33

or Amsterdam, they can lie in their suburban bedrooms and think: remember that American, ten years ago, in Edinburgh? Remember how handsome he was? How perfect, and how good he was in bed? He was the most beautiful man—the hottest sex I've ever had.

It seems so little, so meaningless, so flippant—but it is not, I know. It's worth more than memories of whole relationships; deeper than the knowledge of a loved one. Jamie gives—gave—his lovers these eternal moments; there are some who haven't fetched themselves off since without dreaming of him.

It were four years ago that we first met. He showed up at our doorstep, an unwashed flea-bag, like an orphan out of Dickens. Aye, really—with the exception that he was not a short, stout, sullen figure but tall and blond and muscular like a trapeze artist—a hunk of a man I want to call him; a boy, I must say. I can't think of anything else but a boy.

He'll never grow up; he'll never stop giving. Rough and tumble mischief and that gorgeous smile!

He'd come over from America where he had once fallen in love with an older man who'd used him badly and then chucked him. He'd left in a hurry with no money: a broken heart, a damaged soul—he'd been out on the street, living rough for a month.

At least, that is the story he told, we could never be sure, but did it matter, I thought later? How could we ever have turned him away—such a perfect man, such a wonderful vagabond. He could have lied all he wanted, we'd have taken him in.

We are a house of gypsies and thieves. We're a house of broken wings and burning desires. At least Jamie would mend some, and satisfy others: it was in his eyes that he would, I saw it on the first day.

That's my emblem, my icon of Jamie, that day on the stoop, with an immaculate body no rags could defile; even destitute he looked not like a poor student, but like a supermodel who'd been made up to look like a ragamuffin.

He can't help it. He's made to be looked at, stared at, open-mouthed, gawked at, self-forgettingly—he's just made to be *taken in.*

Of course we took him in, and let him live for free, but he didn't stay long at first. He disappeared again (don't know where to), came back to sleep for a night or two, then disappeared again; and then suddenly he returned weeks later, all cleaned up, with money, and looking for a proper room. He were twice as handsome, if that's possible. His hair was longer back then—much longer, and lighter.

Aye, he is a charmer! He's got one of those smiles. You look at him and you forget what you were about to do. He walks into a room and takes it over. He is a commanding presence, even though he is courteous and shy. He makes straight men vie for his friendship, and gay men—well, cum in their trousers really. All it required: him standing by the window with a drink in his hand, when we had guests, in the living-room—which I call the drawing room, because all our lodgers are drawn there when they are lonely and in need of company. He just stood there, as if he were waiting for someone to come home. Like a housewife in an old movie, fingers tapping on the window sill, anxiously expecting her lover's return.

I did think he wanted someone. He wanted loving, and cuddling, and eternal promises, and red roses; but somehow, they were not for him, he always said. He seemed happy in his role, and when he complained it were just this: everybody's changing around him, and nothing offered the certainty he desired.

Look at him now. Look at him grin now! Everything's changed—most of all he!

He found a job after a long search; it's not easy in this market. It seems, Tim says, all companies want is people with experience in a field almost certainly not taught in school—managing, and database programming, and god knows what with computers and neural networks.

—We aren't preparing the children for anything much any more, says Tim. Small wonder graduates are jobless so long. Small wonder there's more porn actors on the Internet than punters. Small wonder, aye, that the side-streets of Leith are full of pizza puke. Technology's running away. I am a believer in science, but even so I can't keep up, he says. What we teach them now in our *skills* courses is obsolete in five years.

But Jamie were never in danger, with his looks and his charm. Handsome people with winning smiles, American pearly-whites and a washboard to cut yir veggies on always find occupation; it's a law of nature. It were the job he took on what surprised us, because his type would go well with a model agency, or a bar, or a fashion store even, selling overpriced clothes made by child-labour in Bangladesh, and looking fabulous in the process by wearing almost naught.

I thought he'd end up as PA of some rich banker—a *private secretary,* as they used to be called. Yes, Sir: dinner at eight with the prime minister. Yes, Sir: tomorrow, conference in Brighton, but I am sure we can fit in a shag over lunch, seeing as me bum's always primed. I were sure, so sure, in my soberer moments, that he could make it as an actor, but in the end he said he never tried for real, and that there were too many bad actors come out of Scotland already.

Anyroad, now he works at the museum, does research and catalogues, and those labels and audio guides.

We found out he had a degree in English—I cannot imagine him in a school, a university, or to graduate from anything but love-making class. Well, I've never seen him graduate there either, but I hear him *study* well into the night.

He always makes lotsa noise our Jamie, especially when they are good-looking, and hairy, and dark: Greeks and Spaniards, Italians and Syrians. 'Men with flavour', as he calls them.

Next to Jamie's room is ours, Tim and mine, with a big four-poster bed, my writing desk, his computer corner, bookcase, a dining table. Well, it's really a self-contained flat. We had it changed completely, so that I could live—exist—in there on me own, in me chair, and didn't have to call for help at all hours. But in truth, I don't like it here. It's our room; it's Tim and Tim's bedroom—it's not my room at all. Mine's the kitchen. Not because I am an old queen, but because that's where the important things happen, the *real* things. Where people come together and talk, and cry, and share their true selves. I've had more important and deeper conversations over pots of tea at that table in that kitchen, than in

36

my bed, or in this here our room. And we are only ever ourselves when we listen to others—so how can we be happy locked up in our own four walls.

The kitchen for me. Downstairs—I am a downstairs kind of person.

Shall I serve the pudding now, Madam? There goes the bell— His Lordship ringing for tea!

One floor up, directly above, there are three rooms, the first one were taken by Claudio and Lukáš that summer.

Nobody ever stayed in there after they'd left. It needed to rid itself of its memories. What happened in there was too momentous, too much of an upheaval for all, too important. Claudio was crying there, so long and so hard I thought he could not possibly have any tears left. He kept chewing the tissues rather than wiping his face.

It were such a handsome face, and I thought from the first that I knew him—he looked so familiar, right from the start. It all came out later, but I had that sense I'd seen him afore, right from the beginning.

Yes, Mr Dedalus, I had one of my visions, my premonitions, my gut-feelings that he'd come for a reason, and that we would end up changed, and in tears, and that I knew him; not just his type: his very face. The first time I saw him my spine tingled and it still does when I think back.

The room next to theirs were the den of Javier—his nest, his lair.

Javier is from the south of Spain—a bit of a nerd, dour-faced, but nice and hairy and cuddly and warm to look at. He's one of the best-behaved men I've ever met, always friendly, always ready to help.

He's not a student; he's a cook at a Spanish restaurant. He did the most amazing dishes for us on the weekends—a real talent. I wonder where he works now.

Yet within him, Mr Dedalus, lay already the seed of sadness. I observed him sometimes in the kitchen, or when he exercised with his weights (he abhorred gyms), and often when he was watching TV. His rough face, his unyielding hair, his frown—they

37

all seem to say that whatever he was experiencing was not for him.

He was always an observer, and he took notes; and at the end of each lesson, he seemed to draw a conclusion: no, not for me. And at the end of the summer, his conclusion was momentous! Out of kilter, I were, and up the wall—what a shock it were, when it came.

The next room is Aleysha whom we never saw, and who really doesn't like men, or gays, I always thought. She is from Uganda, got herself pregnant two years ago—her boyfriend lives just down the road; found out he were gay after the baby were born. Or admitted it, finally—one never knows, or did she say? Can't recall. And they have been through a lot together. They were trying to find a place to live, they still want to buy—but with this housing market? Prices in Edinburgh have gone through the roof, and even with the recession, nothing's really cheaper now.

I wonder how young people do it—get a job, get settled,—when everything's costing a mint, and jobs, good jobs, are so hard to come by. I am not saying foreigners are taking our jobs—quite the contrary, I'd like more immigration and more tolerance. But I do observe more and more poor local lads—you can tell by the accent still, and the dead eyes; the ones that have been here for generations, and feel run over by a Polish bus.

It's a bit sad to see people who've belonged to the land for so long, to be suddenly outcast or destitute. It takes a long time before *us* and *them* becomes a *we.*

There's one more room on the top floor, which were empty that summer. Flavio used to live there, a bit of a loner, very elegant. In a suit he looked like an Italian gigolo. He was from Brescia—you see I've wanted to look that up in the atlas for a month now.

Tim says go on Google Maps, but I rather not turn on the computer just to look up a city. Now, where's that atlas gone to . . . oh we are in the kitchen. That happens to me some times, that I get so lost in thoughts that I forget where I am—for a moment I thought I were up in our bedroom.

Maybe I should go over to my drawing room, but I tried writing there—I couldn't. I kept seeing Claudio over the chair, crying, eyes beady and swollen, the box of tissues dropping, falling to the floor, his sobs, my tea, the sugar bowl.

He did take more sugar in the end; at the beginning, he had his tea without anything, but then he learned to love it with milk. The daft things you remember.

—You and your fucking tea, I hear Jamie yell, and laugh—his bright, joyful laughter, forever the laughter of an overexcited child.

There, Mr Dedalus, I am doing what you said I should: I am being a mother. I take care of people. I care for them. And yet I don't understand them, and I want nothing more but to do that, to understand, to help not with bland words and meaningless phrases, but with real advice.

I'm not smart enough I always think, but you told me I were. You were wrong. You believed in me for no other reason than to get me into your bed. You were as self-obsessed as all the rest of them. You were the great arranger, the great manager: people with money who run things, the wealthy and influential. In your midst but one who feels, one who knows, one who lives for beauty, hungers after justice, and you crush him mercilessly—no, you were no different.

I watched my charges on all floors, even Aleysha. She must be the worst off, I thought at times, with her baby. She seemed so horribly angry. Tim says she is *marked*; says some women bear their shame and misfortune on the outside. It's written in their faces and grows in their wombs and hearts. They never speak of it. It hardens them, life, and the disappointment. With each unmet challenge, with each dashed hope, they close up more and grow harder and more unapproachable—they turn to stone, and into expressionless craggy outcrops on the coast, where gulls shit on them.

Aleysha spent her life running, but we never talked enough for me to understand if she needed me—wanted me; if she *wanted* me to know. There was some injustice in her homeland, but whatever it was she bore it in silence, with great strength. I know more about the boyfriend, and what he went through, and of course, it pales compared to her ordeal. Those who suffer the most seem to be able to do it in such estimable silence, with such dedication. Those who suffer much less are always the biggest whiners. Gay men are pathetic in that regard, you were right about that Mr Dedalus: we cry with the shrillest voices, injustice! But we are blind to all suffering except our own.

At times it seemed that everyone as passed through our house had been a refugee like Aleysha. I count the gays by virtue of their fate: they are running if not from themselves, then from their parents, mates, or colleagues. Only now, in the last few years, have I met gays who were truly comfortable in their skin, who didn't need help coming out. It's only been ten years since a semblance of justice has taken hold, and fairness—and that only in a few countries.

This year California is starting to teach 'gay history,' and the state is ordering schools to paint gay figures in a positive light. Think of all the dead and tortured, the suicides, the misery; I think of my own childhood. What a different world it were, and how far we have come!

There, old bugger, it weren't all for naught. And I'm not so daft as I look. Pass the bottle.

So that's the house for you, and its inhabitants that fateful summer; to set the scene for the drama of Claudio and Lukáš, who came to change us all and left unaltered. My mythical Slovaks.

Each floor has a bathroom, each bathroom a clunky old boiler; in the basement we do laundry, and there's stairs out into the inner yard, where we should have green plants, only I can't go there and nobody else tends it, so they are all withered. Some lodgers use it to smoke.

That's ye *auld hoose* for you, and that's me little world. I don't get out much, as you can imagine.

The floors are connected by wide round staircases, each with a lift for the benefit of yours truly; a noisy contraption I hate, because it reminds me of my own misfortune, my uselessness, my crippled body and my bruised heart.

On my good days, I ride it with glee. On my bad days, I stay downstairs and scrub the sink, and wait for everyone to leave for work, study, gym, the bars—and return exhausted, refreshed, alone, or with a boy for the night.

I sit by the kitchen, reading, like a doorman.

Doormen, Mr Dedalus, were my favourite thing about New York, when you took me there! They were swell, in their uniforms, their accents, their knowledge of everybody in the building and their habits. I moved into that apartment you kept just for your boys, and I wanted to stay there forever. I had a big bed just for myself, and a view of Central Park, and when you came—once a week, sometimes twice—you were like a father to me, and made me pancakes for breakfast. Don't think I have forgotten. I remember it all. I still go there, to that apartment—you taught me to call it that, rather than a flat.

Do you remember Mr Dedalus, what you used to say—and do? Tha used to spank my bum and say, ain't nothing flat about it, boy! Yes, my round bubble butt. Weren't naught flat about it indeed. Look at it now, rotting in this chair. I am sure it's flat as a board.

We are a gay B&B, but we are open to anyone, of course. We always send new lodgers an email afore they come, and the description of our house on the website—never mind the rainbow flag—includes a note that the landlords are two gay men, so it shouldn't be a surprise to anyone coming here, really! They also have us listed at the community centre, and at the language school, and in both cases it says not just *gay-friendly* but *gay-operated.*

Don't you hate that word, 'gay-friendly,' Mr Dedalus? Who came up with that nonsense? It's like 'pets allowed.'

We do travel, Tim and I: we've been twice around the world in fact. Even businesses that are too big to be either gay or straight—I mean large hotel chains, for example—put up the gay-friendly sign, which then means nothing more than 'we tolerate your sort and won't force you into a double if you asked for a king,'—but it's naught more than that.

It's a disgrace, how everyone's making money off gay people by calling themselves gay-friendly. We only go to really gay places, where you can be sure your money goes to people who really like you, and support the cause—whatever the cause. Tim's got all the opinions about that, I am just carrying the suitcases really—well, figure of speech.

I roll me chair behind the bell-boy, watching his bum wiggle, as it were. There you go—another advantage of a wheelchair. Eternal bum-height.

Tim is very opinionated, and political. I support him, of course, but I don't half understand what he's on about sometimes. He comes home from his school, talking about his children, about youth, Facebook, attention span, narrative arcs and biodiversity. Mostly he rails about what they can't do, what they won't do, his pupils; what they have forgotten to do. Total inability to comprehend and create, only copy and imitate. This is the regurgitation age, he says often to Jamie, who is intrigued by the opinions of a British headmaster, but, like me, often doesn't agree, can't agree, because we don't see the world through the eyes of a teacher, and don't have his experience.

Hundreds of children a year pass through his hands, and he distils from year to year the essence of their change: how each year makes them less attractive as human beings, and more intriguing as insects to study, under Huxley's microscope. He makes references to psychology, he chides Jamie for expecting things to stay the same; he accuses people of having an agenda, turning 'gay' into a political weapon, and then he says,

—It's the age of regurgitation. I too am a child of the regurgitation age. Attention span—are you listening or am I boring you?—attention span with the children in my school is down to minutes. Nobody has creative thought processes, nobody takes up a book and reads and thinks, they just Google it and then bleat out the rubbish others have stolen from somewhere—stealing, don't get me started! What do you think about downloading films and . . . ?

—It's wrong, interjected Claudio once.

—But you do it? accused the headmaster. You all do it!

Jamie nodded.

—Of course! Used to.

—First people said prices needed to go down, now they are down and people still steal . . . are they right? Is copyright

42

doomed? Will we expect everything to be free in the future, and all creativity dead? Does it die, unrewarded? Maybe when replicators arrive and molecular assembly and 3D printing, and two-thirds of the population will be out of work ... and basic food and goods will be free, in that coming utopia the product of creativity will be free. Should be free ... is that their argument? What's yours, Jamie, let's hear it! Why do you steal other people's work? Why do you not respect other people's creativity? You of all people, you work in a museum! You should value music, films, books ... the products of culture.

But Jamie didn't enter discussions like that. He made brief statements that were meant to reflect his convictions indirectly, but were largely meaningless, and then pretended that he had a cock to see to, an arse to fuck, groceries to buy, or,

—Jesus, is it that late? I need to do my laundry. I've got nothing to wear! Not a sock!

And off he would bugger and leave us alone with the fuming headmaster and the politics of replicators and fornicators.

Sorry, got a bit carried away. Where was I? We never made a secret of our convictions is what I wanted to say, and talked to anybody freely. We were known as the gayest boarding house, and people came here *because* of that. For all intents and purposes and all that's holy, anybody coming to our B&B, even if they are in the end assaulted by my husband's virtuous arguments, and by the smell of sex from Jamie's room, and by Aleysha changing nappies, and by Javier playing hard rock at full volume, should well know they are coming to a queer place, with a big bold matron running a tight ship—that'll be me, not Tim; he's ever so much butcher.

It is always a bit of guesswork when a new lodger arrives. Some write ahead, and tell us they are gay themselves, that they *needed* to stay in a gay place, and wanted to make sure—and maybe send a picture. Those are easiest to deal with.

Some you win, some you lose.

Some are just daft buggers calling to annoy us. And then we get the religious freaks calling: abomination! I saw your ad! An abomination! Is it really only 30 quid a night for double? I think we could ... what do you think Harry? It's only for one night. You wouldn't have to do anything. You can sleep in your clothes. Abomination!

Some call ahead, keep repeating they are straight at every opportunity, on the phone, telling you they don't mind staying at a gay B&B, but everything else were booked (it never is, but they love the excuse) and it's only for three nights! Do you mind?

But they themselves are not gay, they stress, once more, but tolerant, so is there an en suite in that room—no, oh that would be a problem, seeing as I am not going to share a shower with a gay man.

No one's actually ever said that, but I can hear them think it. It's as if—Tim puts it that way—the mere presence in our house necessitated emphatic reaffirmation of their masculinity.

The funny thing is, half the 'oh so straight' boys as came here emphasizing their masculinity ended up shagging Jamie—he's got a reputation for turning straight boys, and it's—let me tell you!—well deserved.

Jamie's got what Tim calls universal sex appeal. Women fall for him, and gays in bars—but as if that weren't enough, he's had so many straight affairs it's beyond belief.

Researchers say that twenty percent of men who lead straight lives have occasional sex with men—they are not homosexual; they do it for psychological reasons, or to restore hormonal balance. Now, I am not even sure that Jamie's after *these* twenty percent. He doesn't give up until he's slept with the *really* straight ones. The things I've witnessed in this house!

We had a rugby team stay with us once, who were offensively homophobic when they arrived. Two came in to ask for rooms; we had one big room to let with two beds, one of them an inflatable, and they had sleeping bags, which the rest of them spread on the floor. There were eight of them in all, and I made them a cheap price. They seemed like nice lads, a bit rough, a bit young, but I told them clearly that most of the lodgers were gay, and they didn't say a thing.

Seconds later, I saw them prancing back to the their car, acting all queeny and camp, screaming 'oooh' and walking with one arm

44

held high like a regular diva—so I shouted after them,

—You fucking bastards, you are not staying in this house if you can't respect us!

I rolled out to the edge of the stoop—yelling at them across the street, at eight grown egg chasers, crippled old me,

—You can stay here if you want, for all the week, I have made you a price and it's a good offer. But you will respect me, my husband, my lodgers, and I will not—oh how I wished I could have stood up and stamped my foot—I will not have that sort of behaviour here. Do you hear me? You will respect us! No queer jokes, no prancing about, is that clear?

And you know what happened? They were stunned. They were speechless, and then they yelled 'yes!' all and one of them—one and all I mean. I'd expected them to ignore me, to hit me, to attack me, to wheel me down the street and into the bins—anything! But they stood there, and one by one they wiped their smirks off their handsome, rugged faces and said,

—Yes! All right. We are sorry.

Two lowered their heads, but none snickered. They actually apologized to me! Eight strapping rugger lads! They brought in their bags and god were they ever nice and respectful the entire time they stayed here. They were fair bowled over—really shocked. They did behave! And how polite they suddenly were— two of them made breakfast for all the lodgers, another helped me up the stairs when the lift broke—he carried me all the way to the bed. Still remember the tats on his forearm. (Here's a bit o' news—it were a fib. The lift weren't broken at all . . . he were just such a stud, I just couldn't help mesen'!)

They stayed for six days, was it, and were the nicest lads ever, after that initial mischief. That convinced me, that incident, that we have to stand up for ourselves. If you want respect from anyone you've got to bloody well ask for it. Not hope that times will change and things will get better. You've got to bloody well *make* them better!

Of course, boys will be boys, and rugby players will be pigs: the first night they brought a girl home—and fucked her between them. Eight of them and one girl. Eight young, tall, brutal rugby players with tattoos and beard stubble and one local girl ... eight ... oh, yes ... where was I? It were disgusting! It were ... the poor girl—they just treat them like objects don't they, men are such pigs! So, well, that were on the first night, and the next morning I made it clear that I didn't want that sort of thing going off in my house. They couldn't bring anybody home! Since there was only the one room, it would have been an orgy no matter what, so I said no!—I really put my foot down, as it were.

And of course, I couldn't be sure they weren't raping her— although I found out her name later, and met her even, Mary did, in the pub; and she had been there on her knees of her own free will—but at the time I were scared, I really was. What if they really did rape her, I thought? So I forbade them to bring another girl home the next night, which they said ... Oh I've completely forgot what I wanted to say now! There, Mr Dedalus, tha knows how I can get—you got me all flustered now, what with the rugby lads 'n' all.

Ah yes, about Jamie!

The second night, their room were quiet, real quiet. I swear I thought, they must have their fanny, these growing lads, and they can't have it in here, so they are staying out—there's nobody home. So I thought, well, I'll open the windows, let in a bit of fresh air while they are gone, I am sure they haven't done that; they wouldn't bother. I have a special pole made for the high windows, so I can open and close them from my chair alone without any help.

So I wheeled myself in, absolutely certain that the room were empty. I hadn't heard them come home, and believe me: you do hear a rugby team come home when they *do* come home. Like a horde of buffalo, stampeding, drunk, of course, every bloody night.

So I thought the room would be empty, so I opens the door, I rolls in—and there were Jamie, naked, kneeling on the floor, cock in his right and cock in his left, slurping away like the Madonna on an ice cone—two ice cones, and the two rugby players grinning! I caught my finger in the spokes and screamed! Picture the scene, Mr Dedalus! Dear old me in me wonky chair, fingers bleedin'' (were they?) and screamin'' like a stuck pig, Jamie throwing me a look of surprise—anger, for interrupting, too, I suppose.

Then the lads wheel me out, with their hard cocks bouncing up and down next to me—they weren't embarrassed at all! They weren't to be distracted, were they? Went right back in, locked the door.

Later I heard Jamie getting buggered like there was no tomorrow. No, I were not listening at the door, you didn't have to! The whole house could hear!

That's what I wanted to say—Jamie's like that. He has that angel face that makes straight men lose all their . . . whatever it is that keeps them enjoying other men on weekdays.

I don't know what it is. It's charm. A sort of charm that makes them think, perhaps, that it's like being with a girl, or that it doesn't count—I don't know what it is. Such things were unheard of afore, but the last ten years—I swear, people just don't mind any more, or not so much. There's buggery going on everywhere. Boys will be boys, you know, and at the end of the day, a mouth's a mouth and an arse is an arse. And if it's a pretty arse like Jamie's . . . who can blame them.

Look at all the porn, look at all the straight men doing gay porn. Of course it's for money, but if two lads together were really such a disgusting thing, they wouldn't do it, would they? They say twenty-five percent of men, that's one-fourth, have absolutely no problem engaging in sex with the same sex, exclusively or otherwise. Up to forty-percent do it occasionally, now that people are so relaxed. Forty! Take that, you bible-preachers, and stick it up your Sodom. Where will it end, but? Are we headed for ancient Greece? Are we all going to bugger each other until mating time? Can't say I'd mind. If they'd only started sooner. Oh, I were born far too soon.

Oh well, back to the subject: the funniest thing were that the next night, right, they really *were* out, all of them, except in the morning, Jamie came running down to fetch me, brought me up to his room, and showed me two of the lads in his bed, naked, arms wrapped around each other, still half asleep. They'd dossed down there together, all night, after banging—not him, Jamie said— each other!

There you have the credentials of our little B&B, all laid out, black and white, to see: we even turn the straight boys gay, that's how good we are. With a lodger like Jamie, the straightness just evaporates, and don't need no boozing up neither. Oh and it weren't the same two lads as buggered Jamie—one of them was, the other were their team captain, the one who'd carried me up.

I think sometimes that it's not nature or inclination what makes them straight, many of them—it's just peer pressure. They'd be a lot more bi if it weren't for all the reinforcement they needed— from each other. Men are nothing without the acclamation of other men. They can't exist without being adored—they are much, much vainer than women. So they compete over cars and jobs—but mostly, from puberty, over women, because they are such an easy target. And in the process, they completely forget that they could love each other.

Straight men fight over women, I think, when I am really angry at the world. Women are just possessions; they are vessels to deposit their seed, and trophies ... that is all men want with them. Just read Dostoyevsky, Mr Dedalus always said; women are treated like cattle—and treat themselves like cattle, selling themselves to the highest bidder. Can that skirt be any shorter? Bigger boobs to fetch a better price!

But what if you reject that, what if you dislike that treatment of women—what then? You will be called a wuss and a coward and a queer, or politely a 'sensible man,' or idiotically in *Vogue* 'a new man'—but there aren't any new men, the world isn't changing amongst breeders. Women put on make-up and high heels and choose their prey, and men think with their cocks. So if you don't—if you think with your brain instead—your mates will reject you for it, and despise you.

Men only worship warriors. Our pop culture does. Look at the movies which are 'popular'—that idiotic word! That euphemism for shallow—they are all about men who 'use' women. They claim love, they claim to be 'in love,' they claim to have some kind of affection, but it is only possessiveness, it is only the wish to *own.* They love them only to impregnate them (otherwise they'd be just friends, not wives).

Yes, this is changing, and old Dosto is long dead, as is Mr Dedalus, who put all that daft nonsense in my head in the first place, in the hippie days—but it is changing too slowly. The masses are still made of unthinking straight males. Look at the demographics: it's a world made of straight males, that's it. It's a world made of bleedin" breedin" idiots. I get so angry sometimes, so fucking angry at the world!

And then I calm down, or I have a whisky, and I think, it's good times we live in, but. People aren't so afraid any more of finding out who they really are. Even straight men are softening up, and giving things a try, and exploring their . . . options. According to a recent study, forty-eight percent of heterosexual men in Britain like their prostate stimulated. Bum fun's not just for us then, is it?

Thank god the world is changing, and people are waking up. When I think back how it were in my youth, in them good old days of blatant racism and bigotry! All hiding and lying and pretending! They all said they were wild and free—but they really weren't. They were just conservatives with flower garlands; prudes in hippie costumes. It's taken the Internet to bring it all out, I think, although I don't use it much myself. It's taken the computer for all to see how it really is, life; how we really are, behind the masks, and with our trousers down. It's a good thing, I think, that new lack of privacy, that openness. It's made us all more honest.

So, that's us, was us, at the beginning of that summer, before the Slovaks messed with our heads. A strangely quiet but friendly Javier, a despondent Ugandan woman with her own problems and a useless boyfriend, Jamie the big seducer, Philip the banker-john once a month, Tim's sister Mary (she'll drop by later), and Tim and Tim—that's our *ménage*.

And into this family burst two Slovaks, one of whom was so beautifully draped over the aforementioned chair I am looking at now. I can hear him breathing still, when I close my eyes. He had such a rough day, the poor lad.

How'd you feel if you realized suddenly that all you believed in—well not quite all, I mean . . . it were his fault too, weren't it? At least in part.

I thought then that maybe I should leave him there and go to bed. There was nothing I could do for him. Balm on his soul— how? With his sad eyes, those sad eyes. Squirming muscles.

He had to come to terms with it himself. It were as much his own fault as that of Lukáš . . . It were just all so unexpected!

But aye, like a good mother hen clucking over him, in the end, I brought him his tea, and I didn't desert him. I stayed with him all night: his eyes red, the face blotchy and the hair a fair mess. He was still infinitely sexy, of course. I watched him weep, then sob, then finally, at long last, fall asleep.

PART II

We picked up Claudio and Lukáš from the airport. Tim and I both went, maybe because we were a little apprehensive. I'd slept badly the night before, with one of my premonitions of doom. I get them once a month when I get my useless legs in a twist, so I thought nothing of it. I do think it is just basic courtesy to our lodgers, and if we haven't got anything better to do, why not give them a lift, make them feel special, after they sent such a polite mail to reserve a room?

What a sight they were! We recognized them immediately. We didn't have a photo or anything, not even from their online profiles. It was just ... On the whole flight of a hundred people or so, it could only have been them! They were unmistakable.

First of all, they were tall, and young, and beautiful: one dark, one light. Then they were smiling, almost constantly, and touching each other; a hand on the shoulder, a squeeze, a pat.

And they dressed alike! They both wore jeans and T-shirts, and those flat trainers which used to be called Badminton shoes, which are now back in fashion in all sorts of horrid colours. Now, imagine Lukáš wearing pink ones and Claudio's in dark green, then exactly the same jeans. They'd bought them at the same store in America.

We'd be forgiven, I think, if from the first we took them for a gay couple. Partner look, both with a ravaging smile; cute as pie, as Jamie says; T-shirts tighter than the law allowed, and them pink trainers! They had between them one set of luggage: a large and a small suitcase, part of the same set which they shared. The way they behaved around each other, the way they spoke to each other! We didn't understand a word, but we saw it: the love, the connection, the closeness. I had a brief thought that they might be brothers, but then they were coming to stay at our B&B, our gay B&B! I mean, what else was there to assume, naturally, than that they were a gay couple?

So handsome both of them! A wonderful, charming sweet, gay couple from Eastern Europe. Just the type of open-minded, unencumbered young people you admire from afar; meet by

51

chance, maybe; taking pictures by the Scott Monument; read about on the net, as the 'new generation of gays;' the fresh-faced boys you see on talk shows, but, yourself being far too old, never actually meet, and if you do, then with a pinch of awkwardness which precludes real friendship across the age difference; but, after all, the type of young men who frequently stayed with us, so that we recognized them as such. Young gay men who are in no way ashamed of who they are; boys who love openly and unabashedly, who never hide; not a look, not a caress, not a gesture.

That were it, just as they stood by the baggage claim, a gesture. Lukáš reached over to brush some lint from Claudio's shoulder, then his hair. It was a gesture of complete and tender familiarity, the love between parent and child maybe, between lovers only, and never, never ever between straight friends. I sat and watched, and my heart jumped at the sight of this beautiful team. I don't know why, but team, from the onset, seemed an appropriate word. Tim I think was moved too, that such open affection was possible between men. We'd not known anything like it in our youth.

We observed them, as you do strangers; we were fascinated by them. They constantly looked out for each other, one getting the trolley, the other holding the bags. And then their smiles— like a toothpaste commercial! They were such a fresh and happy breeze blowing in from the East. They brought the sun with them, and warmth and hope! We immediately liked them. We thought they were special, trustworthy—and better than us. Better than our spiteful, ashamed generation. Not prejudiced, not narrow-minded, not cowardly. Their English was fine; we could communicate well from the beginning. Bit odd in grammar and saying 'excuse me' a lot, but they'd do fine in our school. It's a good school, you know—enjoys Europe-wide recognition now. I for one am happy that English is the universal language. I could never wrap me head around French or something like Slovak. It sounds so odd when they talk amongst themselves. Cute, but odd.

We spoke to them on the way in, and of course, since all along we assumed that they were a couple, it never even occurred to us to ask. Straight people do it all the time, assume that everybody has a wife and children. So we treated them like gay lovers. One

52

tends to read into other people's behaviour one's own wishes and aspirations, I am very well aware of that, but they truly did seem like a couple. The more so when they told us later what they'd been up to before, all they had done together over the years. (All which is why it came such a shock when Lukáš freaked out a month later over a trifle.)

At the house, Tim gave them a gay map of Edinburgh; they took it dutifully, glanced at it, and said nothing; they thanked us and I guess that settled it, at least in Tim's mind, and in Jamie's, who came down to check them out, if there ever were any doubt. If you are not gay and somebody hands you a map of all the gay pubs, saunas, restaurants, cruising places; a hand-crafted one by Tim the headmaster, a community map that shouted 'welcome to our world, welcome to gay Edinburgh'—wouldn't you scream? Wouldn't you revolt? Would you at least say,

—Oh wow, thanks mate. But you know, we ain't queer. So here's your lovely little map back. I am sure a lot of work went into that. Ha ha. Sorry—we won't have any need for it.

They took it. They looked at it. They saw the rainbow flag and the picture of a muscular torso; they saw the two circles with arrows interlocked, and they read the big Futura typescript; but they said nothing.

No, Mr Dedalus, I am not *that* deluded. Didn't assume naught without proof, I did. I would never have just assumed under other circumstances, but how could one—it were inescapable!

We watched them unpack, showed them how the wi-fi worked, took them out for dinner. We don't speak Slovak, so we didn't understand anything they said in private; but we observed their expressive, open body language, and that were just amazing. It was clear, it was so obvious! Two wonderful, beautiful young men in love!

They constantly did things for each other: one missing a memory stick, the other getting up to fetch it. I brought a bowl of fruit, cut and peeled—some oranges and apples. Lukáš took it, but did not eat. He reached over the pile of cables and computers, and gave it first to Claudio, who looked up, looked into his mate's eyes, smiled, said thank you—all too elaborate, too caring.

Two straight buggers—two men without a deep connection, without love, without the most amazing friendship—would they care so? Would they fuss so over a bowl of fruit? Would there be between them so palpable a kindness?

When only one slice were left, it stayed there, and then (we watched and didn't believe our eyes) Lukáš took it and fed it to his friend. He said something funny, and Claudio laughed, opened his mouth, and in went the apples slice.

Could there be any doubt? It were all settled, and Jamie made sure gay Edinburgh knew it the first night: a hot couple of Slovaks had moved in at the Manor Place B&B! Fucking hot! Like right out of a porn flick!

Then I caught them on the second day: Lukáš reclining on the pile of cushions in the living room, watching a film on his notebook, and Claudio's head on his chest, eyes closed. They didn't move apart when I came in; they weren't ashamed to be caught in such closeness. Even if, as Tim said on the stairs, they didn't know it themselves yet.

Sod the absent kisses. Maybe that weren't done in Slovakia.

We went to bed to the sounds of Mendelssohn's Scottish Symphony from the television, but we weren't watching the programme at all. We just listened to the elating music, I think, each of us with the new arrivals afore our mind's eye. These magnificent young men, so in love.

They had money—there was money, and time, and dedication. They came fully equipped with rucksacks and even a tent, and announced on the third night that they would first do a 'grand tour of Scotland.'

Now, the highland adventures always come at the end of a stay. They are always the result of some familiarity, or being sick of the city, and always involve some planning—some help from Tim and me, or the school. But not the Slovaks.

On the Saturday they landed, on the Monday morning they were gone for two weeks, and we heard not a thing from them. They paid for their room, but they just left the excess luggage there; that too were a surprise.

Young men their age, self-confessedly unemployed, always on

a budget, don't rent a room and then use it to leave a big and a small suitcase. Yet it did not seem to matter to them.

They acted like they had a fair bit of money, like they didn't have to worry about spending an extra hundred here and there—a bit like posh folk, when they talked. Even when we went out and they paid, they did not suggest to split the bill. Students always do, but the Slovaks, surprisingly, were generous from the onset, and easy about money.

—Well, I reckon Eastern Europe has caught up with the rest of the continent, said Tim, no less surprised than I.

Money is always the problem with young lodgers. They have forever too little, and spend it on the wrong things. Too often they can't pay the rent, but they can afford ten drinks in an evening, or to take their lovers to the pictures. Money distorts everything: every relationship, every dealing. It denigrates friendship, it destroys affairs. It makes perfectly sensible young men with perfectly straight teeth look like common whores. For example, just because Philip were a rich banker and gave Jamie some money now and then—too much, we thought, but it wasn't for us to object—Jamie looked like a hustler, even though the true reason Philip came back and Jamie welcomed him was pure animal attraction. They were both hot!

They fucked like beasts. They growled and snarled at each other; they ate each other alive, and Jamie pounded him so hard we feared for the bed. Philip's screams filled the whole house. Without the money exchanged, that strange 'tip' with which Philip made sure that his homosexual escapades remained a business transaction rather than a confirmation of his true desires, they made it all seem contrite, and base. Money matters, you see, too much. Money made my life a mess, because I turned my back on it, and money makes everybody's life a misery. We never discover our true selves, our honest natures, because they are always hidden under the notes, beneath mountains of meaningless cash. Tim would say we've made money itself important, and erotic—a tool to deceive and hide, and to hurt others.

Not so with Claudio and Lukáš. They didn't seem to care; they didn't seem to notice it. Money makes life a mess for those who expect too much from it. Claudio and Lukáš had no expectations,

55

and then I saw that it were true, much later. They indeed expected nothing more from life, that all that was important for them was the here and now—and their love. Only I were wrong. It weren't the here and now—it were the past that concerned them. A terrible past.

Anyroad, posh or not, they were gone for two weeks, and we were left wondering what exactly was going off between the lads. Because you see, it still bothered us. They didn't kiss, they didn't hug, they didn't quite behave like lovers either. They made none of the gay comments.

They seemed in love, yet they didn't feel like *one of us.* So we wondered. And of course the younger lads like Jamie wondered if one or both of them were available!

The confusion were perfect in every detail. One could see it even as they left on Monday morning, as they stood in their room to pack. What would you expect two young men to do? Each occupied with his own bag, each in charge of his own life, each busy counting his own knickers—but not them. He made a list, Claudio did, and Lukáš checked it against the contents of the rucksack. All their lives for two weeks contained in their one large red rucksack. There was a jointedness, a union there that was not easily overlooked. It was more even than I have seen with most couples.

I had a thought that maybe they had some kind of military history together, when I saw them pack. That they had fought side-by-side, and seen death and—but where? They were much too young for any war to have moulded them, to have forged them into one. There were a dependence that seemed warm and cosy, and a happy circumstance. I've worked in TV programming for thirty years and not once have I seen such intimacy between men portrayed. It were truly unique—it shone through everything they did together.

—Our gay boys gone? said Javier, just come home from work the day the Slovaks had left.

He'd met them briefly, and drawn all the same conclusions: gay couple, hot as hell.

—The blond one's quite a looker. The other one—Javier raised his arm, held the palm level, then shook it—so, so. But together— yummy! I say!

I smiled graciously. 'I say' was Javier's perennial imitation of Englishness. Only he said it with a Spanish accent.

—They might be something else.

—Like what?

He stood there surprised. Apparently it hadn't occurred to him yet.

—They might be related.

—Related? What, you mean brothers or cousins? No!

He had his work clothes on and was itching to get out.

—Javier?

—Yes, mama?

Only he were allowed to call me that.

—Javier, can you keep an eye on them, please.

—What, me? What for? They are lovers ... what do ... ¿por qué?

—Keep an eye on them, please, when they get back.

Involuntarily, I looked up—a whole floor higher.

—Oh, you mean Jamie? You mean Jamie will try ... He'll seduce one of them. Or both!

He laughed dismissively, then shrugged his shoulders.

—Cou'be. I would take the blond one. I guess Jamie too. You too worried, mama. First you tell me to watch Jamie—nobody can watch Jamie, nobody can control him. Now you want me check on the Slovaks. I tell you something ...

He came over, bent down, kissed me on the cheek.

—You *musstop* worry about your boys. They grown up. Jamie's a man. He is responsible for his own actions. They Slovak are how old?

—Twenty-six, seven.

—You see? What you want look after them? They are adults. They are ...

—I know, I know ... I know! But from where I am standing— sitting; from my older perspective ...

— ... we all just boys. Incompetent, loud, always horny.

I nodded.

—I tell you about horny, mama Tim. I will get laid tonight!

—With whom? Have you met someone?

He patted his trouser pocket, then pulled out a USB stick.

—I got new download.

—You have a date with a porno?

—Of course. So much more handsome. So much less trouble. I got rendezvous with my five friends.

He raised his right hand and wiggled his fingers. I didn't smile—I couldn't. The way my boys spoke about sex just for fun, about being alone . . . about jerking off. But Javier gave me another jagged kiss, and ran up the stairs; seconds later I heard the door slam shut.

That's it then, I thought. Alone again. Back then I weren't such an insomniac, but that's how the drinking started. I were alone, worried, sulking. Tim were in Oxford at a conference, Jamie were banging some boy in his room (yes, oh, yes, oh wow, oh come on, fuck my ass . . .). I turned up the volume on the television. *The story of life begins* . . . Yes, Mr Attenborough. We know. It don't begin up Jamie's roomy arse now, does it? Or maybe it does? Should I try vodka for a change? They sell Absolut now: buy one get one free. Jamie had a one-night stand with an Absolut sales agent. Tall, blond Swedish kid. They fucked in the living room, talking all the way through: Absolut Cock! Absolut Arse! Absolut Buttlicker—and giggling like girls when Jamie shot over the lad's face.

That always did strike me as unfair, how Jamie could have so much fun during sex. When I had it, back in the days, it were always so much more serious. One *did* it—it was important. It were a statement, the end of an effort, the main event—not recreation, not a snack in-between. One concentrated on it. One didn't jump up, as Jamie did now, playfully, and say,

—Wait! I'll put on a video! Let's try that position! Can you fuck me like that? Where's your phone—can you film me while you bang me?

Ratatam, ratata, Mr Dedalus. Can you believe how times have changed? We were still the forbidden couple, thee and I, back in them days, man plus man, old plus young! There were laws

58

against us, and our sort of frolicking. Now people fuck in the street and get married—or at least partnered. Can you believe how it's all changed?

Every man turning fifty any time in the last sixty years must tell himself: Oh god, I was born too soon; look what they are doing now! Next thing you know, we'll have full equality, and a gay prime minister. Well, we're halfway there anyroad.

Voracious, that's the word Mr Dedalus; that's what you were. You were rich and voracious; you couldn't get enough of anything.

Maybe that's why I left you. On account—as you liked to say with your imitation of a southern drawl—on account of your voraciousness. Your voraciality—voracity.

When I am drunk, making up words is fun: they make sense, they express summat. When I am sober, they seem silly.

That book you read to me on the sun deck of that ship—he must have been drunk half the time, that writer. Irish, was he? Most people prefer books that have no soul. I like the wild ones. What I have read since you left me—I left you, pardon; *I left you*—not a single one. No' a fuckin' single book.

I keep telling Tim I've read them all, when he asks, but I haven't. I can honestly say that my only intellectual occupation is to sneak out of bed and sit here in my chair, watching the neighbour's mutt shite all over the pavement. Mr Tallisker is my witness. Oh, it's Mr Glenmorangie tonight, I begs your pardon.

All the lovers . . . that have gone before! One bottle, two bottle, three bottle. How's it go? One bottle of summat, two bottle of summat, three sailors pissing on deck, four sailors pissing on each other, Jamie pissing on the boy upstairs.

Yes, they've moved to the bathroom, the shower is running. What Jamie doesn't realize (or does realize, and I don't realize he realizes) is that there's an airing duct that leads through the whole *auld hoose,* and starts right above my head, in the corner there—so you can hear all the voices, and the one-night stand kneeling and saying,

—Yeah, piss on me, piss on me!

I open the window a little and shout,

—Good evening, Mrs Erskine! Lovely evening, innit?

She can't hear me, deaf old cow. The dog barks back.

59

—Oh yeah (gargling sound), oh yeah—fuckin' give me that piss!

When Claudio and Lukáš returned from their grand tour of the Highlands, they were sun-burnt and weathered; they looked years older and thinner.

Sun in Scotland in the early summer, yes, and up and down the heather and bracken, and climbing Ben Nevis, we supposed. They had arrived hearty and healthy, if somewhat pale, at the airport, and now they returned from the Highlands as if they had been to a Club Med for a year—a Club Med without food, by all appearances. It were shocking, the change. Not emaciated, not sick, but that were the first impression. Then you looked closely, and saw that all the cute plumpness in Claudio's face were gone, and Lukáš, even though less tanned, looked like a bloody fashion model, shed half a stone at least.

—Hot Slovak couple back from the Highlands, Jamie announced in the bars, looking even hotter than before! Lean and hot! Get your cocks ready, boys!

I were a bit worried initially, clucking hen and all, but they were all happy faces, and then I realized that they had conquered something. That is how they looked, like mountaineers having scaled some impossible peak. We weren't to know, were we, that they did that all the time? They went everywhere and challenged themselves, climbed every mountain, swam in lakes, hiked in the jungle—it was their life, what kept them in synch. It added another dimension to our guesswork.

We city dwellers and couch potatoes, creatures of seclusion in dark bars and stuffy rooms—an afternoon out on the heath was the most we came to nature. Two hours in the gym was as much exercise as Jamie took, plus his occasional cycling and running. But here were two rugged adventurers, two hardened explorers. They were at home in nature, they loved it. (We can be together without having to talk much—we both don't like talking, is what Lukáš said much later, when so many things had become so much clearer, when the shroud had been lifted.)

They had wanted to see the Highlands, they had said, so we all imagined them driving a car around and looking at the scenery. Now we were wondering if they had driven anywhere, or just walked the distance. They had done everything, and been everywhere, which in their estimation, Tim and I thought, was just that: a tour round Scotland. To us, it seemed like Livingston had returned from Africa! Salute our victorious explorers! Magnificent men! Good lads! Queen and country.

Well, I suppose not.

So their tales began the night of their return, in the drawing room, all assembled and looking at the pictures on their notebooks. I had made tea for everyone and added rum, and we had finger-food left over from one of Javier's catering dos: little breads with roast beef and radish, shrimps and egg, like a regular dinner party. There were even some bubbly.

They had, for starters, crossed the bridge on foot; walked, in fact, in the first two days all the way to Inverkeithing and even farther. By the water, along the shore they insisted. Always by the water! Where? By the railway line more likely, and was there a place in Scotland where you did not see water? And only from there hitch-hiked to St. Andrews, with a girl—a woman, Claudio interjected—a girl, Lukáš insisted, and began to describe her.

There were pictures of them, on the bridge, gesticulating. Being general silly-buggers; playing dangerously, extending limbs over the railing; grinning, laughing, standing legs apart over the rails at Kirkcaldy; and next to a rusting boat, smiling; then again next to a coil, a tangled pile of weathered rope like teenagers. And they looked it: wild, high-spirited, jaunty young men, still paler in those pictures, still fleshier in their cheeks. One could not conceive of them as grown men—mere lads, out on an adventure, their smiles too broad to be true! They said they'd planned all this for a long time. They said it had been their dream.

Yet there were something odd about the pictures, and I didn't see it immediately. There were one with a twig in Lukáš's mouth, their arms around each other's waists, next to tracks in an unnamed town. (It must be Burntisland, because you can see Edinburgh across the water, and the train station is right there.) They said they made it that far, and from there took the train to Kirkcaldy.

Could they have really walked that far? There were gaps in their narration, and pictures in the wrong order, and their English . . .

Jamie looked suspicious, later too, when they said they had run around Cromarty Firth in a morning, just for fun, to relax. Relax on a trip that consisted of nothing but walking and hiking and swimming and more walking and climbing and . . . Run for fun, like city folk? Daft!

Surely, I thought, they were bragging, exaggerating, with everything—but not to impress us, but for their own benefit.

Their stories were intertwined, reinforcing each other. One started, the other continued; one walked, the other ran; one hiked, the other climbed; one had a look at the ruins, the other stood there for an afternoon in contemplation.

They never boasted against each other; it were never a race for the top—it were always a we, an escalating we with some distant goal. They tried to convince, it seemed—but that I only thought much, much later—each other of their happiness, of the intensity of the adventure. As if living it were not enough, they relived it in each other's magnifications.

They reminded me of that children's game, where you put one hand on top of the other, everyone in a circle, until something happens, but I don't know what. You shout something, and then the lowermost hand must withdraw; this is how they appeared. Exaggeration maybe, to make their own adventures more real, more believable to themselves—to make the memory last?

And yet, their bodies proved that they had truly exerted themselves. Their bodies were proof that all might be true, that at least they had been there, done that—much more I imagine than your average bugger tries on a trip round the North.

Then came the pictures of towns, of ruins, of narrow streets; of patrician houses too which they could not believe to exist there. It were St. Andrews, of course, old and posh and imposing. Did they think Scotland were all huts and hovels?

Lukáš said, —Like London almost, so big houses.

They had slept in a room with seven others, in a hostel, and there were a picture of all of them—three Asian faces, and the curious look of what they said were a Russian lad—staring straight at Claudio while the picture were taken. I looked long at the face, the plum, broad face of that Russian, until I knew what that look was: pride. The man in the photograph was proud to be standing next to Claudio. Because Claudio was so handsome? Because the Russian too had recognized him?

The more weight he lost, the more he tanned, the more familiar he looked. The Russian brimmed with pride as if he'd his picture taken with some famous film star. In the end it were so obvious! How could we have missed it?

Nobody mentioned the school, the university, the royals— only we British seem to care about where they learn their table manners. There were only two pictures of the church, but some of aircraft, and they had taken an extra trip to see the base.

—But it was rain then, a whole day, and we stay in.

There was mention of Claudio reading and Lukáš disappearing for an evening. They exchanged looks and a few sentences in Slovak, then laughed, and Claudio gave him the thumbs-up.

We asked what it were about, but they only said it were naught important, nothing to interest us, and Lukáš went a bit red in the face. Jamie glanced at me knowingly, it seemed, but what could he know? He only imagined things! I did too: a threesome, with the Russian maybe, or had Lukáš scored on his own?

I asked him to go back, show me the picture of the Russian again, but Jamie made a joke, and they clicked forward instead. I'd wanted to make sure that I had been right. There was something odd in the Russian's expression, something unnatural for such a setting.

They went on to Dundee, Aberdeen, then in a bus straight across and through the national park to Inverness. There were pictures of them standing on a stone, leaning away from each other, fingers of two hands locked. And pictures of them pissing in front of a signpost, but looking back into the camera—they skipped quickly over that one. They got off at some place—Grantown, Tim reckoned, but didn't interrupt—and tasted whisky.

There were a picture of the owner of a shop, blind drunk at three in the afternoon. Again, it were always 'we did this,' and 'we did that,' and never 'here is Lukáš in Grantown,' or 'that's Claudio at the church of . . . ' The places, the actual names did not matter. Their travel was not one of tourism. They were not sight-seers.

63

They were not in that stage where one follows blindly a guidebook and takes delight in learning things about the places one visits, like Tim and I do. Well, like Tim does, and I listen. They were in each picture just happy to be there, not caring much where *there* was.

I had a thought then, that they were happy to be away from home, just glad to be away together—and yet the pictures weren't those of a honeymooning couple. They weren't pictures which said: oh, look at us in Naples, so in love.

Until then they had regretted, they said, not taking a rental car, but in that whisky shop it became clear that one could not tour Scotland driving. One would have to miss out on so much excitement, like being gorgeous, young, and drunk in the early afternoon. I looked up on the shelf while they talked, and was tempted, but I didn't let on.

There were more pictures, an endless sequence as they went through Inverness and stayed in a B&B Tim and I knew well. It had Tudor lilies on everything from the carpet, wallpaper, to the dishes in the dining room; even the flower bed and the mailbox had lilies. It had been run too by a gay couple. One of them had recently died; we had received a post card. There's the Slovaks in another gay hotel! It didn't seem odd then, but later, as I thought back, I puzzled over it.

A man interrupted us with a message from the school; he goes round to all the 'affiliates' and posts notices. Only in our case, he hands it to me, I think because he reckons I can't see the notice on the board—or because we give him whisky.

There was an excuse now, after all this talk of Spey, and Tim fetched the bottle. We all had one—Claudio with a strained face, as if remembering something from their trip. It went through my mind then, in a flash I saw it: they had drunk a lot and fallen over each other in the tent, eager cocks rubbing against each other. Had they been sleeping in a tent that night?

Does it matter, Mr. Dedalus? Here's to your health! One minute I think they are already a gay couple, the next I imagine them falling in love, over and over again.

The story of their highland adventure was such an occasion: at the church, by the sea, in the heather and bracken. I saw them fall in love over and over again, discovering themselves, which were of course wrong—as you rightly remind me, Mr Dedalus—because they have been together for years.

Whatever intimacy there were between those lads, it weren't new, it weren't wild, it weren't—it wasn't! I know, I know, it wasn't—the sort that turns my fantasies into scripts for porn movies.

Do porn movies have scripts?

Oh, let's have another one Mr Dedalus! On the house! Slangevar! Tim taught them that word that evening, and then 'slecher,' when he spilled a drink over Claudio's arm, an hour later, and some more words they could never use in polite society.

Tim, my dear husband, was quite taken in by all the talk of the Highlands, delivered so enticingly by such handsome faces and lean bodies, so unconsciously graceful, with such friendly smiles and imposing gestures.

I imagined them leaving the booze shop with their hands down each other's trousers, palms on each other's bums, hard-ons, uncontrollable lust. They seemed such as they returned from the wilderness north: lusty, horny, full of mountaineering testosterone, and I could not conceive of them as anything else but lovers who fucked each other across the moors at every opportunity.

There's a tree—I'll suck your cock.

There's a boat—let's do it on deck; and by the river, and by the loch.

It were all in my head of course, as I listened to them talk.

They went to Loch Ness, and said they walked around it in two days, sleeping by the shore for a night, in their tent, hoping to catch the monster. In my mind, I added up the extra days they said they spent as extensions of their two-week journey: it would have taken a month to complete if it all were true. But I guess much can be done in evenings, mornings, over noon.

They weren't like us. They didn't have four-hour dinners or drive to Dunbar for a spot of lunch; they hiked and walked and ate sandwiches on the way.

So yes, it was possible—but it was so remote from our own experience, this incredible activity. When Tim and I went on vacation—not only now, when we were younger, too—we saw four or five things and spent the remainder sitting about, having drinks and gossiping. What Claudio and Lukáš did in two weeks would take us a year to achieve, or longer.

They were nature lovers with heart and soul, behaved too as if the outdoors had just been made for them. I should have been offended; I usually am when I see on TV the people who play golf, race cars, raft down rivers or drill picks into rock faces. It all seems to be primeval, this need to impress one's lack of achievement onto nature, to destroy and form, to conquer and subdue—I have more respect for things natural, I stand more and watch, and observe. But maybe I too would ascend and traverse and scale and cross if I could get out of this fucking chair!

They were such scalers and crossers, such ascenders and traversers! They saw a lake and had to walk around it (run, in fact, half the distance) or swim through it, and spend an extra day just to complete the circuit. They saw a mountain—a little later, Ben Nevis—and had to climb it.

Yet as I had another whisky and Mr Dedalus returned to stay for the night, and Tim told me to stop now or be sleepy (and drunk) all afternoon, I imagined them hiking around Loch Ness, chasing each other's snakes, in the water (wasn't it freezing!) and certainly in the tent at night. I saw them making love to each other at every opportunity—they were so virile, so mobile, so impossibly young and carefree.

They had enough with one drink, and we cleared the empty plates, but there were more pictures of them on the Isle of Skye. They had loved it, they said, standing at 'the end of the world.' The weather had been ominous, with the deep hanging clouds. But isn't the sky always hanging low in Scotland, isn't it always an oppressive sky? They didn't think so. They thought it was different and glorious, that it enveloped one if one let it, that it was 'spectacular' (the word did not come easy to their tongues, Tim taught them in syllables). They thought one could sleep outside, almost. They did again, in their tent, at Uig, with their heads poking out, looking into the star-filled sky.

I imagined them kissing for hours, entirely oblivious to the real stars, and only seeing those in each other eyes.

Yes, Mr Dedalus, I hear you! Stop imagining things! But when I were young, when I could still walk, when I were a lad like them—what would I have done with a mate like Claudio, a friend like Lukáš? How could one not be in love with either one of them? Shut up and let me tell my story. Back into your grave!

Can it be helped that I am guilty of lusting after them both—fly open, cock out? In these constellations, to sum up, for the benefit of those who can't be with us tonight (that's you, Dedalus, old fag): Lukáš and Claudio, always lovers, always gentle, always sweet with each other. A lot of kissing, of tender embrace, of lowering their trousers slowly and discovering each other's bodies. Of little nothings whispered in their ears; of hands grabbing pricks firmly, but with care; of buttocks not ravaged nor devoured, but contemplated and worshipped; of fingers rubbing gently spittle in and opening him up, so as not to hurt. Then of cocks, sliding in with all the circumspection such deserves, with all the gentle motion, never to offend, rip, snag, tear, wound. Then sliding in and out not yet in wild, obliterating passion, but with sentimental fray—am I hurting you? Is it too fast, too long, too big? Can you take it? Do you want me inside you? Tell me, honestly, my lover—do you want me inside you? And from the first, I have imagined Lukáš fucking Claudio, and never once the other way round.

Later, with more alcohol, after longer pauses, I envisaged them in the claws of Jamie, under his spell. In his lair: both naked, spanked; their buttocks red, their cocks hard and dripping; their mouths kissing, wet, spitting into each other; and Jamie—brutal, hard, broad-shouldered Jamie—standing behind them, all blond muscle from across the pond, wild and untamed, saying,

—Now which one of you little fairies shall I fuck first?

More pictures were shown. I almost dropped my whisky glass. Jamie suddenly looked at me as if he knew I were fantasizing about him too. Am I guilty of turning them into objects of my desire—when desire is all I have left? Is there guilt in wanting, and what is guilt, I ask; and again: why can I only have these thoughts—so beautiful, so eloquent—alone at night? Do you hear me, Mr Dedalus? What have you turned me into? A night-walker, a darkness-stalker, a debaucher (not much debauching going on though, is there?) of young Slovaks. I felt a sudden faintness, a premonition—a dark shadow passing through the room. Then it were gone, and I were back, cursing myself, listening, glowering—and trying to sit up straight in my wheelchair.

There was a picture of them in swimming trunks, about to lunge into a lake. The water looked freezing. I had another vision then, a quick and fearless one: that I had seen Claudio naked afore! That his body was known to me, somehow—I was sure of it now.

In the remotest corner of my brain, Claudio and I had been together, I knew. He had been naked, and I had been, too. But where? How? It were just one of these faces, I told myself, for how on earth could I have met him before? What was he to me? A lodger come from afar, a young lad from another world? And yet—I stared at the handsome muscular figure standing on a stone, his arms wrapped around himself, shivering—what had they expected?—and I knew that I had seen that body before.

—Tea anyone? said Tim and we paused.

I were miles away still when the tea come. And I weren't alone with my imaginings. Javier came home from work, joined us, downed a large double and refilled his glass, cursing his boss and the weather (it had again started to rain), then sat down. We listened again with open eyes, with eager eyes, with hands—in Jamie's case, twice—on our cocks. But not too obvious, because we just weren't sure. Even when they talked longer in their broken English, one didn't get the impression of listening to gay lads. There was something lacking, some flippancy: the snide remarks, the irony, the exaggerated hand-gestures, the rolling of the eyes. It weren't there. Have you ever heard gays speak of holidays, of adventure, and not mention a man—somewhere? A landlord's son? A post man? A farmer? That hunk in Sitges, that gorgeous boy in a Barcelona night club, that young guy they saw on the train to Paris? Some irrelevant detail, irrelevant to the story, but of course, not irrelevant to them (to us!) to spice things up.

They never commented at all on the people they had met.

With the exception of the girl-woman who gave them a lift, and the proprietor of the whisky den, there were no other people in their adventure. There certainly were no men, no muscular deckhand on the ferry, no waiter with dreamy eyes, no Canadian hiker with a sexy beard. If it were Jamie, we would have seen a series of men he had met on the road; but with the Slovaks it were always and everywhere exclusively them, just the two boys. That is what made them so un-gay: their quiet privacy as a couple.

Javier listened, and agreed I think, and saw it much sooner and clearer than I did. It was in the photographs. Tim was too enchanted to see it; Jamie only thought about them wrestling naked or fucking under the stars of Skye. We were sat round the fire in the living room, and listened to the Slovaks recount their adventures, and couldn't help but think we were listening to a honeymoon. Everything was we—we this, we that—and never he this and I that. They did everything together! And yet, there was nothing gay about them when they spoke. Neither was there the usual brutality of straight men: the mention of death, sport, killing, racing.

Then, slowly, I broke through the fog. In two weeks, and the account thereof, there were not a single separation; as they showed the pictures again (for Javier's benefit we went back to Kirkcaldy; it were after midnight, but nobody wanted them to stop), then I saw it—exactly the instant Javier noticed it too, but he had only seen them for minutes. I had watched a hundred pictures for hours now. I knew Javier had understood it immediately, because he gave me that look, but he didn't say it out loud. As the images of Fort William and Ben Nevis came on screen, when they showed the series of pictures of their climb—they had taken the longest, most arduous route up—I saw it too, and noticed Javier looking at me. And then even Jamie started up, turned to me with watery, shocked eyes, and I made a sign not to speak. It were so clear in his expression, that he had clocked it—we knew now; only Tim remained in the dark.

He were too entranced, too mesmerized. Tim looked not just at the boys, but also at nature, because he would be there—he would want to be outdoors, and on the mountain, and by that sea—if it weren't such a bother to either leave me at home or take me along. Tim were the only one in the end who didn't catch

69

on; who didn't see that there were two, three hundred pictures, and not a single one of them showed either Claudio or Lukáš, or either one with someone else, alone. There were no 'Claudio with a guy we met at . . . ' or a 'Lukáš and the captain of the ferry.' They were always together, in each picture. Asking strangers to take them, I imagined, but then there came one image where Claudio's face was blurred. Lukáš said,

—You can delete that, and Claudio answered,

—Yes, I setting automatic wrong.

That explained it. Tim looked at me, and I at him, and then he too saw the light. We were thinking the exact same thing: two weeks of trekking and hiking and climbing and even rowing (there were pictures of them in a boat) and they had only taken shots of themselves, always of the pair, and as they talked, they said 'there is us at . . . ' and 'this is we climbing . . . ' and 'this is we in tent.' There were many of those, both of them at rest, after an active day, lying next to each other, even leaning against each other. Show me two straight boys who take pictures of themselves together, all the time! On the top of Ben Nevis were the cutest. Lukáš supporting himself against a stone structure: a funeral pyre I joked; some kind of altar, said Javier almost out the door; a summit shelter merely, said Tim, who I assume has been there— in any case, a pile of rocks. And to his right was Claudio, appearing shorter and weaker than he really is, and his head on tall Lukáš's shoulder, in a curious expression that said, 'he's brought me up here; he's my rock, I can lean on him.' It spoke volumes to us, that picture, but Claudio took away all the magic when he exclaimed bashfully,

—Oh I was so tired after climb! It were so long climb!

—It was! Not 'were,' roared Tim, uncharacteristically, then at me, —You are teaching them bad English! You must be more careful!

We knew a little more now about them, about their relationship, but what did we know? That they were a gay couple who didn't behave at all like a gay couple? That they were a straight couple who acted gay, did everything together, took always pictures of themselves, never apart, seemed to reaffirm constantly that they

70

were a we, and not two mates merely.

How could two straight friends seem so entangled, so dependant on each other, so clearly in love? How could a gay couple seem so straight? It was an entirely new observation. They were in a limbo between our world, and the world of straight people—and if one is your hell, and the other your heaven, they were in purgatory. That evening the word came into my head: purgatory. I had no idea how close to the truth I was with it.

They had returned via Glasgow. They had stopped to visit a friend, they said, but there were no pictures of him or her and we didn't know who their friend was and we never found out.

We were all curious, for it were the only mention of them relating to an outsider. Did they have gay buddies in Glasgow? Did they have family there, school pals? They hitched a ride in a van and suddenly Tim said they shouldn't be doing that (he had said nothing earlier), that it were dangerous.

—You shouldn't do that, travel with strangers, it's not safe here in Scotland, he reprimanded them. In my mind I saw the newspaper headlines: Slovak gay couple murdered in Fife. Why Fife exactly, I don't know; it should have been Stirling at most, or that stop on the motorway where they had found the girl dismembered a few years back. Also that Tim should be so concerned was odd. They were two tall, brawny lads. What could happen to them?

Presently we were restless and distraught, and it seemed that everybody wanted to leave.

We had expected the evening to clear things up, to make things known, to bring us closer and to lift veils; to make them part of our *auld hoose*, of our cabinet of homo curios. But they were only farther away now, in the strangest limbo. We understood nothing. We observed. We smiled, but too tightly, maybe too obsessively, too nosily, and somehow, we did not bond. Not the way you'd expect to bond with a gay couple. The usual kinship based on erotic banter and shared experiences were lacking entirely.

We dispersed a while after midnight, the fact alone that everybody *wanted* to turn in sign enough that summat were oddly amiss. A night like this should have ended in innuendo, in Jamie's attempt to get one of them off to bed—or both—or at

71

least inquire into their sex life.

I mean, two weeks on the road!

But there were nothing, and it seemed everyone was glad to get away from them. Tim and I went to bed, and Javier met us on the stairs. He had changed his clothes to go out dancing, he said, but we knew he were more likely to go to the park. He likes the anonymity there, the darkness, the wild desires, and the smell of jasmine. I told him to be careful, then listened, waiting for Jamie. Sure enough he were next—out the door the flighty bird, another night searching for adventure. I rolled back to turn off the lights and stared at where we all had sat, unable to see much except for shadows, outlines, questions lingering over the scene and still a thick fog.

We brushed our teeth together, Tim and I, in silence; and then in bed we lay next to each other, arms folded, staring at the ceiling, none of us reading or speaking a word, until Tim said,

—Isn't it romantic, the two boys?

—Yes, I said, so young and handsome and in love . . .

I didn't want to talk about my doubts, and that I were no wiser, that I didn't know what bugged me. I wanted to keep imagining them as a gay couple, even though deep down I knew already that they weren't. I wanted to be with them in their tent on the heath. I wanted to touch them. I wanted them to be real and on my side of the fence. I wanted to know them.

—Are you so sure they are in love?

—They must be, Tim, I said, with all my feigned conviction. They must be. Don't you listen to them talk? They are . . .

—Yes I know.

— . . . such a perfect couple. Such a romantic couple, two young men. Claudio's fit like a butcher's dog. Both are . . . so fit and healthy. Did you see the colour of their skin? Did you see how tanned and lean they are?

It seemed a perfectly good argument, to focus on their skin, rather than on their curious, inexplicable relationship. I didn't want to brood.

My husband grunted. I said loud, louder than needed, to drive away my doubts,

—Can you imagine them *not* making love after a day of climbing,

72

hiking, lying next to each other in the tent—it's impossible. The way they talk ... their youthful bodies ... They were made for loving each other, they were made for ...

— ... outdoor romance! I think you are getting carried away.

—Yes, yes, I said, but honestly ... I turned to Tim, painfully aware of my broken body and his old limbs, letting my eyes rest on his white mane.

—Be honest, Tim, don't you find them hopelessly romantic? Don't you think they are just like a couple in a trashy romance? They go so well together, so perfectly! The sweetest, softest, simplest, manliest men you have ever met, and watch how they treat each other! It's ... it's unreal!

He gave me a kiss. A kiss to say, yes, darling, but we are romantic too; and once we were young; and in any case you are spinning stories around every young man you fancy and baby you shouldn't get too excited because—and this he said out loud,

—I think there is something wrong though.

—What do you mean?

—There is something wrong about their relationship. Something's off.

We fell quiet. I was almost asleep. Suddenly Tim's voice was in my ear again,

—They touch each other like brothers, not lovers. I don't think they are in love. It might even be the opposite.

I stared at the ceiling, into the swollen darkness. My lust and curiosity were abruptly gone, my excitement evaporated. I felt empty inside. The opposite?

After their return from the land of the kilt and the caber, Claudio disappeared for two days to 'do something for his uncle.' On Thursday, just in time for instruction at school, he were back. He said nothing about that trip—not a word.

That Friday Jamie stayed in. Tim and I were in the living room reading when he came in. It were oft like this back then: he would take a nap around seven, eight, then rise around eleven, shower, dress up for a night on the town, looking like a million pounds, then come to us, say 'how do I look?'—his last, rather unnecessary boost of confidence—and then disappear out into the night after

73

receiving our adoring compliments.

He was different now. He came in with his hair ruffled and wearing a dirty T-shirt. He stopped in the door, looking at me, at Tim.

—Where are the Slovak boys?

We said we didn't know.

—Not going out tonight Jamie?

—Nah!

And then he joined us, for the first time in months on a Friday night. He seemed subdued and content. He sat down with the e-reader the museum had given him, and read.

—I've just discovered that I have a mind! I'll be reading lots more now, and stay in more.

Tim frowned, then murmured,

—What's going on?

I think we both thought he were having us on, but then Jamie sat quietly, concentrating on the text except for a few glances left and right, and out the window, and towards the door always; and I were baffled until I realized he was waiting for them. He wanted them back. We had so quickly become used to observing their every movement that our lives seemed empty and without purpose when we could not. I felt the same.

—I think they've gone out for the night. They left at eight, but didn't say . . .

Jamie said,

—Who?

But it were affected, his answer. He knew very well who I was talking about. He went back to read his book, and suddenly he looked up and said,

—You know I saw them yesterday? Lukáš was drying Claudio's hair!

He had not been reading at all. Like me he were thinking of them constantly.

—Drying his hair?

—Like girlfriends. Like sisters. Claudio sat on the bed, and Lukáš was towelling his friend's hair.

—So?

—So? It's a bit intimate for two guys who are apparently

74

straight.

—Don't forget they've grown up together.

—Well, yeah. But it still—it feels a bit weird.

And that was it. But I could see by his wandering eyes that once again he weren't really concentrating on his reading. He were mesmerized by the Slovaks as much as I were.

An hour later, Tim and I about ready to doss down, we heard the front door. Javier burst into the room, looked towards the fire, nodded to Jamie, stared at an empty space next to me on the sofa, then shrugged.

—Slovak boys no here? Ah well, *buenas noches* everybody, he sang and then ran up the stairs afore any of us could react.

—What's up with him? said Jamie, not really expecting an answer.

Aye, what's up with us, I thought. We just sat there, together, but there was an awkwardness, an emptiness inside us, and a sense of anticipation. Something was coming. I knew something was up.

Tim went to bed, and Jamie left five minutes after, saying to me,

—It's Fitzgerald.

I gave him a blank stare.

—The quote. 'I've just discovered that I have a mind!' It's F. Scott Fitzgerald.

He smiled broadly and sauntered out with the confidence of someone who'd just won a battle.

And as usual I were alone again. I put down the magazine I had been holding and breathed in the silence and the cold (the fire was low) and felt them: the portents of change. That's from a book too, Mr Dedalus—your book. One of the few things I remember. The portents of change. An omen! All right, Mr Dedalus, enough already with the suspense.

But Mr Dedalus weren't there that night, and neither was Mr Macallan. Shite and onions! What a night of succumbulation!

It seemed wrong to drink. I was waiting for something. I had to be alert, I thought, for when it arrived. What it was, I could not grasp. It was an idea more than an event, but that was the beginning. From that day on—no, from the evening of pictures—everyone in our *auld hoose* started behaving strangely. The two Slovaks kept us all enthralled, and for two months that summer, everything revolved around them, all the time.

Aleysha, the only lass in our circle apart from Mary, laughed at us. She stopped by the next morning to pick up records from her room, announcing that she would still pay rent for another month, that she would stay here most nights because they hadn't found a place to live, that in fact, she may not want to live with her floozie, who was erratic, depressed. When I told her about the guessing game, she came alive.

—That's ridiculous! she screamed, spilling her coffee onto her blouse. That's ridiculous. Why are all-you obsessed with it? What does it matter? All you gays are so obsessed with it! Just because all-you are like that, it doesn't mean all-us are! You are obsessed; all-you should leave them alone!

Of course, she had a point, I thought when she borrowed the vacuum and went upstairs. What did it matter? And yet it were a nagging question.

I am being honest, brutally honest, when I say it wouldn't have mattered if they hadn't been so adorable; one always wonders more about the handsome people. If they had been bland, withdrawn, boring, ugly even, yes, then I am sure we wouldn't have tried so desperately. But they were such a delight to watch, so engrossing, so endearing. One wanted to catch them *in flagrante*; one was tempted to spy on them at all hours.

Like the captivating presence of a very handsome student in a classroom when you are a teacher; like the colleague at the office who you dream of at night, but are not allowed to fall in love with; like a friend's partner you fancy, but can't touch. They were temptation, omnipresent. Yet I didn't want them for myself, neither one of them—I just wanted them together. I wanted confirmation that their love was true and pure and gay and joyful and all it is supposed to be in a trashy romance. I just wanted to see, to bear witness. Maybe, aye, we also wanted to know (I knew I was not alone) if we had a chance. No, that's wrong. I, Tim, we would never have a chance. Jamie, maybe; or Javier, but he was too old. So Jamie, yes—maybe all I was waiting for was whether Jamie would be able to seduce them. I don't know.

Aleysha saw right through me but, and that's why she laughed so hard, because she weren't affected at all. She had enough on her plate with the baby and her weirdie boyfriend. Did she want him as a father? She didn't know. Did he want to be a father to the baby? She thought yes; but then she had caught him with another man, and even though this was the UK, something inside her, she said, something 'African, and mystical, all-you cannot understand' told her that her son shouldn't be brought up by a gay man.

I should have been offended, or eager to convince her otherwise, but I just didn't have the energy.

It had always bothered me that she didn't confide in any of us; that she seemed even disgusted by the idea of homosexuality, I thought. But the moment Claudio and Lukáš arrived, I didn't care any longer. I didn't feel hurt; I didn't feel ignored. Aleysha just faded into the background, and so did her baby. Even when Lukáš put up with her.

But that was later. In the early days, Lukáš was such an enigma, even more than his friend. Maybe because he was taller, thinner, more the gentleman.

One day, I found him sitting in the kitchen, holding a photograph in his hands. When I rolled in, he quickly tried to hide it, but between almost knocking over his drink and fidgeting with the wallet, it dropped to the floor, sailing through the air and landing right by the side of my wheelchair.

I reached down to pick it up. It were a picture of a young man with baseball hat and sun glasses, standing next to an aeroplane. A small two-seater, single-propeller affair, with, Lukáš said after he got over his initial shyness, a German registration. Again he waffled, turned almost red.

The picture was curious: crumpled, carried around in his wallet, it were almost like a picture of a soldier gone to war, a picture his sweetheart would carry around. I held it and looked at it, and then at Lukáš—he blushed even more. In the instant, I was convinced that this were his secret, the bugger was gay after all, and carried his lover's picture around in his wallet. I smiled.

—Who's this? I asked.

He didn't speak immediately, and when he did, it was not about the instructor, the pilot, whose name he didn't mention—I think, or I cannot recall it—but about the plane, about a flying day he'd enjoyed. The first and only time he'd been on a plane. A friend had arranged it: they'd flown in Austria, over endless fields of grass, wheat and rapeseed, and small villages with little churches, over lakes and castles, towards the Alps and back to a small airfield by the Danube.

There was a tremble in his voice, and emotion, when he finally said that the pilot was *such a nice guy*, really; *such a wonderful guy*; and that he had had so much fun that day; that he had enjoyed it immensely, he said,

—The best day of my life!

Now, come on? A lad on his first flight, touched and moved, maybe. But carrying around a picture of the handsome pilot? He were delish, I am not saying he weren't—but that's not a thing straight boys do? Is it?

In my head, the picture formed: bound somehow to Claudio, but in love with another.

Maybe the pilot were straight! Unfulfilled love. Desire he had to hide from Claudio.

Ah—there you have it!

Maybe I should write one of those gay romances myself. I've got the characters all in front of me.

It were a Sunday then when they first denied it, after a long night's sleep, a quick breakfast with home-baked parkin, and that talk with Aleysha in the kitchen. The first Sunday after their return from the Highlands, and it were bloody cold—a *snell* wind in true Scottish fashion—and we wrapped up warm.

We showed them the town, told them what to visit and what to avoid, where to get drunk, and how to order a whisky properly; how to say 'awreet' and 'aye;' what goes into a haggis, what a tartan was, where they could get kilts made (they never did, thank god) and how bagpipes worked. And that you should never call a Scotsman 'English,' and that you best not talk about their claim to nationhood, unless you *wanted* to get into a fight.

In the late afternoon, the large sun at last drenching the town in welcome warmth, we took them to the castle, during which Claudio pushed my chair and Lukáš rather reluctantly read from the guide book I had given him. It didn't seem necessary to him, and I had to remind him to 'use the book.'

I think we wanted them to read more, to improve their English, which was daft: read they could back home, they should be talking as much as possible. So each time he had to open it anew and search for the right page. Of course, Tim had to contradict everything it said there, in the proper Scots manner: nobody could know the real Edinburgh but a true Scotsman—certainly not some snotty guide book writer from London.

—It worse, said Lukáš, reading the back cover of the book. It is German writer, and the guide is translation.

—Curiouser and curiouser, I muttered, and laughed, wondering why we even owned such a book, and why Tim had given it to me to give to the Slovaks. Tim scowled, said something about 'havering,' but didn't explain what it meant when Claudio asked, then sulked for a while. I don't remember exactly why. Some teacher, my husband.

Lukáš read a few more lines when nobody spoke, and then put the book away unobtrusively. When we were at the wall where the cannon stands, looking out over the whole city, Claudio behind me, treating me with so much circumspection, they stood very close. In the corner of my eye, I saw them hold hands for a moment, Claudio and Lukáš. Only it weren't holding hands like lovers, it were a squeeze—quick, furtive, reassuring, and yet . . . ? It were another of those gestures which just did not fit. When Tim turned around, they even seemed to move apart.

I decided they were in the closet, that they were playing games with each other. Just then, finally, they opened up a little. Well, we pried them open, when our visit was concluded, and the sun had disappeared again behind a black wall of clouds. Everyone was cold and wanted to go home, and we were waiting for the lift.

—So you decided to take one last trip together before finding a job? And to improve your English?

Both affirmed the question. Tim looked at me quizzically, not quite understanding why I asked.

Why did I ask? It's simple. That squeeze of the hand pushed me over the edge, and maybe Aleysha's taunt, and the picture of the pilot. I decided I wanted to know, to hear it from their own mouths, put an end to it. There were summat about them that just weren't right, and I needed to get to the bottom of it, for my own peace of mind. The small gestures were obvious to anyone who looked, and they couldn't have been ashamed of being gay in a house where it was clearly more an offence to be straight.

I had an inventory in my mind already, a list of things I had seen them do, and which niggled away at my soul.

Lukáš had pulled up a chair once, like a proper lad does for a girl on a date. When they ate, Claudio would ask his friend if he needed anything, and then get up to bring salt. Even before sitting down, one of them would always make sure the other had everything he needed—at breakfast for example. On another occasion I had found Lukáš in the room, putting on some new bed covers for both of their beds, and while I stayed there talking to him, he had folded both their clothes and put them in the cupboard. That's not normal for two straight friends! You don't fold your mate's undies unless you like to lick what's underneath. And then they dried each other's hair, for Pete's sake!

So that was the dilemma: all them queer things going on, and yet they clearly didn't seem queer.

People are so much more open these days, and even young men are in touch with their feelings, and not afraid to hug. I know it's a different world, a feminine, soft world, where men can kiss and hold hands—but this were different! They stayed in a room with two beds, which had been very close together, but instantly they'd moved them apart. Why, if they were lovers? Afraid to be discovered? And then we knew from Jamie that they were out the second night in a straight club, and Lukáš had been seen chatting up a girl.

Jamie, our oldest and horniest lodger, knows these things, because—as always with new arrivals—he had followed the cutest one around, and was generous with his offer of assistance. And if Jamie says a guy is straight, then he is.

He has such a charming nature, that forever youthful, all-American brat. But Claudio so far hadn't shown the slightest

80

bit of interest in Jamie, and in his book, that's a big insult, and a definite sign of being a determined breeder. Even so, if they were a committed couple, wouldn't he ignore him too? Or were I asking too much?

I were flummoxed. It were over me *heid;* over me pretty *heid*.

—Have you taken many trips together?

I knew they had already told us, but Lukáš again listed countries: twenty altogether. He mentioned long-term stays, summers in the sun, winters in Lapland. The cursory mention of rock-climbing adventure vacations seemed obscene, recited in the confines of a lift cabin, Lukáš's hand holding my wheelchair steady.

—You really like the great outdoors, don't you?

I had to explain 'great outdoors' for them.

—Nature, yes. We love nature, said Claudio. That why we go to Highland in beginning, we always want it to see—to see *it*.

As always, it were a 'we.' I don't think so far I had heard either of them say 'I'.

—So, I said, hesitantly, and adding up the summers and winters, the countries and places Lukáš had mentioned—you aren't that young any more?

Most of the lodgers who came for English courses were between twenty and twenty-four.

—We are twenty-seven.

It were an odd statement, talking like they were twins. But as it turned out, they were both twenty-seven. Even so, I would have expected one answer from each.

—You've seen their passports, said Tim, haven't you?

I didn't answer him. I hadn't—I had completely forgotten to register them as I should have. When they arrived, they'd been such a presence, such a pleasant shock, I had completely forgotten to take down their details.

The lift finally came and Claudio pushed me in. It takes minutes to get down to the parking lot from the top of Edinburgh castle. It must be the slowest disabled lift in the entire United Kingdom.

—Isn't it a bit late to start university?

Or had I read their letter wrong? No, they had said that they wanted to improve their English and tour Scotland *before* going

81

to uni.

—It is because we working before.

—Working? Before you went to university?

—Yes. What we are doing is called a—he looked desperately for a translation—something like 'self-support scholarship.' It means you must working for four years, and then you get scholarship from government if you interrupt. It is 'further education,' he said, stilted as if reading it from a pamphlet and didn't quite know what he was saying.

I nodded, although not quite sure what a government had to gain from removing people from the job market, interrupting their careers, and sticking them into already crowded institutions of higher learning.

—What did you do before?

—Work, you mean? After school we worked at a lumber yard, then at a restaurant, then in bank. But not good pay. And not good work.

They looked at each other, obviously remembering their shared experience.

—Quite a chequered career, I laughed, before having to explain 'chequered.'

They looked embarrassed at each other.

—And you went to the same school?

—Of course. Since we were fifteen. We have been together since then.

From my chair I looked up, first at Claudio, then at Lukáš.

—You have been together for twelve years?

They nodded.

—You've done everything together? School, work, travel . . .

—We always sharing an apartment. Yes. We always together, said Lukáš.

—So you have been living together for twelve years? asked Tim, suddenly interested. He finally saw what I were trying to get at, that I wanted to get to bottom of things.

They nodded. But Lukáš started and added,

—Except for the army.

—You didn't serve in the same regiment?

—Yes, but we share a room with . . . many other . . .

82

He tried to think of the number, but I saw his point. They had stayed together during army service too. They had really never been apart.

—But ... I began, unsure of whether to ask this or not, if it was too early maybe, and too direct.

The arrival of the lift on the parking level spared me the decision, for the moment.

They wheeled me to our old banger, wheelchair clattering over the uneven pavement, and helped me into the driver's seat, then got in the back together. Tim doesn't like to drive, or he says so, to give me a sense of achievement. I don't like driving, but I don't want to look like I'm giving up the means of my independence.

When I saw Lukáš putting on his seat belt and then showing it to Claudio, making sure he too was buckled in—like one does with a child, with such a loving and intimate gesture, I just couldn't help it. I put the key in the ignition, but froze there.

—So you grew up together, and you have been living together and working together for twelve years, travelling everywhere together, doing everything together. It's so nice to see a gay couple so committed.

In the overhead mirror, I saw them nod, then look at each other.

—We are not ... gay, Claudio said softly.

I pretended to be really surprised.

—You are not lovers?

They didn't quite catch the meaning. Curiously enough, I found over the years, 'lovers' is a word that nonnative speakers rarely understand in the right sense.

—You are sure you are not gay? You sound like a gay couple ...

They both shook their heads emphatically, so I quickly added,

— ... that's not gay.

They laughed, first a bit louder, then more reserved, and then it turned into a strange cackle.

—A gay couple that's not gay. Yes, that it, said Claudio, with an admirable lack of embarrassment. Yes, that it exactly.

It was like I had given him the right tool to express something he hadn't been able to express so far, at least not in English.

—Okay.

83

Tim turned towards them, looked at each of them in succession.

—You are not gay?

They said 'no,' at the same time, then Claudio said,

—I am sorry, and smiled wanly, suddenly seeming shy and uncomfortable, while Lukáš demonstratively stared out the window.

That was it, their first clear denial. Curiously, I didn't feel any relief. It hadn't settled anything, nothing was clearer, and when I thought about it, my head was spinning. I had my answer now, but clearly it were useless. It only made the riddle bigger: if they weren't gay, then ... what were they? What was all the intimacy about? Were they an altogether new breed of straight man, of male bonding—femininely intimate but stubbornly hetero? Bollocks! They must suck each other's cocks. They simply must. It couldn't just be us queers reading erotic undertones into their courtship dance!

—I must admit I have never met a couple of men who were so ... intimate with each other, and weren't also in love.

They did not answer. We crossed Princes Street and New Town. I wanted to take them to Portobello for a pint and some pub grub, picking up Jamie on the way. It was a thing we did on Sunday evenings, and it felt right to go on now, to push further, now that we had part of the answer.

When I stopped the car in front of our house, wheels caressing the kerb, in my deliberate precision, Tim frowning his usual frown, Claudio got out first to fetch the wheelchair from the boot and Lukáš stayed seated. Claudio was wearing a singlet, and his biceps shimmered golden in the night.

After the doors had closed, Lukáš lent forward, in a clear attempt to avoid his friend overhearing him, and said,

—Maybe we are in love. But we don't have ...

And there he stopped as the boot opened. The head withdrew but came back again a second later, even closer, adding,

— ... with each other.

I didn't hear the missing word or words in between, but I imagine he said 'sex.' We don't have 'sex' with each other. *Maybe we are in love, but we don't have sex.* A nonsexual gay couple.

Here's a new twist to get your knickers in. Bollocks, bollocks, bollocks! Young lads like these, how could they not shag each other? Come on!

Before I could even think of an answer, he was out of the car. Too late I called to Claudio not to take the wheelchair out. I would wait in the car, I didn't need it.

—You only have to go inside and fetch Jamie, and whoever is in the kitchen and wants to come. Put the chair back. Tell them we are going to Portobello, they'll know!

Another night has come, Mr Dedalus, of solitude and fright and anger and self-recrimination and disconfirmation and dissolution and destitution; and rather than clearing my head with a walk—a walk, ha! Aye, wishful—I am seeking solace in the bottle again. I am your messenger, and you are with me. I am your thrush, your throstle—your bobbing word throstle; your spy and spittle. You are inside me, after all these years. I am still bound to you.

But here the truth is: there is no carnal. Never been, if you believe it. *There is no carnal.* No, we are not gay. Maybe we are in love, but there is no carnal. Don't you hate all the labels, the words, the label-words, can't you just let them be? I can't. They fascinate me! Like Rafael's cock. And you know this: even straight men get aroused by big hard cocks.

Tim says I have an Oedipus flex cornflakes, only I don't remember my mothers, and when they came, despite the cold, they were always rather cuddly. Red face again, too much John Barleycorn—cure for the red nose, as it said in your book. Only thing I remember, John Barleycorn inside me. Dun for the nun. Piebald for the bachelors. All bachelors we was, on the ship, the yacht.

That's my boy, come aboard. Anchored in Grenada, you said you were in the mood for black cock, so I went out and got you some. Hedonism in the seventies. No AIDS then, just prudish pretence. Brave men, all of them as came to your boat. Handsome men too. Remember T and C? Oh, how you squealed. And I sat there, not amused, jealous, forgotten. You kept me on, kept boy, 'cos I kept you sane, and kept you company when you weren't high or stuffed with cock from either end. Oh, Mr Dedalus. The drama!

So there. I were never amused, and never abused, to my eternal chagrin. Not even in boarding school, which lasted me less than two years, on account of me being not the smartest; but Newcastle, Newcastle, where is thy sting!

And as for Oedipus plex: do I want to kill my mother and sleep with my father? I really don't think so. I can't even remember the blighter. I'd rather kill you, Mr Dedalus, but you are already rotting. I soon will be too.

I was afraid of you, and your money, and your demands, and your impulsiveness. Fear is always worse when you're young. It's very much like pain, once you get used to it ... But tell that to a nineteen year old. I knew nothing—nothing of the world, except how to fold your shirts and bring you a daiquiri.

More cocktails.

More cocks and more tails, lickerish tails.

But I were pure, as pure goes. Too pure for my own good. And what for? To rot in a wheelchair, trapped in a frowsty *auld hoose*, with a man who pities me.

He sleeps with me, we love each other, but really, honestly, bugger—it's naught else but pity. My life, crippled. Had I stayed with you, had I slept with you, I'd be in Barbados now, asking for another wad of cum from Felipe. Do they call them Felipe these days ...? We had so many!

Is that deck chair free? Do you think anybody will suspect we are lovers, if I rub oil on your back, Mr Dedalus? I am sure Stephen Fry will; he's got an eye for lads in tights.

Mr Fry has developed a persona that is larger than England herself, that lollops precariously around her weather-beaten shores, that, were it to examine my loch, would drain its waters and expose the monster: the monster of guilt, of despair, or self-pity. It comes inland only when the East wind blows, and after you pay your license fee and lived through seven reruns of *Footballers' Wives*.

But, my dear Mr Dedalus, on your yacht on your way to Santa Lucia, another bum-boy in your cabin—how many have you had, over the years, after me, and what have you done to them? You had a great wish for us—for all of us.

Were I special in any way? Were I your favourite? What would have happened if I had stayed, if I had said yes? How many have replaced me year after year? How many have you dismasted on desolate seas . . . ?

Back to Portobello.

First gear, old crate, off we go.

What did Claudio mean? A gay couple not gay, but in love — but not physical.

There is no carnal.

I'm all for mystery and a few secrets, but this is just . . .

Can I interest you in a lager, Stephen?

That evening by the beach, with a bit of boozing going, but nothing excessive, over pints of beer and fish and chips, and those marvellous wasabi peanuts what have become all the rage, we all heard their story.

Jamie was there with his new flame clinging to his muscled chest and giving a laboured smile: a jagged, disinterested frown and squinting eyes—I am sure he would have liked to be alone with Jamie in bed. It were a Glasgow lad, face like a bag of spanners if you asked me, with broad shoulders and a massive tattoo on his arm, a motley canvas of flesh, skull and bones in the middle and snakes around it, and on the other side a cock and balls.

Once in a very while Jamie picks up these rough types, which aren't really his style. I cannot even remember the lad's name, but he didn't help, with his distracting moves, his interjections, his somewhat annoying way of trying to speak about things he were more familiar with, and his fondling, his persistent possessiveness, his pride, I assume, of having been chosen by Jamie.

It's an act of charity on Jamie's behalf. Maybe if you can have all the most handsome men on the planet, it must feel like absolution to favour at times the ugly. Not that he were ugly, but he were not refined—not the *finesse* we've come to expect in Jamie's lovers.

Of course, in the following days he was soon replaced by another young man with spectacles, more Jamie's type; invariably a little shorter, a little more masculine, not blond, and a bit acrobatic, with a semblance of intellectual interests, even if they were only superficial: pretend-nerds with pretty arses.

The tat hunk went for a slosh when Claudio and Lukáš opened up after another beer, and spoke, increasingly fluently with each sip, about their childhood. It was hard to believe at first, and it really took us a while to take in, that they had grown up in poverty. Not working-class households like mine; not council estates, but real, abject poverty in the East of Slovakia, over a hundred kilometres away from the next big town, in a village without running water, or, until they were eight, electricity.

—There was nothing there, Lukáš said again and again.

Nothing. Villages of a hundred people or less, living on a pittance. Dilapidated farmhouses whose crumbling grey shingles were sliding off one by one after the rains, whose roofs were forever collapsing, whose walls were sinking, surrounded by relics of Communist mismanagement. Rusting tractors and discarded farm equipment. He spoke of bands of thieves and beggars, of a girl raped for a loaf of bread. Of dreams also—of the West, Western Europe, the EU, emigration, the prosperity at their doorstep, and yet out of reach.

I mean, you don't think about that nowadays, in Britain. You don't consciously think about poverty and poor people. You see a few homeless in the street here and there and wonder how they get through the winter, but you don't call it *poverty*. Sure, Tim says it is a problem here, too, but I wonder how it can be, if I look at what people buy at Tesco's—carts full to the brim with shopping, car boots full of stuff nobody needs. You hear about single mothers in the council estates being a bit hard up, about junkies, and young people out of work, but not widespread, systemic poverty? Not about no electricity, wells to be dug and drying up, people stealing to feed their children.

What the boys told us came as quite a shock. Have you heard of people gathering grass to make a salad? They were foraging, as kids, in the woods around their village—foraging! Hunters and gatherers, that's what it sounded like. Hunters? Poachers, really. It's not something you can relate to easily, or understand, is it, Mr Dedalus? Not in this day and age. Not here, amidst all our affluence. Not you and I, on our cruise ship.

Oh my god, why did I have to remember all that now? The shrimp cocktails, the hundred dollar tips, the time you bought me

88

my first cigar and how much it cost!

I sat in Portobello in my wheelchair with a mountain of guilt weighing me down, bending the spokes.

Claudio's father owned a small farmstead and a fish pond. Lukáš's parents were both retired and living on less than twenty quid a month. Claudio had a brother in the army and a sister who was killed in a motorcycle accident when he was very young. He seemed very reluctant to talk about her.

Lukáš had four brothers and sisters, all still at home. A brother now had a car—the family had never had one before. They were better off now, with all the children grown up and working, but their childhood . . .

A new explanation began to stew in my mind: the shared experience of dire poverty is what has made them such close friends. They had their memories, which were so different from everybody else's here, and that's what made them appear so unique.

After two pints it seemed like a perfectly rational explanation. They were just talking. It was just a pub, and cold at that, but as we listened to them speak about the simple childhood, the fight to survive, the farm work, the games in the forest, the hunting and poaching of animals, it seemed like a fairytale to us city boys, like an entirely impossible story. And yet, there they were, seductive and proud in the very flesh—proof.

Anyroad, they'd known each other literally forever, and their young lives were marked by extremes. They'd gone through the same school together, about an hour's walk away from their village, on foot, every day.

They'd stolen chickens together and got in trouble with the law in other ways. The image of two boys emerged who had been pals since their earliest childhood days, who had never existed without each other, who had learned about life in a world that was both imminently present, intense, and yet strangely out of touch and remote—receding, I am sure, even farther as they toured the world.

Exactly! If they were so poor, how could they afford all their vacations? I thought of asking, but the right moment never came. Plus, it would have sounded nosey, like an accusation.

89

So they grew up, and did their military service, then went back to the village and took stock of their lives. It didn't seem to have occurred to them even then that they could go separate ways.

—Ah, a good old-fashioned boyhood friendship, said Tim. Like in the old days!

It dawned brilliantly on me that there must exist a type of friendship between boys that doesn't involve torturing things, getting drunk, or playing with each other's willies. All of a sudden, I were insanely jealous of them, and I think Jamie too.

They had something one didn't have to find and fight for, it seemed; something grand and natural that were a part of them, that would never leave them. They were as intimate as two men can be, without having done anything to make that intimacy happen, and without doing anything to destroy it; they were just friends. Their state of friendship seemed to be ordained by the forces of nature; a passive, content state unassailable by events or emotions.

But the idyll didn't last. When they returned to the village, they soon realized that life would either split them up, or they would have to make compromises to stay together. That's when it became complicated, and according to Jamie 'plain weird.' Why would two straight lads opt to stay together? School days over, puberty survived, army service done, why go out of their way to remain a couple?

There were a long silence after their almost hour-long recollections of winters in complete seclusion (roads impassable), or teachers sharing a buttered bread between four of the poorest pupils; of buildings torn down as a new age dawned; of suicides, of the end of Communism and the vacuum it had left. Then of rebuilding too, of growing abundance, of better circumstances, at least for part of the country. Their parents had been too old to get new and better jobs, so both families seemed to be waiting for the children to grow up and work.

—So we have work first, we have to, get work, and only then we can travel. And we can now go university, because when we are seventeen, eighteen—no choice. Lukáš emptied his pint quickly, as if to put an end to his part of the story; as if to say 'I am going to tell you no more.'

Claudio was more embarrassed throughout, I noticed.

—Do you go back often? asked Jamie, reading my mind.

Lukáš said 'sometimes' and Claudio 'never,' but both spoke simultaneously, so we laughed. It was obvious they would rather stay away.

—After my sister die, he was only person which matter in my life, said Claudio, sounding very mature and honest.

Yet when their eyes tried to meet after that sentence, they couldn't.

I watched the spectacle, as did Jamie and Tim, and we were rather moved. We saw it all: there was something left unsaid, or the memory just too overwhelming, or the joy that all that was behind them too grand to contemplate. Whatever it was, from that point on, only Claudio spoke. Lukáš had related most of their childhood story, most of their wild days, their stealing and lying, their setting a barn on fire and looking under a girl's skirt; all that had been Lukáš talking, and Claudio sitting there, looking at his mate with a strange expression. At times I thought it was love, or longing. But it might have just been respect. As if he alone would have never done the things they managed together. Maybe, I thought at that point, that was the nature of their relationship— that they pushed or pulled each other along.

Then, of course, Claudio was the sensitive one. He was easier to talk to in general. Lukáš was always more quiet—quite a bit mysterious too—as if he were hiding something.

Lukáš relaxed a little when Claudio spoke. He told us how they'd travelled abroad, and you should have seen his eyes light up. They been to Rome together, and to Barcelona, to Paris and of course Vienna, Salzburg, Munich, but also to Iceland, the US, to Vietnam and Japan.

We sat there listening to Claudio talk of fountains and mountains, between sentences glancing over to Lukáš as if he were asking 'is it okay if I tell them?' Such silent affirmations passed between them, such strange meaningful glances, which nobody could decipher.

They'd been to Nepal, trekking for three days, staying overnight at a monastery where by accident they extinguished some eternal flame; a cursing monk had came out with a modern

91

lighter, turned the gas back on and grinned. A round of laughter distracted us for a moment from the burning question.

—So how'd you get the money for all the travel? asked Jamie's tat hunk bluntly. That's exactly what I had thought earlier, but didn't dare ask. Jamie jerked, but when I smiled, he relaxed.

It was Lukáš who answered, very decidedly, but avoiding eye contact with his friend. The waiter brought another round. Jamie flirted with him, and got slapped for it—lightly—by a tattooed arm.

—Claudio's got rich uncle in Bratislava!

Suddenly everybody looked at Claudio, who only nodded as if he were ashamed.

—That's where we get the money.

We looked back at Lukáš. Claudio drank from his beer, a gesture meant to signal us: no big deal. Let's move on. I could sense he didn't want it mentioned.

It negated all the talk of poverty; it made them seem like liars.

Where had the uncle been when they were kids? Had he come in later? Returned from abroad, after the fall of Communism?

More questions! The Glaswegian, I could tell, wanted to say something, but Jamie put a hand on his arm, and for a while they were busy with their inelegant courtship. It were more a crude fumbling; I could tell from the first it wouldn't last.

What you reckon, Mr Dedalus? Rich uncle, eh? Found one like I did. Mine were ever so swank—yes you were, don't deny it! So what was he then, a real uncle? A sugar daddy? One of them had a sugar daddy? Claudio then, for sure. I can't imagine Lukáš in that role. Because, honestly, if he'd had a rich uncle, why all the stories of poverty in their childhood? Or did the uncle strike it rich when Communism fell? Corrupt party official? Then why did they not say so? Wouldn't their parents have been better off too? It didn't make sense!

My wonderful new theory out of the window. But maybe they simply had omitted that part. The childhood were long ago, so was the poverty. It didn't seem so improbable now.

There were a rich uncle, there were salvation, a lifeline.

But then we were back to the earlier conundrum: why did

they stay together? Why would Claudio's rich uncle pay for both of them? Why did they stay a couple? For it were very clear, regardless, ultimately, of their sexuality, that they were a couple. A couple of sorts. I saw that Jamie must have been thinking along the same lines. He said,

—Ha, so you both live off the old uncle now?

It would make sense, if there was money. That could bind Lukáš to Claudio—comfort, security. Two toy boys of a rich old man? Both of them, together then, having done unspeakable things, sold their manhood, their self-respect and were now tied in a pact of eternal damnation? Bollocks. The money then? People as grow up poor find it hard to let go, don't they? Like me, Mr Dedalus, innit? I found it hard to turn my back on prawn cocktails and lobster bisque, didn't I? But I did.

Claudio was about to speak, when the annoying Glaswegian announced that he was cold—no wonder, sitting there in a singlet just to show off his tats—and wanted to split. He pulled Jamie away, and moments later a motorcycle revved up, a big red monster of a machine. My heart leapt. I was worried every time I saw one of these, and now with Jamie on the back, clinging to that piece of rough. Claudio and Lukáš stared at the motorcycle as if they were seeing a ghost.

We paid and went to the car in silence. Tim drove us back, 'cos I had had far too much to drink. Red nose again, and beaming face; the motherly glow. I sat brooding, and a bit annoyed that I was no closer to solving the mystery.

They had been everywhere together—that is the strange part. How many young men last a decade living in each other's drawers? And why the constant travelling, the constant challenging each other with ever higher peaks and deeper lakes, and farther countries?

They weren't rich, even if Claudio's uncle paid for the plane or train tickets. And yet the hotels they mentioned were never the cheapest, and then there were the adventure holidays. They had gone trekking in Iceland for a month, later showed us pictures online of both of them sitting in a hot spring pool in Hokkaido. I went to a travel agent the other week and even the cheapest offer is a over a thousand quid for a week. Uncle or not, it just doesn't

93

add up, either way, for two young lads in and out of work, from poor families, to travel so extensively and exotically.

I would have loved to travel myself. I never had the chance, but. I came back from my grand oceanic tour of the world as a kept boy and got run over by a fucking car on my way to buy fags. How's that for a biography? Grew up, went round the world, sat in a wheelchair.

What a preposterous thing life is. I were eager and young, handsome, all the world ahead of me, all the chances. I could have been something, in the media, on the telly. I had the wits and the looks, and the charm, and even a soupçon of talent—talent of sorts. It always had been my dream. But it weren't to be.

At least I've got Tim to look after me. In a world where gay relationships last weeks or months at most, he and I are really a miracle, and I am grateful to have him.

So, anyroad, we accepted them: they were close friends as went around the world together, friends who'd done everything for each other; but they weren't gay. Didn't stick each other's todgers up each other's bums. So what. Not everybody can be perfect. Not every man experiences the bliss of anal sex in his life. Some are positively afraid to let anyone near their nether entrance. Lunatics, if you ask me. So much fun to be had on that end. But, joke aside, no matter how much they looked the part— no matter how much we wanted them to be—they were just two mates, whose friendship resembled more a love affair than many gay relationships do. Who had grown up together poor. Who had a rich uncle. Who held hands at times and loved each other.

There were still something missing—something big and ominous.

It felt a bit like we had assembled a puzzle, but the centre were glaringly absent.

We'd only done the clouds and the grass and the water around it, but not the middle. Not the faces.

Hurray magoog, mahoney lovely, madaarling. Welcome to the club! Portobello dinna solve anything. Rich uncle, fuck me, Mr Dedalus, farting rich uncle, sober not I! Not tonight! Macallan's my uncle, and Johnny Barleycorn my lover, and a wheelchair is my home.

Me butt's itching and me liver's on fire! There she goes with pooping Tim. Fucking Tiny Tim the mutt. Shite and onions! I think the dog is actually called 'Tim'—adding *insultation* to *injuration!* The scraggy old bitch!

Fuck me, I am pissed. We had wine for lunch; then drinks at four, when we taught Lukáš how to sink a whisky in a pint; then the dinner, then Portobello—did we have dinner? Bugger me and call me Nellie, what a day! And you expect me to make sense of these Slovash ... Slovarashians. Why is it so ... involved?

Issabit complicated, innit, all that guessing? And should we be doing it, digging in other people's lives as we dig up each other's arses?

Could just be friends, but cannae believe that! My Slovaks. Something's up! I feel it in me bones! In love my arse! In my arse love. Love my arse!

What was it that bothered me? What? That they were cute together? That they were so fucking handsome? That Claudio seemed more gay than Lukáš? That Lukáš I thought were fibbing. I were sure now that one of them at least were lying! Put my finger on it! Put where? What? Help! What finger on it? Where? There is something there, some *ting I dinnaken!*

I've gone all Scottish again. Must be the whisky.

They are just weird. They are not normal. Fucking straight lads ain't normal in the head.

How I hate that word, *normal.*

Strange people are comforting; they are real; *normal* people on the other hand are like zombies, menacing shells of flesh with no redeeming features. They watch TV all day and worry about their lawns; they fret about things they don't understand, and repeat only opinions they read in the papers, on the Inter-bloody-net; they have no original thoughts.

It's a fucking disaster, the world we live in.

Normal people, their views, their opinions, their daft view of the world, their salvation crap—you know where it comes from, Mr Dedalus? From that deep recess, that dark cloud that follows us everywhere, that abyss full of hatred and fear. We are always only two steps away from falling into it; yet they—normal, hateful,

95

hollow people—they delight in playing on its rim. Frolicking. Frolistering. Fistering. Fisting. Mind-fisting each other instead of trying a single original thought. Grin and bear, grin and bear.

Up yours, you boring normal weirdos!

But they aren't normal, now, are they, my Slovaks? Anything but! I say! What the fuck is going on? Top up my glass while you are at it, handsome! When ya ready, luv!

Hip hip hurrah! Shag me senseless and I'll roll you to nirvana, Mr Dedalus.

Did you expect that when we sailed the seven seas? Did you expect it when in Sydney I got lost for a fortnight and a week, and you found me at a party, stoned, sleeping with a long-haired American who insisted he was Joan Baez's son?

I knew it then, that the world is a strange place, that we who dare, that we who aren't not quite *normal*, who leave the house-with-a-lawn and then two-point-four-weeones-on-a-seesaw dream behind, we as aren't philoprogenitive—Tim's word, not mine, but a canny one—we who have the guts to stand up and say: I am so bloody weird and different, I don't understand even myself—we rule, in truth, and you know why, Mr Dedalus? Why we rule the world? It's very simple. Only our stories get told! Nobody wants to read about normal people! Nobody wants to watch a movie about the boring sods, the daft, church pew-crouching, puking middle-class buggers. Not anymore!

So we win. We win! We are the fucking arse-champions! We who have the key to the kingdom of freakishness. Blessed the meek of mind, blessed the wee of cock, blessed the soddin' bastards as missed out on everything!

That's why I didn't mind Joan Baez's son—wasn't he much too old, and he smelled of burnt tyres!—shaggin' me, and being stoned, and even being arrested.

Thirty years later and I wish I could remember what we were nicked for! It seemed so momentous, that time in Sydney. It weren't even a city back then, Australia not even a country in the seventies, not a real one at least, with no identity. It were just somebody's lawn with bones sticking out of the ground here and there. I'd imagine aborigines, and all the animals they exterminated, but I am not smart enough for them politics of retribution. Or is it reconciliation? All the rage!

Tim says outrageous wrongs have been done there—outrageous! I touched a kangaroo. I saw a wombat, and a koala. Three weeks in paradise, and then back on the boat ... Oops, excuse me! Sphincter control not what it were.

You didn't take me to Ayer's Rock! What's it called now? Would you like another one? I think there's another bottle of same kicking about the house.

What did you do, Mr Dedalus, while I got laid with brawny Americans and skinny Aussies—or the other way round—on Bondi beach? While I were on my knees in prayer before the Cock of Shawn? Weren't there a Sergio somewhere? Who was he? And where, Mr Dedalus, were you?

Oh yes—mining! You wore a suit and spoke with a deliberate Texan accent, and purchased a mine somewhere in the dusty North. And then you caught up with me, plucked me from the dens of iniquity, from the bedrooms of the sad and debauched, rescued me from the Vegemite Ripper! How I hated that foul shit! Your house by the harbour but! What a harbour! Its own boat service back to town! Captain in striped tights steering, tip of cock visible, me salivating, fish jumping. And we went back on your yacht, and popped over to the Kiwis, where you bought a forest, a fucking entire forest!

What a life we had, aye—you and I, Mr Dedalus, hoping every step of the way we would finally fall in love with each other.

PART III

Claudio came home from school early one day—sleek-combed, preppy, delightful in the way his chest stretched the too-small T-shirt—and found me in the kitchen.

When you are stuck in a wheelchair, people find you, not the other way round. I could get around more, if we would install a ramp outside, but it's a convenient excuse not to.

There, I've said it. Tim's wanted to do it a hundred times—make a ramp so I can reach the pavement on me own—but I told him no. It ain't worth the bother. And the truth is, I do like the world coming to me, sat on my throne. I know I said I wanted to travel, but that were afore the wheelchair. Aye, I don't like to travel in a wheelchair; it's a terrible nuisance.

I know disabled people do all kinds of things—heroic things even—them special Olympics and all—but that's not for me. I like to be in my kitchen, and have the world pass me by.

I like watching, observing, studying; it's in my nature. And digging.

Aye, that's where Claudio found me one day—what day? A few days later. I can't tell exactly which day, because of the whisky. It were *after* Portobello, that's for sure. And we only went to Portobello once with the Slovaks, because the discussion had been so intense, and the Glaswegian so annoying, and the shock over what they told us of their youth so great that nobody wanted to return there.

I had *perused* the computer, as Tim likes to say, the resources of the magical Internet, and found out about Eastern Slovakia, the poverty, the desolation. I had also stumbled upon an article about poverty in the UK which shocked me.

In our midst, in my own neighbourhood, people living on a few hundred quid a month. 3.5 million children living in poverty, the highest rate of any industrialized country!

There were a documentary running on telly that showed it; that opened my eyes. One day I drove down to the council estates and looked around, and seen it—the squalor. I could suddenly imagine that something like that, an upbringing under such circumstances, would forge a friendship bound to survive. Would make them feel quite different from the rest of the world.

Claudio said hello, took a drink from the fridge, and then stood there, looking at me intensely, but without his usual, winning smile. I asked him if anything were amiss, and if he enjoyed his time in Scotland, if he were learning enough at school, and if he thought it a good school. He made a bit of small talk, that was it. I went back to what I were doing, unable to shake off the feeling that summat were bothering him, when suddenly he got very serious and asked me about the wheelchair and how it happened; so I told him. Just a little; not the whole truth. It were just a stupid traffic accident, I said, and I didn't want to talk about it.

He listened politely, shocked maybe, or disappointed—that it were naught special after all, just another accident—or maybe pissed that I didn't tell him it in all the gory detail. And then he told me *his* story: that he'd had a sister, a younger sister, who had been killed by a motorcyclist who'd never been caught—a hit-and-run. I taught him the expression 'hit and run.' He found it curious, that saying, because there was no hitting and no running involved. So I explained 'hit' in that sense, and 'run' as in 'shooting off.' Claudio's English weren't quite good enough to tell emotional stories, and then he watered up halfway through, so I didn't understand some of what he said. But he'd lost a sister, and it seems he'd never quite got over that. She must have meant a lot to him, that much I gathered.

I hated my wheelchair so much that instant! I wanted to get up and hug him, comfort him. It's those moments, those emotional moments when my disability hurts most.

I don't know why he told me. It's one of these things: he saw me in the chair, and remembered his dead sister. He wanted to know what it meant to live in a wheelchair, what it felt like. He wanted to know what it would have been like, if his sister had lived. He liked wheeling me about, he said, pushing my chair, even though I didn't need him to, because he wanted to *know* the feeling.

Apparently, he said, she'd survived for a few days in a coma, and he had been by her bedside all the time, talking to her, asking her to hear him, to come back! The doctors had told the family that even if she made it, she would never walk again, she would

99

be paralysed, even unable to function—lack of oxygen in the brain, something about the spine.

That must be why Claudio was so nice to me from the start—always offered to do the shopping, always helped with the laundry—and that in turn must be why I decided so early on that he was the *gay* one, the sensible, caring one. *One of us.* Well, that and the fact that he slept with Jamie. But no, that came later. And it did complicate things, not between Claudio and Lukáš, curiously, as one would have thought, but for the rest of us.

One time I found the two lads standing close to each other doing the dishes: one scrubbing, the other rinsing and drying. They didn't hear me roll in, and I caught Claudio smelling Lukáš's neck and then the shoulder. I thought at first they were about to make love, and prepared to retreat, but I had misread the scene entirely. Claudio said something to his friend, then Lukáš raised his arm and smelled himself, and they laughed.

—Do you need to do laundry? I asked them.

They turned round quite startled.

—I already make pile by the washing machine, said Claudio. But now I see he needs wash this too. He smell like pig!

Lukáš, the big serving plate in hand, kicked him in the shin, and Claudio sank laughing to his knees.

The boys were just fooling around, I realized, but still! The way Claudio had smelled him, it were more intimate than I can imagine straight boys would be. But maybe the world is changing. Maybe that's it: men in general aren't so stiff any more.

—Give me both your shirts and I'll start the wash. Yours too, Claudio. You have a stain on the sleeve!

Claudio looked down and saw it. Without embarrassment or hesitation, both pulled off their shirts and tossed them into my lap.

—And while you are at it, those jeans too. You've worn those since you arrived.

They looked at each other, then stripped. The gesture was remarkable. It was so natural. Gays are usually so much more body-conscious; and yet I doubt even two straight men would strip in front of an old queen in a wheelchair—or maybe the wheelchair rendered me harmless? I don't know; I have too many hang-ups. It is me as thinks too much. What else do you do in a wheelchair but think and malinger? Plus, all the guesswork was confusing me by then. I didn't know what to think anymore.

Anyroad, Claudio and Lukáš just stripped, then looked at each other's chest for a second. Suddenly Lukáš reached with his hand to his mouth, wet two fingers with spittle, then rubbed a spot on Claudio's chest, very close to the left nipple.

—When did you last shower? You have egg on your chest, man.

Claudio looked down on his own chest. He did not object to the intimate gesture in any way. He did not push the hand away. It was as if he was used to being touched by his friend—by men. They looked perfect together in the fainting light of the Scottish evening. Both had natural bodies, not overly developed. Lukáš had love-handles any queen would have been ashamed of, but his stomach were excessively flat and naturally defined. He was pale, and his chest sprouted a few dark hairs. I doubt he'd ever seen a gym from the inside. Claudio were different. Not exactly ripped, but with a harder muscle tone, thin waist, broad shoulders, well-developed pecs, and clearly visible abs. At first I thought he was hairless. Then I saw that he shaved. There was a fine carpet of recent regrowth all over, even the legs. Swimmers shave, don't they? I was about to ask if he swam, when suddenly Claudio punched his friend in the stomach.

—You need work out more! he said, still speaking English as I rolled away from them towards the laundry room. —You are skinny goat!

As I rolled out of sight, they switched to Slovak again. I heard them wrestling, fighting, yelling, running; I heard the table moving and a chair toppling, and when I came back, Claudio had Lukáš pinned down on the floor, rubbing his biceps under his shins—but not hard; gentle, even. Nevertheless, it's not a thing you see gay guys do often, that playful aggressiveness of young males, that juvenile-primeval combat training. So I thought, there you have it, straight as a die, they must be, despite everything. Only then—the sun was behind them in the window, so the moment it happened, their faces blocked out the light and I saw only contours—Claudio bent down and kissed Lukáš on the lips, short enough to be dismissed as a joke, yet long enough to be, aye, romantic, afore jumping up and running away, past me, up the stairs and into their room. Lukáš dashed after him, his tread lighter on the stairs, and the door banged shut a second time.

What were they doing in the room? What had that kiss been? I had seen it clearly! There had been feeling behind it, some kind of caring, some romance . . . so after all, they were lovers then. Or was I just too old to understand it? They said they weren't gay, but can you believe men? Men never talk about their feelings honestly, they just can't. It's so confusing, a coming out, and for some it takes longer. Gay young lads always say they are bi, or curious, while they are searching.

Me in my old days, here in this forsaken place, having all my prejudices turned on their head! I didn't know what to think any longer. Were they playing a game, trying to fool us? Were they gay after all, and only acting—straight-acting? Was it the foreign country that made them cautious? Or were they fooling themselves? Were they just bound by secrecy, by hiding themselves from each other?

Banging me head against the wall, that's what I were doing. Daft buggers, messing with my house, with my friends, with me.

I were so lost and befuddled, I needed outside help. I went over to the clinic for me physio that week, and talked it over with Alan, sweet English lad with a lazy eye and sanative logorrhoea, if you let him, and big hands, and good with them. There's naught to be done with my useless stalks, try as he may. Even after all these years, all we do is move them a little about so the blood circulates, so they don't wither while they're still attached.

Alan said I should back off; I shouldn't worry. I should give Claudio time.

—'E needs to find himself, thassall.

Yes, I thought, that's all. They need to find themselves. Drop it. Let them be what they are, let them shag who they want.

—Issnot so clear any more, you know. Young people. Half of them call themselves *bisexual* now, until they settle down. Issall the rage.

Yes, all the rage. Isn't it splendid, sexuality changing? No

102

more taboos. No more need to come out, really. And no more need to choose sides, either. I guess that's appealing to some. No thinking—they just *do*.

I don't like going to the hospital at all. It seems fatuous, the whole affair: the nurses, the doctors, the therapist, and for what? We've long established that I can't feel anything; what I do feel, I imagine. They are gone, cut down in their prime, never to be useful again, my wee stumps. They are my punishment for a year of abandon to lust, for a year and a half of pleasure with you, Mr Dedalus. I paid the price for running off with you: now I can't run.

I don't complain—or rather, I don't complain in public. I've got my window, my chair, Macallan and an almost Scottish capacity for self-pity. And that'll have to do.

We all expect so much from life, and get so little; perhaps that's why Claudio and Lukáš were so fascinating. They seemed to expect nothing, but had everything. They had each other, more intimately than any man can have another. They took each other for granted, as if they were perfectly sure they could never be separated.

—Ouch! I shouted as Alan rammed a chair against my elbow. Clumsy giant.

—I am sorry. Did I 'urt you?

I rubbed the spot, but gave up soon. Pain doesn't matter much to me. In a way, I am grateful for every jolt I can feel, where I can still feel it.

—You know you could 'ave a baby, if ya wanted to! said Alan, wiping his oily hands after rubbing me down.

—A baby?

—Issall the talk. They've gone and created artificial sperm and eggs, and you can 'ave your DNAs put into them artificial sperms and eggs, an' 'ave a child.

—Here at the clinic? Here?

—Thassright, 'ere at the university. So same-sex couples can 'ave offspring now. We've beaten nature, at last.

—Or rather, again. Won't be much left of the old bitch, soon, I reckon.

—No, Alan laughed boisterously. Ha ha, no! Issnot just 'ere, they are saying there's a few universities what can do it now. In

103

a few years, it'll be standard procedure, like checking for them inheritance diseases.

—Yes, Alan, but the science is one thing. Don't forget the world is still largely full of daft buggers worshipping holy books and keeping their womenfolk veiled or locked up! And especially when it comes to procreation! Straights will claim that as their last frontier, you know! You can have marriage, but you can't make wee ones! All male-female breeding still in their minds, god bless. Oh, can you imagine what the god-squad will say?

—You reckon it'll be a problem then?

—But of course it will. For Pete's sake, how do you expect them to react to a child with two genetic mothers or fathers? Brood of the Devil, they'll shout. Unnatural, they will claim. These people don't understand our human, scientific destiny. They will insist, again, like always, that it ain't *natural*. Defining of course *natural* as whatever the buggers are *used* to. For them as still believe in miracles it's all heaven and hell and good and evil. Combining two female DNAs to make a baby is no less natural than sperm-swims-to-egg and all that evolutionary breeding crap. Our science, what we create, as humans, it's as much evolution as what the old bitch Nature came up with, only better! Much better. No disease, errors, no accidents, no unwanted children. No lazy eyes! Think about it, no lazy eyes!

—Are you making fun of me?

—No, no, just . . .

—Thass no' you talking anyways. Thass your Tim.

—Well what if it is? He's the smarter one.

—Ha, I knew it! You reckon he'll wanna have a child with you? A wee one made out of Tim and Tim? Little Timmy?

—Only it's going to be a better world. A baby, Tim and I—oh no! We're too old. But Jamie, Javier, our Slovaks? Maybe. I can think of so many couples. It will be a blessing.

—It will. For those as can't have children, it'll be a blessing.

—Only the god-crowd will protest. They'll bomb the clinics, like they now do with abortion. They'll call us freaks. They'll ostracise those born of two same-sex parents. Not just those— all 'unnatural' births. We'll live in a world soon split along those lines: science adopters and science rejecters. We'll have to redraw half the map. And we'll have to defuse the maniacs. Oh yes, it's a blessing, but the god-freaks will put up a fight.

—Yes. Probably. They'll put up a fight. Bugger that there's still so many of 'em around, innit?

I thought of Claudio. Wouldn't it be perfect, combining his DNA with his friend's? I pictured the baby, while Alan helped me back in the chair, and then I thought about it the whole afternoon. A baby made from two male DNAs, and what a fucking weird world we live in, how much more complicated everything were getting. It's not just mojito or daiquiri any more, you know—the choices are getting more and more difficult.

Claudio—hunky, full body-shaving, always-smiling, adorable, sexy, blond Claudio with the thick biceps and the straight blue vein, and the golden hair on his forearms; pensive, sensitive, quiet Claudio with the supreme DNA—was the one who ended the dance of the fruit bowl. We have a big wooden bowl in the kitchen, which is always to be full of fresh fruit. When there is less than three pieces left, he as takes the next fruit has to go to market and refill it. It's a house rule, and I don't know who came up with it. Tim must have, telling everyone that I need lotsa fruit, lotsa vitamins *for my condition*.

How I hate having a *condition*. As if being queer weren't enough!

I'm probably the one as needs the least fruit, seeing that I can only wheel myself about and have me vitamins in big jars anyway. It's the young boys who come here, who are out night after night screwing the locals, who need to replenish their energy stores. But I guess fresh fruit don't count as energy. And *I* don't count, really; just an excuse to make up a rule. Just a nuisance on wheels, with a duster and a wet cloth.

Anyroad, it is supposed to be always full, yon bowl, which of course it never is. It gets depleted day by day, until only three apples or three oranges or any combination of three is left (usually, and why three, who knows?), and yours truly is the one as rolls off to the super with Tim and buys some more. Or I call Tim to bring some home after work.

But not since Claudio and Lukáš arrived. Since the very first day of their return from the Highlands, since their romantic sojourn, I like to think, in the heather, when we explained to them how it works, the pile of fruit stayed the same height.

It's Claudio who made sure, I discovered; every day after school he stopped by the grocer's and bought a small amount of fruit, even exotic stuff, like mango and papaya and kumquat—first time I ever seen one of those yellow buggers. He bought blueberries in a little basket, and raspberries, and a huge melon too; summat different every day. None of our lodgers ever went to so much trouble, showed so much care and love. Fancy buying fruit, just as they were supposed to, young lads! We could be forgiven for thinking they were gay. Everybody thought they were gay—even Tim's sister at first! They were just too ... nice! Straight boys aren't nice, she said; they don't think of buying bloody fruit! They are rough and inconsiderate and stupid and wild and ... different, even at twenty-seven. Or maybe that's when they start to mature?

They don't do laundry for each other or buy fruit for their fellow lodgers! They don't spend almost every evening indoors, playing computer games, or reading or watching TV with their heads snugly on each other's chests! They don't, at that age, chase each other rough and tumble round the kitchen table and end it with a sweet kiss.

—Why do you think they are here, Tim? I asked, even afore he had parked the car by the bench.

We were driving up to Oban to visit his mother, and help with the cleaning of the old hotel she was still running almost entirely without help, at eighty-three. We put his sister in charge of the B&B. Not that there was much to do. There were no new reservations, no change of lodgers, no plumber coming.

We had stopped, as we always do, for fish and chips. Although we must have bought our dinner there a hundred times, I cannae remember the name of the shop or the town—I think it's Callander, but I can't be sure. You see, we drive up north, and my accent goes all Gaelic.

We bought our grub and stopped at the usual spot by the next big lake—Loch Lugnaig is it? I'd have to look it up to be sure. That's the thing with familiar places: you live there, you dwell amongst them, as Tim would say; you *inhabit* them, and they become so familiar you forget their names. It's really the deepest of intimacies, when you don't need a name any more. That's why couples call each other nicknames, or nothing at all; why you drop the greeting in e-mails to people you really feel comfortable with. And that's why by using his name, I startled my husband, my confidant, my lover of three decades, the plastic bag with deep-fried cholesterol bombs on his knees, his fingers on the handle, ready to get out.

—Why do you think they are here? I asked again when he turned towards me.

—You mean Claudio and Lukáš?

—Yes.

He shrugged off the question and wiggled out of the car, carefully embracing the bags. What elaborate thoughts for such a simple inquiry—but then again, why did I ask? I had brooded on it all the way, at least since Stirling. It had occurred to me after deliberating the fruit bowl issue, and realizing how different they were after all, our brawny adventurers.

Tim helped me into the chair, then pushed me down to the water's edge, where we always sit and eat. It's the most beautiful spot in Scotland, and it's nowhere near any touristy sites. It's just one of a thousand elongated lochs, but at sunset, on a beautiful summer's day, it is pure magic. Even though, we were the only people about. Fish were jumping; the midges were starting to come out. Tim put the bag and box of food on my lap and opened the drinks.

—Claudio called them *midgets*. Flying *midgets*.

—What? Oh I see! Ha!

When he had talked about their bicycle tour, and how they had been pestered by insects, we had taught him the word 'midges,' but a few minutes later, he had turned them into midgets. Of course, we bent over laughing at the 'attack of the flying midgets by the lake.'

—Not just a few, Claudio had said, there were midgets all over us!

And then we were 'swatting midgets' and 'scraping midgets off the windscreen,' until somebody told the story of the midget-

107

tossing competition, and we calmed down. I had seen only then that Claudio had been very embarrassed over his mistake.

—So, I repeated with a mouthful of chips dipped in mayo, chewing slowly, gazing over the black water; why do you think they have come here, Tim?

It's one of the greatest pleasures of being old and ugly and disabled. You can have a pile of chips with mayo and ketchup and not feel a shred of guilt. As long as you are alone! Last time we had Jamie with us and he couldn't 'believe you are eating all that! That's pure fat!'

—Well, to learn English. They said so. They came to learn English.

That's exactly the answer I expected from Tim, one hundred percent the right answer. Careful analysis. Recalling the facts; reclaiming reason. They were here to learn English. Well of course they were here to learn bloody English!

We ate in silence for a while, watching the fish jump higher and higher as the insects swarmed and the sun turned red. Scotland is full of insects in summer. I thought of Claudio and Lukáš camping, wrapped up in their sleeping bags so as not to get bitten. No, I thought of them in the same sleeping bag. Two men in a tent.

What a convenient excuse midges would make for a fumble.

—I mean, everything happens for a reason in life. There are, I believe, no coincidences. I mean . . . life is nothing but coincidences, but . . . you know what I mean.

—I don't. Do you want white pudding?

—No, listen. Did you buy any? You didn't buy any!

—Oh, yes—but I thought I had.

—We are getting old.

He gave me a look, a glowering look that was at once angry and loving. Yes, we were getting old—but we were getting old together. We'd spent thirty years in love.

—Anyway, think about it. They said they aren't gay. Why did they end up in our B&B? If they aren't gay, then why are they so close, so intimate? Not just emotionally, also physically! Or I mean both. They touch each other. I saw them kiss, really kiss, lips on lips. After brawling. I mean, play-fighting, chasing each other—you know, about the kitchen.

—Really? Kissing?

—Yes. Not tongues. But not a taunt either. True affection. At least . . .

—I think we need to give them time. Perhaps that's what they are doing . . . finding themselves, you know. Finding out who they are. Maybe that's why they are here.

—That's exactly what I have been thinking. Maybe this is the end of their relationship, maybe they know that they have to change. Getting on thirty, marriage or not, children or not, give up their friendship, and if not . . . how can they continue?

—Yes. I see.

—And you know what happens to men when they marry: they become stale and conservative, and aggressive, to protect their brood. And clearly, they don't want that. Maybe, Tim, they have come here to find out once and for all, if they could be lovers; if they could lead an *alternative* life. Perhaps this is meant to be a test? Perhaps they are running away, perhaps at full speed, from their life together. Perhaps—I am just saying—perhaps, just maybe, they *need* us. That's why they chose a gay place to stay. That's why they chose us—because they need us.

—Need us?

—Subconsciously, you know? Perhaps they came to a gay place on purpose, so we could help them . . . come out. Maybe they even selected our house specifically, after reading about it on the net. So they could see what it would be like, living together as man and man. Maybe they want to stay together, gay or not, and are here to find out if they can, find out once and for all if that is a way of life. That's what they are doing, yes.

I could tell by his look that it had occurred to Tim before, that he had had the same thoughts. We are very attuned to each other. Invariably, he keeps them to himself, but I can't. I need them confirmed, my harebrained theories. I can't sleep if I don't talk about my thoughts.

—It may be, but we mustn't meddle! We ought to be careful. You mustn't put any pressure on them.

—I mustn't put pressure?

—Yes. You do get ahead of yourself at times. You do tend to . . . bully people. You need . . .

—Bully, me?

— ... to give ... Yes, Tim, you can be a bit ... direct; a bit forceful, when you get your teeth into something. A bit obsessive even. You know that yourself. Don't forget they are very young.

I suppose he were right. One doesn't like to hear these things about oneself, but yes. Maybe ...

—They aren't actually *that* young, he continued, which is the point that surprises me most. If they were twenty, one would understand all the searching, the lack of ... position. People used to fight wars at age twenty, and have families, and responsibilities. These two are almost thirty, and they haven't quite made their mark in anything. They are still ... What I mean is ...

—I think it may be ... it is almost as if ...

— ... it's almost as if,

We looked at each other—having, as so often, said the same thing at the same time—and smiled. Over time, we really had become *one*. And as always, I let him say it.

—It's almost as if their relationship, their being together, had kept them from growing older, as if their love had prevented them from maturing.

—Maybe that's what love is supposed to do, I said, taking his hand. Keep you young inside.

Tim pursed his lips; a sure sign that he wasn't altogether happy with his own conclusions. He didn't follow my lead. He weren't in a romantic mood.

—And yet, Lukáš seems awfully mature.

Strangely enough, I had thought Claudio the more grown-up. I thought of his hard, shaved body; the pubic hair sticking out—the shape of his butt in the white cotton when I had seen him last. But then I had in my mind made him gay, and more in touch with his feelings, whereas Lukáš—sinister, that was the word.

—Sinister.

—What?

—Sinister. That's what I am looking for. Lukáš, a bit—he's a bit dark. I don't mean the hair, it's just a coincidence. But he is much more serious. Much more ... yes, sinister—their relationship. I were brooding about it yesterday, and today in the car. There is something sinister about them.

—Sinister? Oh, I don't know! Are you sure?

110

He offered me half his fish, but I couldn't eat any more. I threw a handful of chips into the grass to the right, and a few moments later a whole posse of gulls had descended upon them, sounding awfully like squabbling children. That made me think of Alan and the artificial eggs and sperm, and I had the impulse to bring that up. To actually ask Tim if he would be interested ... but no. Even if he were interested ... what would I do with a child in the house? Me, a wasted cripple in a wheelchair? I am not fit for child-rearing.

—I suppose, what you mean, said Tim when he finished eating; I suppose what you mean is, that they have come here by some serendipitous force. What you believe in, that there is a reason they came not just to a gay B&B, not just for them—but for us. That they somehow chose us without knowing.

—No. Yes. No, I said, having not really thought about it that way. The thing is, Tim, I get the feeling that there is something behind all this ... something more than this guessing game. That there is ... oh, I don't know. It's just me. I am being difficult.

—No, no. I feel that too.

—You do? What do you feel?

—I feel ... not sinister, or even serious—not that. But I think that they are hiding something, both of them. That there is something they are not telling us. But I don't know if they want it buried—if it needs burying at all—or if they need help uncovering it. I am not so sure it's really about their being gay. It seems more ... The thing is, I hate to pry. I hate to ... it has to come out naturally.

—What I feel is ... yes, I know what you mean. What I feel is, that they are maybe not honest with each other. That they are living a lie.

—Living a lie? You mean being gay—and not admitting it?

—No, not necessarily. It's as if there is something momentous there, something incalculable. As if there were a huge lie at the bottom of it all that they couldn't cope with. Maybe one of them has made advances and was rebuffed. Maybe Lukáš beat up Claudio in the past.

—Why not the other way round?

—I don't know. A feeling ...

The gulls had devoured all the food and were stalking up and

111

down at the water's edge, staring with their expressionless eyes. Suddenly I felt a chill. We stopped talking, because frankly, there were nothing to talk about. It was all just feelings and guesswork and circumstance, and really, when you thought about it, not our business. They were just lodgers. They were guests in our house. But I have ne'er been able to think of lodgers as anything else but me bairns.

We watched the sun set. It were about ten thirty, still light: that mysterious northerly glow tourists fall in love with, and which I miss so much during the winter months.

—I could never live with a lie, I said after a while.

Tim's last words had stewed unconsciously in my mind. I said again,

—I could never live with a lie for long.

Tim looked up. He appeared frightened and unwilling to talk further.

—Are you tired? I asked

—No, no. What do you mean . . . a lie?

—Well you know. If their lives . . . if there were some grand deceit, some hurtful lie. If one of them kept something from his lover . . . I mean friend—from his friend. If their relationship—any relationship—were built on a lie. I couldn't cope with that. Say, if you found out very late, that all you believed was false, that all you had done in your life were based on some wrong—some wrong assumption. Something somebody had told you, or not told you, and all your feelings for that person were formed by that . . . lie. And then, after years—years later, really, you found out that it weren't true. Oh, it's awful! I would—it would destroy me.

Tim didn't answer, and when I reached again for his hand, he instead bent down and picked up some stones, then tried to make them skip on the water's surface. It was the first time he'd ever done that. But he didn't say a thing. It was almost as if he avoided looking at me. A shiver went down my spine. The gulls started up, making an eerie, threatening noise. I wanted to leave.

The last stone skipped four times. I applauded, then reached over in one last attempt, and took hold of his hand. It were ice cold. He just stared out onto the loch. All around us was suddenly a swarm of midges. I waved my hand, but gave up when Tim

112

seemed to move, ready to leave.

—That's why I love you so, I said. That's why I love you Tim, because you and I have no secrets.

—Yes ... quite.

—We've told each other everything; we support each other in all things. The other day at the hospital, Alan said—we talked about something—he said I sounded like you. Sometimes I think I am just repeating your words. We've always been so frank with each other. I couldn't live in a relationship where one had to hide and be careful, and keep things from each other. You've been so good to me.

—Perhaps we are too old for games and lies, he said, then clearing his throat, I thought, rather awkwardly, and shouting— almost too loud, and coughing—'those damn *midgets*!'

It were a week after our return from Oban; a week of the Slovaks getting used to school, establishing a routine; and for Jamie to pass an exam in his job, to get better pay. A week of dumping the Glaswegian, of moping and accusing everybody of having driven him away, but being of course rather grateful that we had done so. It were a week of the usual housework for me, and being a general dogsbody, and rather a shock for Mary, who thought that a *nasty* had moved into the flat above hers, and her test results had been mixed up at the hospital, and for two hours and a half, she were slowly and miserably dying of cancer. A week during which we had to turn away seven people at the door, because for the first time in years, we were fully booked all the way to the autumn. It were a week of strange emotions for me, trying after Tim's admonition, to let off and tread carefully, that we found ourselves in the kitchen again on a Friday night: the boys from Slovakia, Jamie, and Javier, the older, quieter Spanish house mate, who'd just quit his job at a dodgy restaurant—a job he had hated anyroad, was glad to be rid of and was in a mood to celebrate and show the world that he didn't care tuppence.

If there is a meaning to the word 'straight-acting,' Javier is the dictionary definition of it. I don't think I've ever seen a single effeminate gesture or heard a raised pitch in his voice. He is so perfectly serious and even dour—frumpy said Tim when he first met him—he can pass as straight anywhere ... and there I go again peddling stereotypes. Surely there are more effeminate straight men in the world than butch gays. That is to say ... what do I want to say? I get so muddled, Mr Dedalus. But I must tell it like it were.

Any-bally-how-n-road, even Jamie didn't think Javier gay, until he tried him and 'made him scream for more.'

I think the two of them were fuck-buddies then, on an on-and-off basis, boning each other occasionally, meaning that Jamie knocked on Javier's doors in the wee hours of the morning, when the poor cook finally could go to sleep, but his majesty, the American gym god, had come home from the bars empty-handed.

All that were long afore the change, of course. Jamie's big change, mine—everybody's. Jamie used to be like that: angry when he didn't pull, when he came home hard-cocked and defeated by his own ego—mainly because he hadn't found anyone good-looking, or rather worthy enough.

There were a general consensus that day that one did not want to stay in, that the house were too cold and too boring, and that there was no booze left—truth being that we had hidden it from Mary before driving to Oban, and forgotten to bring it up again. All the bottles were in the drum of the broken washer-dryer. But I felt like going out, and so I let them wheel me, wearing a red hat—whose?—on my head and a whistle. (Where on earth had the whistle come from? It was one of those loud, metal ones they use at the boat races.)

We behaved like teenagers, and made faces at the people in the street, then Jamie ran my chair into the gutter and I almost tumbled out, big blob rolling in the ditch, like Patsy getting out of the car—that calmed us down a bit; knee all scraped and bloody.

And then Tim, having found my note on the door, came running after us, and took charge, and we were civil again, in the presence of the headmaster. He did this to everybody: instil a natural sense of 'better behave!'

We went to a pub just two blocks from the corner of the square, and had pints of 80 Shilling all round. The place were full of office boys at one end and working men on the other. In between were a few tables with the odd assortment of early drinkers like us. Tim

114

and her fairy god-children. Or rather, the crew of the queer B&B, plus the handsome Eastern Europeans. I swear one of the blokes in Armani recognized Claudio, but left, almost the moment he did. Had I had the use of my legs, I would have gone after him and pinned him down. He did recognize him!

For a while we talked about school; how the Slovaks were settling in, what their classmates were like, and what they were learning. They found the staff very rude, the extra payments for books and credits *a bit stiff*—'nother idiom to teach them—the classrooms badly aired, but the teacher, a young woman from Sheffield, worth all the trouble! Lukáš winked, laughed, tried out an 'aye?' For a second, it seemed he had forgotten we were all gay. Or was it a joke that had fizzled? It were an utterly awkward moment! Jamie gave me and Tim a strange look, and I had to agree. But then, they seemed to focus on the female teacher more to reaffirm their straight credibility than from real interest; they both made a comment about her knockers, but when Javier asked, Claudio couldn't even remember the colour of her hair.

Since Javier hadn't been with the boys, and was the only other nonnative (the *colonial* Jamie, just like in the old days, not quite counting as a *foreigner*—isn't it strange that this hasn't changed?) in the round, it were naught special, we thought, that they showed an interest in him, that they wanted to know where he was from. They said they had been only to Barcelona, not further down.

He told his story in the course of two pints: how he had left the south of Spain because he was tired of the seasonal work, the tourists, the bad quality of everything, including the sardines; the religious old folk, the stupid right-wingers, all the black immigrants, the trouble with the police harassing gays in bars and finally—but he put it as if it didn't matter at all—his mutually abusive relationship with a shoe store clerk who tried beating him for looking at other men.

—Tried, but I hit him back. Spanish men, he said rather effusively, are just like Latin men; they don't want to love any one, they only want to *possess*. They want to own you, like they would own a dog or a woman. And they hate themselves for being gay, all and one of them. They think they aren't real men if they suck cock. They are sick—all the baggage of centuries. What they call

115

fuego, the fire of love, is only the hormones while they fuck you; as soon as that has cooled, they are jealous, selfish, spoiled, and so arrogant! Ay, hijo, so bloody cocky!

Claudio were a bit taken aback. He said something in Slovak, and then, rather cryptically, we thought,

—But you are a man too!

And then Javier did the first queer thing ever: he threw his head and arm back, exposing his neck, and said loud enough for some of the office boys to turn round to our watch our table,

—Are you sure, darling?

We laughed, Claudio somewhat embarrassed at the outburst he'd caused, but we settled down again. Javier kept an eye on Claudio—so intensely I knew he really wanted to hit on him, but weren't sure what to do next. I noticed how nervous he was suddenly.

They brought nibbles, and Jamie ordered something to eat; I can't remember what.

I told them about my friend Susan, who had moved to Sydney, Australia, and worked for a gay and lesbian helpline. She had written to say that most of the calls they got at work there were,

—Hold your breath—guess, from whom?

—People trying to commit suicide.

—No.

—People running out of condoms!

—No! Don't be facetious, Jamie.

—Well, tell them, they'll never guess.

—Lesbians. Lesbian couples, beating each other. Domestic violence between lesbian lovers.

—You are kidding? said Jamie, smirking, and not taking me seriously at all.

—No, that's what she said. They had a huge problem with violent lezzers.

—What a strange place the world is, said Javier. I always think men are much more violent.

—Yes, of course. Straight men—and lesbians.

Tim drank, then said,

—Do you know that almost a fourth of women claim to like or love other women to the point that they could enter a long-term

116

relationship? Yet . . .

—Yeah, but . . .

—No, let me finish! While men, even when gay, are much less likely to admit to liking or loving other men. Including gays! We did a nationwide study that showed men are much more likely to have sex with each other than to admit to their feelings. Men are . . .

A young man in a pinstripe suit suddenly appeared standing behind Tim, with a beer in his hand. He were smiling broadly, and looked already drunk.

—Well that's because men are pigs—they fuck anything, anywhere.

I think we were tempted to take him seriously, to include him in our conversation, for about five seconds as Tim turned round; then the man's smile fell, and with the utmost menace, and perfectly in earnest, he said,

—But iss no' right! Issagainst nature! Fucking perverts!

Jamie and Javier rose simultaneously and moved in his direction when from the bar thundered a sonorous voice,

—Hey! You there! Out! I told you not to come in here again!

We turned to look, but whoever it was had disappeared behind the cashier; then we saw the back of a burly feller head towards the back.

The man in the pinstripe said,

—Fucking faggots!

But before Jamie could get close enough to—well, hit him, I suppose—the heckler was gone, out the door, doing a bunk.

Through this interlude, and by virtue merely of our seating arrangement, I watched Lukáš more than anyone else. He had at first a look of surprise, then fear, and then, when Jamie showed himself so decisive and unafraid, even an expression of kind admiration, as if the last thing he would have expected from Jamie the slut were Jamie the hero: Jamie, standing up for himself and others.

But then he gave Claudio a look that was so pained, so utterly full of shared knowledge and emotion that for a while I felt quite uncomfortable.

Quietly brooding I formed a new theory, which lasted about

half a pint: that they were gay after all, but had been bullied, beaten, maybe lost a friend, and thereafter chose to hide from the world. Yes, maybe summat like that.

With more beer, the pub emptying of punters and filling again with the evening crowd (the office boys just throwing off their jackets to mark the transition, and ordering sandwiches), we ended up talking about courage, Jamie and Javier's actions still lingering, I suppose in our subconscious, even though the weird heckler were long forgotten, and the mood was light and jovial again. Javier was still checking out Claudio when no one was looking—his eyes glued to the biceps, the thighs, the line of his cheek.

I think it was Javier explaining why you could get laid with a man everywhere in Spain, but gay identities were still rare and people didn't embrace the separate lifestyle. Yes, Spain had changed, and Madrid Pride was a hoot, and they had gay marriage and all, but gays still were not respected. His argument was that Spanish men are ultimately cowards,

—Cowards *sin cojones,* who fuck in every dark alley of Madrid, but would never kiss you in broad daylight. They are so macho the bring their girls into the darkrooms of the gay bars. They all say they are bi, just because they are fucking cowards!

I were afraid then the conversation was going in circles, but the 'kissing in broad daylight' started a round of arguments about kissing in public, and men—straight men kissing—as the University of Bath had shown in their survey, which we all thought was biased by the fact that the men were too young. Men in their twenties, said Tim, are too young to be either straight or gay, they were still finding themselves (he looked at the Slovaks).

—They are barely able to control their urges in any direction, and using them as a yardstick for society as a whole is hardly appropriate. You see, there is the generation gap, wider than ever, and then kissing and kissing are two different things. Kissing a man for fun, for gay chicken—is that what they call it?—or for sex; or kissing, like Tim and I kiss, because we have been together so long, and it's a real sign of affection and commitment.

He leaned over and kissed me. I hate the term commitment. It always reminds me of jail—or a lunatic asylum. I thought of the

Slovaks kissing.

—It comes easier, when you are with a lover, to kiss in public. When you are together as long as wheelie here and I it becomes quite natural. At least . . .

—Yes, but would you do it at ASDA? That's the question! Would you kiss in a supermarket, in the checkout line, or in a doctor's office. Or . . .

—Oh, we? I said. We've kissed everywhere, including bus queues. But you have a point. Gay men are still too afraid—too afraid to be in public. It's cool on TV like that German soap—Christian and Oliver—cute as pie and making out, but that's TV. In real life, it's still a conscious act; it's still an act of rebellion! And there is always somebody objecting, or applauding, or attacking. Nobody notices straight couples kissing, but queers still turn heads.

Claudio was nodding, then said,

—You cannot do in our country! They kill you. Or in Russia. They kill you!

Yet with all that talk about snogging, and with 'rebellion!' as his obvious clue, handsome Jamie suddenly grinned, grabbed Javier and planted a wet one on him until one of the office boys over by the door whistled and Jamie, tongue still in the Spaniard's mouth, gave the whistler the finger. Somebody behind us laughed, and a few people jeered.

—You see, said Tim. There's kissing and then there's *kissing*. And it certainly doesn't go unnoticed.

I feared for a moment that Jamie had forgotten we were in a *normal* pub, but in the minds of the very young and attractive the distinctions don't matter as much anymore. And in the mind of Jamie, I guess, courage is everything. How I admire him for that—his spontaneous bravery.

They finally broke the kiss and took applause from a group of girls at the bar. Jamie, always the consummate show-master, rose a little without standing up and gave a bow. He wouldn't draw so much attention, of course, if he weren't such a bloody handsome bugger! Jamie gazed provocatively over at the office boys, and the one who had whistled threw him a kiss—but it were more of a tease and not real affection. Nonetheless, Jamie were about to get

119

up—to make a move on him, I suppose—when one of the girls came over and kissed Jamie on the cheek, said something like that it were nice to see boys kissing; and then she noticed Claudio and Lukáš, both flushed from the alcohol but with the customary cool about them, even a bit shy, and suddenly even stiffer than usual, and pretending, or really concentrating hard to follow the conversation.

—Now you two!

She was obviously tipsy. They took a second too long to realize what she meant, then said almost simultaneously,

—Oh no, we are not!

—Come on boys, said Javier, it doesn't matter if you are or not. Prove the University of bloody Bath right! Straight men kiss too! Bloody 89% of them! I say! It's just fun. Show us then, how straight boys kiss!

—Yeah, giggled the girl. Show us how straight blokes kiss! I wanna see!

She waved for her friend to come closer. I noticed Tim shift uncomfortably on his chair. There was a palpable tension suddenly, and the headmaster was ready to intervene, like in school, should something go wrong. I tried reaching out for his hand, but he didn't notice it.

The waiter brought another round of beer, and for a moment, our minds were elsewhere. Everybody drank, but the girl still stood there, and kept telling them to kiss. Lukáš shook his head and smiled uncomfortably, trying to dissuade her. He refused to let go of the glass; he held onto it like onto a safety buoy.

—Come on ye two, show us how straight lads kiss then!

She said it with such a heavy Scottish accent that I heard Tim mumble,

—They won't understand.

He was about to get up and intervene.

—You kissed at the house, I said to Claudio, but I doubt he heard me.

—I want kiss *you*, said Lukáš to the lass, but his voice was drowned out by the girl shouting something over her shoulder. Her friend came at last, plus another girl with a very short skirt, and the three started clapping, yelling,

—We wanna see ye snog, we want to see you snog—until, in a gesture that took us all by surprise, Claudio reached over, with his big brawny arm, pulled Lukáš closer, and kissed him smack on the lips.

It was short, too short to have any meaning, but with a sudden burst of hands clapping and the girls doing an exaggerated dance, it achieved what I think it had been meant to do: it disarmed the situation, relieved the tension, and sent the drunk girls back to their bar stools. Lukáš said something in Slovak. Javier told him to say it in English, and it was this: that they should get up now and 'look after' the girls, show them that they weren't really gay, and maybe ... you know ... get laid for the night. It was, after all, a Friday.

Again Lukáš smiled uncomfortably, giving each of us in the round an apologetic look. It was a perfectly normal thing to say for a heterosexual man, I suppose, but it seemed like an insult to all of us. And he knew that. It shouldn't have, of course, but he apologized, with his eyes, for having tried to be himself. It was curious that he and Claudio were so intimate in private, and yet here, in this pub, they seemed like any other couple of straight lads.

Javier got up, walked over to Lukáš's chair with playful annoyance and an exaggerated swagger, said,

—You do that stud, *vamos,* go pick up a girl or two! and lifted the Slovak out of his seat, pushed him away, towards the bar, and sat down next to Claudio.

For a moment, nobody was sure what he had in mind. Tim looked even more concerned, ready to jump up. Jamie grinned— he had an inkling, I think.

Lukáš stood there, gobsmacked, and with his hands idle reached for his beer. Without his friend he didn't make a move in the girls' direction, but instead came over and sat down in Javier's chair. He was a little red in the face, and seemed almost angry. And by the time he had sat down, still clutching his pint, Javier and Claudio were kissing—*really* kissing. Intense, romantic, all-out snogging, tongues and all, flicking over lips, and holding each other, arms all the way around the back, pulling the other in, and forgetting the world around them. Claudio sighed demonstratively.

121

We had been so busy watching Lukáš, that we had missed the start; now we stared with open mouths.

Jamie said,

—Wow! and from across the room came again a whistle.

They stopped long enough for Claudio to grin and Javier to say,

—I can tell he was a good kisser. He have those nice thick lips. Very sensual. You like kissing Spanish men?

Claudio was a little embarrassed at first, searching perhaps for a witty answer in the foreign idiom, but then he grabbed the Spaniard himself and before their mouths touched again said rather curiously,

—I like sunshine!

And then ... they didn't stop. It weren't a quick gesture, a daring display of *rebellion*, and they weren't drunk. They weren't just kissing—they were making out.

They touched the sides of each other's heads; and Javier had his hand on Claudio's thick bicep, pressing down hard, and then his hand on his thigh—and they were still kissing.

Claudio touched Javier's chest, slid his hand in his collar—and they just kept on kissing!

The office boys looked away now, shaking their heads in feigned disgust. Men in groups always do that, to preserve their dignity and banish the memories of their own adolescent adventures, or just to act like bloody immature wankers, or because they secretly want to try what they see, to make sure nobody would suspect them of ever having wondered what it would feel like to snog a boy.

Nobody in their right mind can seriously be disgusted seeing two humans kiss.

Javier and Claudio now had their arms around each other. They passed the point where it could have been shrugged off as a cool stunt of gay chicken. They were kissing each other, almost oblivious to the world, and just kept on kissing, for the sheer— and visible, on both ends; and audible—enjoyment of it.

I watched Jamie closely when I came to my senses again, reluctant to look away: there was a new-found respect in his eyes for the Spaniard, and maybe rekindled interest in the Slovak. There was also a bulge in his pants he tried to hide by shifting

122

his legs and putting his mobile phone from one side to the other.

Claudio was miraculous to watch, he seemed perfectly in his element. More even than with Lukáš, he seemed like a full-blooded, sensuous being, not giving superficial affection, but a part of his soul.

The girls showed no more interest—kissing were okay, maybe, making out too much; the office boys were now lost in their own bar games; only the whistler threw glances in the direction of the kissing couple—no, not at all! He were really looking at Jamie. But Jamie had forgotten he was there. Instead he turned to Lukáš and said,

—Should we kiss too?

He was warned off with a very clear shake of the head.

—No! No! Lukáš said strongly, then even tried to break the kissing boys up, saying

—All right, that's enough Claudio!

But his friend was too far gone exploring the sensual Iberian mouth.

After a long and rather strange silence—and I imagine to Lukáš's greatest relief—the show was over; the kiss broke. Claudio's eyes were strained and a little wet. His face were flushed and glowing; his chest were positively heaving.

There were some applause somewhere in the back of the pub, but I am not sure if it were meant for them. I was glad it was over, but I had enjoyed it of course. And now I wondered what it all meant.

Javier put a hand on Claudio's pecs and rubbed the hard flesh.

—You know, even if you aren't, you *should* be gay—I am not saying you are!

Apparently, I was not the only one trying to be careful.

—But you are an excellent kisser! Wow, hijo! You are so fucking hot! You've got more *fuego* in you than a thousand Spaniards!

I caught Tim staring at the bulge in Claudio's crotch. Javier wiped his lips, but stopped half-way, then licked them. He seemed a bit spaced out, and when Jamie looked at him, winking, and maybe not without a certain jealousy, he averted his eyes. Tim, usually taking his beers slowly and in tiny sips, emptied the half-full pint in front of him in one go, then put the glass down with a thud.

Claudio said nothing, but smiled enigmatically, and then, his eyes still low, looked for the first time since the inception of the spectacle over to his friend, batting his eyelids as if—yes—pleading forgiveness, as if checking that he hadn't overstepped some boundary, and whether he were still welcome. It were a clear indication that there was some alpha-male stuff going on there too. It was such a curious look that Jamie noticed it too, and together we puzzled over it a few days later during our tête-à-tête in the kitchen.

Lukáš acknowledged his friend, but abruptly he looked at his watch, decided that it were time to split, and rose from his chair. He put a twenty pound note on the table. We all stared at it. His glass was still almost full, and so was Claudio's. When had he had the time to drink, snogging away like that? But without hesitation, Claudio got up also and followed Lukáš out the door, leaving the four of us quite without a proper ending to the evening. Tim, always the man in charge, was the first to rise with a

—Well?

and at last the rest of us began to move. Javier was still on a cloud, and Jamie didn't look much more present.

Strangely and entirely unexpected, Claudio and Lukáš were waiting outside, leaning against the wall, and not speaking.

We all walked home in a curious procession: Tim ahead like a steam engine smoking his pipe, while Claudio pushed my chair right behind, like the wheels on the locomotive, Lukáš walking a little behind, talking. At first he said something in Slovak, but then in English, and addressing Javier and Jamie, and then clearly me, because he touched the handle of the wheelchair when he spoke. He said over and over again,

—It was just fun. It was just for fun! It was not for real!

And his face was still red.

We heard them argue in their room for a little while that night. Not very angry, and with long pauses, but all in Slovak. I wish I knew what it were about. I think I know now, but when it happened, at the time, it were all very bewildering.

There you go, Mr Dedalus. That were the highlight of that week. Not being afraid of the big black sheep.

It seems all so long ago now, and so preposterously emotional—charged with *unnecessary* emotion. We were all barking up the wrong tree! And it weren't our business, but we made it the focus of all our thoughts.

The whole summer that year revolved about nothing else. It was as if the Slovaks had come to show us up, to tear us down, to make us grovel and feel guilty.

As a child, I had a friend by the name of Paul, who was from a Jewish family. We were eighteen. We went out to a pub with two girls; I can't remember their names. One worked at the post office, and she reminded me a lot of a film star, the way she moved with an inbred elegance, although she weren't especially attractive. Anyroad, at some point we were talking about kissing, and Paul asks his girl what it feels like to kiss a guy—this was ages ago, remember; in the early seventies—he said he wanted to know, with the beard stubble, and the harder chin, and the different smells.

Mind you, I don't need to tell you, Mr Dedalus, those were different times. People still smoked in pubs! She looked at him, slightly intrigued, I remember, and instead of describing it, she pointed at me, and said jokingly,

—Why don't you just kiss Tim, then you'll know! He's cute! Why don't you kiss Tim?

And he did. I am sure she'd meant it purely as a joke, but he just grabbed me and kissed me, in front of everybody. Then he wiped his mouth and said, ah, so, that's it, or something like it, and left me with a boner. He went to the toilet—I assume to rinse his mouth, the stupid fuck—and left me there with the giggling girls. I made no protest, I didn't show any disgust, it had all happened too quickly. But then one of the girls said,

—Did ya like it then? Did ya?

I should have just said something funny, like

—Oh yeah, it weren't half bad!

and shrugged it off, but I turned sullen and angry, and they kept on nettling me,

—Did ya like it then? Did ya really like it? How were it? Were it good?

and by the end of the night, everybody in the pub knew I were gay. It just got out of hand, somehow, because I didn't know how to handle it. I couldn't pretend. I couldn't . . . and after that kiss, somehow, I wanted people to know. I'd been kissed by a boy. Fake and false and everything, but I'd been kissed.

Well there you have it, I've never told you that, Mr Dedalus. That's why I left home and went to London, and met you, and ended up on a ship with my cock up Rafael's arse—that's how my whole life got started, or rather derailed, as it were, with yon daft kiss!

The pub doesn't even exist any more. It's a penny store now. The pub, the place, the very *locus*—where all my life changed has been obliterated by the forces of . . . by the sands of time. The sands of time, yes. Don't it sound grand? Oh I am such a drama queen!

So of course, after Claudio kissed Javier, that intimate, public scene of almost pornographic quality, I had all kinds of hot flashes, and I didn't leave the house for a week.

I remember thinking afterwards that Claudio had been too enthusiastic, had perhaps *acted*. Not far from the truth then. Not as stupid as I look! I sat at home, thinking of you, Mr Dedalus, and how I wouldnae be here today in this fucking wheelchair if it weren't for you, and how I would have never met you, if it weren't for going to London, and how I would never have gone to London if it weren't for that kiss, that stupid kiss by a curious straight bloke, after which, in my home town, I couldn't show my face. Paul, who'd started it, just shrugged it off. He told everybody why he'd done it. He'd wanted to know, he said, how it felt to snog a man, and that were it. He'd just wanted to bally know how it felt.

Oh, it's easy for them—for them as only have to pretend. Nobody called him a queer; nobody sent him packing. He still lives there, married, with children, and for all I know he's still snogging boys in the shed.

A strange thought occurred to me just now: after he kissed me,

126

what did he do in the toilet, really? And for so long! He must have been twenty minutes, leaving me with the girls. While I was being outed, and ridiculed and bullied, while my life at home ended with a bang and a smack—was he vomiting? Washing his mouth out with soap, the asshole? Or were he rubbing one off?

Mind you, I were quite a looker at eighteen, you understand. I wouldn't hold it against him.

The kiss made them famous. Was it the girls who gossiped, or Jamie, or both? I don't know. But people started coming round the house. Friends and acquaintances we hadn't seen or met in years; young lads who said they knew Jamie or Javier from the bars, or some of our former lodgers they wanted to get in touch with; and people without excuses, asking about the Slovaks.

At first I thought they were real—maybe from the school, maybe here for an appointment, to do homework together—but soon I clocked what they were really up to.

Some brought gifts, some stayed for tea, hoping to catch a glimpse of the mysterious couple. Even youngsters came, eighteen, twenty years old, who'd overheard a conversation, who—said one—had read it on a blog, or on a Facebook post. But nobody, the pimplish boy insisted, had seen any pictures, so he had come to see for himself, to 'check it out,' he said, with an Australian accent. Asked if it were 'all-right to have a look-see,' and wouldn't I take it personal, *mate*, and please excuse the interruption—when I told him they weren't here, or that we didn't have any Slovaks at all!

One has to protect one's lodgers' privacy. Matron Tim, broom in hand, chasing off the stalkers!

Two girls showed up also, rather forthcoming with information, rather badly done up with strange make-up around the eyes, saying that her—that is, the redhead's—brother had mentioned Klaus or Claudio, she couldn't remember, whom he'd heard about from a friend who was gay, whom he'd seen shaggin' in the park—she just blurted it out like that!—and that they didn't have a problem with gays, but they wanted to know. Know what? Brats. Off! Off you go! Leave us alone you nosy bitch!

For a fortnight though, it seemed all Edinburgh was obsessed with their secret, if there were one. Whole Edinburgh was out

127

to discover the Slovaks; and rumours started about them being famous, and in movies, and singers, and really, really cute; and that they lived in our B&B to avoid the press, and the paparazzi; and that they were rich, that they had money and one of them were the son of a Russian oligarch—of that guy who owns the football club, and all matter of nonsense—until Jamie spread the word in the bars that they had left, and anyway, they'd just been plain friends, and hadn't any money at all. And as for *olligarks*, you cow—you don't even know how to spell it!

Tim's sister dropped in. She likes her drink too, so we have to hide the booze from her, as I've said. You can't leave Mary alone with a bottle, and we usually go to the pub together, and talk about her addiction to cigarettes and television—the shopping channel in particular.

She had gone over the limit on all her credit cards again, buying fitness equipment and cooking utensils, and miracle cure for ailments she didn't have, making a down-payment on a trip to Madeira she would never take. It's a proper disease they say—a *disorder*. Once she bought a camper van! She can't drive, and she certainly isn't one for camping! Yet she is a smart woman, you can talk to her and she will listen and, amazingly, she will have something meaningful to say almost on every occasion. Or at least something comforting. Anyroad, I like talking to her. Wasted as I am, we two get along like a house on fire.

Like now, after she'd pushed me round the church gardens three times, asked if I had 'done me business,' then got us the best table in the pub and two pints. I told her about Claudio and Lukáš, and she said,

—Well, there is something there tha' issnae right!

It didn't sound like much of an insight, but it was, really, because she went on to say,

—Some trauma!

—Trauma?

—Yes. Something traumatic.

—You mean dramatic?

—No, I mean traumatic—an old wound, aye? Can ye nae feel it? There's a lot between them left unsaid.

—What do you mean can't I feel it? You haven't even met them. How can you ...

—Based on what ye are telling me. I am only listening. I hear you!

—Are you psychic now?

—Oh, don't be so daft. There's trauma. There's something in their past which has shifted their roles.

—Shifted their roles? What are you on about?

—Yes. Made them into different beings. Normal straight blokes behave differently, and gay boys behave differently. So there has to be something that makes them behave the way they do. And in my experience ...

—In your *experience?*

Mary has been on disability benefits for twenty years. Before that she was a secretary and a bar maid. What experience?

—Yes, well, I watch a lot of telly. People do go on talk shows ye know. Ye can learn a lot off the telly.

I shook my head.

—Well, ye wanted my opinion. This is it: there was a single traumatic event ...

—Rubbish! I interjected. Just rubbish! They are just good friends! What trauma?

—Good friends my bony arse! If they are just good friends, why did you bring them up? Why does it bother ye then? Why do ye think there's a mystery to solve in the first place?

—Because ...

—Because ... ?

—Because there is! 'Cos I can feel it! There's summat ...

—Oh! Are you psychic then?

—I feel it in me bones.

—Hae ye got psychic bones?

I almost slapped her, but she had that smile on her face, that all-knowing womanly smile, and a grin, now, and suddenly I knew she were right. Trauma.

—Ye and yir boys! Ye auld fairy!

I gave her some money.

—They are too old to be snogging and cuddling. Teenage boys do that, aye, but they are grown men. Two men can be friends,

129

nae doubt, friends to die for each other, know what I mean—but that's history. That's friendships forged in war. Fightin' buddies. Where would they hae been fightin'? Young men without women around them. Sooner or later—and twenty-seven is late—women come between them, and they's off breedin' and doing their bit to overpopulate the planet. So if yir boys are not queer . . .

—Well, they say they are not.

— . . . if yir boys are not queer, then, if I am looking at this right, she said, earnestly stuffing the bills into her pocket, it's all about a lass!

—About a girl?

—Aye, about a girl. Mark ma words! she said theatrically, her unkempt, oily grey hair falling into her eyes, to be wiped away with a majestic gesture—then she sniffed twice and lit another cigarette. It's all about a girl!

—Are ya sure?

—I am absolutely sure! Think about it. If they *are* straight— let's assume that for a moment—then only a girl couldae upset them so badly, thrown them so out of kilter. Men are—forgive me, straight men—are simple! They only get excited about three things: fighting, which includes sport; cars, or gadgets; and women. It's tanks, tools or tits. And they never change, really, but if they do—really change—it's because of a woman. There's a woman somewhere in there. There's got ta be! Find her. Find the woman, and ye'll know their secret.

—*Cherchez la femme,* then?

—Aye. Off ye go *cherching.*

After the kissing incident, we didn't see Claudio or Lukáš for a few days. They weren't gone, exactly—they just were *not there.* They didn't come down to the living room or the kitchen. They made no noise in their rooms. I spoke to Claudio for only a moment on the stairs; he said they had a lot of homework. He said he needed to concentrate.

And yet I saw him leaning by the window, sitting on the sill in only his jeans, his flat stomach reflecting the morning light. I saw him in front of the house, sitting on the stoop in the afternoon sun, daydreaming. I saw him with friends from school, all boys;

and I saw him alone, in a pub, playing with his mobile. I saw him standing by the builder's skip at the end of the road, believing himself unobserved, and smoking a hurried cigarette—he didn't in the house or in front of Lukáš. And every time I saw him alone, he seemed unbearably sad.

I saw Lukáš too during those days, also alone. I went to visit a friend in hospital when I ran across him in the casualty waiting room. At first I thought he were hurt, but he'd only come with a fellow student who'd been in an accident. Anyroad, I had five minutes, and I stayed there, looking at him through the glass.

Then it hit me: he had the same expression of sadness, the same face like a slapped arse. He was lonely, lost. His eyes were sad. Yet I'd never seen that when he were with Claudio; together they were always cheerful. Even in company with others, they always seemed happy. But alone—alone in a crowd, or really alone—they seemed burdened with their fate, their very being seemed to drag them down. I told Tim about the meeting, and he said, *de profundis!*

So I thought, ah well, it's really a painful coming out. They are gay all right, those lads, they just won't face it! They just need time, and maybe a little push. Never mind what Tim said, I thought; I'll help them.

I looked at Lukáš: dark hair, fine long face, noble features; it occurred to me: aristocratic. But sad. The unbearable sadness of the homosexual male, before he learns to accept who he is. Gays all have that sadness about them, when they are alone.

It's funny really how 'gay' came to mean homosexual—it's just the *wrong* word! Most of us carry around a heavy burden. Regrets. The loss of so much—and we never quite know what we gain. That's why there's drag queens. That's why we need all the make-up!

Then, a day or two later, Lukáš took me by the hand and pulled me into a corner of the landing, where the broom cupboard is. I could feel that he had the sudden urge to explain himself; and when it did come out of him like a painful birth, like water from a rock—an urgent *emanation*—I hardly knew what he was saying, and why he needed to say it to me, and with so much insistence.

131

I tried to get him to sit down in the living-room, make some tea, talk in peace, but he wouldn't hear of it. When he spoke, he looked about anxiously as if to make sure that we weren't overheard, but nonetheless he said it, deliberately, and slowly, as if he had prepared his speech very, very carefully.

—Claudio is not homosexual! He kissing the Spanish man only for fun! Not what you think! He is not homosexual!

I wanted to get away, readily believing that this was all he had to say, that he just wanted to make sure, at the same time realizing that this must have irritated him for days, that Lukáš, in fact, was still embarrassed by the scene at the bar, that it had gnawed at him all this time.

—Okay, I said, trying to get away, he's not gay! Keep ya hair on!

He seemed to relax a little, and let go of my arm. He put his hands on the frame of the wheelchair however, so that I couldn't roll away.

—I can explain why you think we gay. I explain!

He swallowed.

—Go on . . .

He said again,

—I explain!

But it was obvious he still needed a few moments to collect himself.

His eyelids flickered when I looked straight at him, then he turned away, breathed heavily for a few seconds. His agitation, his flushed face, made him all the more attractive.

At last he said,

—Men are always bullies, loud, and violent. Some only inside, but they always are. They must do violent—they have to. They make baby and have to protect babies, it is in natural! In evolution.

He mispronounced that last word so badly I thought I misheard. But then he went on,

—They fight over women, because of DNA! Because they are like that! They fight, always, and want to have a woman. Own and destroy. Look at sports! In Slovakia is crazy about hockey, but go to hockey game! Animal on the ice, and animal watcher. The spec . . . spectacle?

—Spectators?

132

—Yes, spectator, like silly animal too, and aggressive. Football is already violence but hockey have weapon too, have hockey stick. Sports is same as war. You go see hockey game in Slovakia, is like a fight. Sport is war—that's why men like it, but so dumb, so dumb! Dumb like box of hair! It's a . . . a . . .

—A substitute for war. An outlet for the aggressiveness of men? Clan and tribe and all that, and fighting over women, and each other, full of anger . . . I know, dear.

He looked reproachfully at me, almost a bit menacing. I decided not to play the queen, and not call him 'dear.' But he didn't mention it. He weren't to be distracted from his prepared speech.

—Yes. And men always need outside object, because inside they are worthless, you understand?

—Worthless?

—Yes. They cannot have baby.

—Because they cannot bear children—they cannot give life? That's very philosophical. You are . . .

—I don't know why. I am not smart. I only know Claudio and I, we are *not* like that. We don't bully. We don't like sports—to watch I mean. Watch sports is stupid. But if you don't participate in their games, their aggression, you are outsider always. In the world, you see, all is man, all is *for male.* All the world is made by men.

—But surely, there are sensible young men. Not everyone is an animal. Not every male is a brute. When you remove them from their mates, their cliques, their gangs, they become quite . . .

—Yes, maybe. But I thinking maybe only on surface. Inside, men are always . . . incomplete. So they make a world full of aggression, to complete what they missing. Our whole world, all government, sports, education—all produce aggressive bully, to make the pain in men go away. Nine out of ten men, even if they are open-mind and revolutionary when young, once they marry, they become conservative: they must provide for children, protect, so they become conservative bully. Threaten others, make fun, destroy. Men hate women, in truth, most do. Maybe you gays, maybe you are only honest people. The world would look different if making only by women, but it is all men: all competition, aggression, bullying, hurt . . . look how women are treated in marriage, many marriage: like cattle still, look in India—we going there to see, and it was horrible. Many places in the world still treating women like cattle. And in Islam country, they treat them worse—like children, never grow up, and kick them around like dogs. And rape, so many women raped, when young, and even in marriage. Half marriages are violent, or would be violent if women don't obey. I feeling always ashamed often, to be man. To be aggressive, to be competition . . .

—Competitive, I said, but it felt wrong to correct him, so I said it under my breath.

I had the image of a veiled woman in a hut in my mind, and a toothless, ugly man beating her. Ashamed to be a man—he was telling me something he was convinced of, something profound, something he felt was very important to who he was, what had formed him, disturbed him, the font of his sensitivities, essential to what they were, together, he and his Claudio. And at the same time I had this despicable thought: oh, come on, what a sissy. What a pansy! What is he on about?

—That is why you think Claudio and I are homosexual, because we not bully, not watch sports, and are not aggressive and brutal and . . . and we don't make joke and don't go out to get girls. That why we go staying in gay place, and we don't spending much time together with girls. I mean—we together. When we are with girls, it is alone, we go away for that. Because when with girls, we are different. But that is why we look for places gay, because we fit in better. Sometimes we going to gay bar just for drinking, because in straight bar—we stick out. We are *softy*. In Slovakia, we get bully, because we don't like dirty joke, and talk dirty about women, and endless talk about stupid sports. People—drunk, stupid people—who cannot even run a kilometre or hit a ball at all, sitting in pub and calling football players dirty names. It is all outside abject men need to feel complete: aggression, war, fighting, muscles, even. We don't like aggressive, and we don't like treat women like abject!

—Objects, I corrected, involuntarily, when I heard his pronunciation.

—Yes, abject—sex abject. At home, in normal pub, is always fight, and people boasting, and very—how you say—people were

134

cruel—no, crude I mean, very rough. In many place of men it is the same, like being in the army. We had terrible time in army, terrible: that is why we like hiking alone, and go on long nature vacation, and not we playing in team sports—we trying, but in sports, everybody who is not bully—gay, women, weak—you know, sissy—we are coward, we are not tough enough, you understand? It is not our inside, not what inside us, you see? It is not being our nature to be so like normal men, we all feeling and they trammel us. Trammel our feeling.

—Trample? They trample . . .

—Yes. 'Trample' is not German? I think it were German.

—It may be, but it's English too. If that's what you mean. You can't say 'were' by the way, it's 'was German.'

—But you say 'were' always—often I mean. I hear you say 'were.'

—That's because of where I am from—it's wrong; it's a dialect. I try not to, but sometimes it slips out. Don't copy me! My English is messed up. You should talk to Tim more.

He smiled. I did too, but a bit embarrassed. There, Mr Dedalus. Now I am blushing, because you didn't quite manage what you set out to do: extinguish the Yorkshire lad in me, and make me a man of the world. And living with Tim did the rest. And moving to Scotland, and picking up the language of so many lodgers. There were a time when I said 'g'day' to everybody!

Lukáš interrupted my thoughts.

—The world, it ravaging, it no place for weak people. *It is* no place for weak peoples; only bully men, from soldiers, to banker, to politicians—all taking all by force—grab, grab, you know? Be brutal and take as much as you can. Grab, grab, greed, greed, and bully! Women make sex symbol, and gay are killed, because world is ruled by bullies. Men who respect only power and aggression, not love and con . . . com . . . I forget, 'súcit,' how you say 'súcit?' Mitleid?

—I don't know. What does it mean?

—It mean when you know what other man feels. When you care about . . .

—Ah . . . compassion?

—Yes, compassion. *Com-pa-ssion.* I must remember word . . .

135

That's why you think Claudio and I different—because we have compassions, and we don't like to be bully. And that's why we staying gay place sometimes, because it more ... soft, because gay friends is more compassion, and not so ... Where we come from, in Slovakia—maybe everywhere—men are so ... shallow. So hard to find real friend! It more ... real. People with compassions are more real. They live, you know.

—Compassion, not compassions. I don't think gay people are any less shallow, on the whole, on the contrary: the majority ...

—Maybe not less shallow. But at least, not aggression—aggressive.

I looked into his eyes. For an instant, I thought he had revealed the secret of life to me—at least a great truth, something all-encompassing and permanent. I felt that I understood him completely, and his relationship with Claudio. But the sensation was only temporary. Surely, being compassionate and sensitive has nothing to do with the gender you prefer. And yet there was a truth hidden in there, in his outburst. He was railing against *a type* of male: the chauvinists, the machos, the homophobic grey-haired bible-wielding arseholes who still fill our parliaments, our government offices, our banks and law firms; the alpha-males who torture and maim and penetrate and lie and steal to get to the top. I could feel his anger at the world, but then he smiled, and I saw that it were only himself he tried to explain, his and Claudio's life he tried to make sense of.

—But you must understand, we don't have sex with men! Not with each other, never have. We are not lover, not gay lovers. We are just—we just don't fit in! I think sometimes there is no place for us.

I had an impulse to caress him, to hug him, the lost child, the forlorn soldier of compassion, but something told me he would have pushed me away. Then he said with renewed intensity,

—We had enough violence in our life already. Now we don't bully. Now we are compassion. I am sorry my English is so bad still! You know what I meaning though, you know?

I nodded.

—We are soft and useless. We have broken—we are broken!

—You are broken, how?

136

—Yes, we are broken.

—Yes, but . . .

He didn't understand that I was asking him a question, and just nodded, said again, 'broken, broken,' when suddenly there was a noise from the floor above, and he let go of me and ran away.

I stayed motionless until the front door fell shut. Javier passed me and smiled. I wiped something—I think the balustrade, or a handle—just a motion, to give me a reason to be there. I was so surprised by Lukáš's verbal attack, I remained there for many minutes, pondering, and rather stunned. He had seemed like a preacher in the pulpit; but now that he were gone, I was unsure of what exactly he had revealed, or if he had said anything important at all. And then I had this image of a man banging his head against the wall, frustrated by the stupidity of the world.

For the first time in my life I thought: well now, straight boys feel it too. There are straight men too who feel that our macho, winner-takes-all, survival of the fittest male unculture, our testosterone capitalism was all wrong. There were straight males after all, who were embracing *feminine* values. Why they had to be feminine these values, I don't know. But they'd been trampled into the mud, ridiculed, just like the rest of us. Show a bit of weakness and they'll walk right over you.

I told Tim that night in bed what had happened. He said at first that there must be some strange rage in Lukáš, some inexplicable aggression. But then we focused on the denial, his insistence that his mate weren't gay, and Tim said,

—Did he wait all this time to tell you? Why is it so important? The kiss in the bar was weeks ago—when was it? Why did he wait all this time?

—I don't know. It seemed very important to him that I should know—that I should understand Claudio weren't gay. He was very . . . intense when he spoke.

Tim made out the light, then said,

—They had a fight that night. They fought for a long time, remember? Raised voices you know—I wish I knew what it was about.

—I know.

137

—You know?

—No, I mean . . . I'd like to know too. I'd like to know what they fought about.

—Yes. But he's a thinker though. He mightn't be able to express it in English, so well, but he's smart all right. He's definitely onto ideas. He is forming concepts. I wish half the students in my school were that wise. All they seem to do is click on Like buttons. This is the age where ideas are dying . . . the great thinkers. Well, anyway, so I see—there is hope. Hope coming from the East. It'll be the East that will revive our mindless Western hedonism then. Thank god for EU expansion then. They'll bring in some new blood.

He turned towards me, and I could feel he wanted to say more. He put a hand on my chest, very gently.

—You know, all that anger against the male world . . . There is something violent lurking in their past. Something . . . All that generalizing, those generalizations about straight men, they are ludicrous of course. There are always exceptions with men, men who are more sensitive and clean. Not like Latinos or Spaniards, men who shoot each other on sight, out of shame, rather than loving each other. And they are just that, generalizations, meaningless, I mean, lots of gay men are possessive and aggressive and lots of straight lads are sensitive and caring. He's talking about young men growing up, about their games, their crude virility, calling girls cum-dumpsters—where did I read that? Respecting nothing, shooting dogs and cats for fun and baulking at the mere mention of tenderness. He is talking of youth, of the uncouth male, and their stupidity—the source of all trouble in the world. Men before they are polished, worn down, by female influence and life and the realization that maleness, unadulterated maleness, only breeds violence.

He continued,

—Maybe Slovakia is like that. Maybe they really never met a nice straight bloke—or a violent father? A brother? Were they both bullied in school? Abused by a teacher? There is something that turned these two boys against the world of men, something that . . .

—God you do sound like a school teacher!

—Well I am. I am. I can't help it. When I see children, young

138

men, with problems, I wonder what the problem is. The cure. There has to be a reason for the way they are.

He pulled up the blanket the way he does when we are ready to doss down. But abruptly he spoke again.

—Could it be that . . .

—You realize we are obsessed with them? Obsessed!

— . . . they . . . What?

—Tim, honey! We are obsessed with them! We talk of nothing else. For weeks now. They have . . . taken over the whole house! Javier is in love with Claudio, you can tell. In lust at least. They have us all in thrall . . . ! And have you noticed another thing . . . ?

I just had to say it. It were on my mind, after several nights, it had been lurking in the back of my mind.

—I noticed you are drinking less? That it?

—I am trying to, but that's not what I mean.

—What then?

—Have you noticed that you and I, we are talking more? We used to talk a lot less. Ever since they arrived, we've . . . Remember by the loch, and almost every night now in bed? Remember how we were before they arrived? We barely said good night to each other any more. Don't you feel you and I have become closer?

—Because of them? You really think so?

—I think so. You even call me during the day now. You've never done this before.

—Yes but . . . because of Claudio and Lukáš?

—Yes. They have an influence on everybody they meet. They invite curiosity. And they change the world around them. They are like . . . like a vortex, like a black hole . . . travelling . . .

—A vortex? You are watching too much *Doctor Who*!

—No, I mean, they suck in everything, and change it, and it comes out all new at the other end. Don't you think so?

—I don't know. They certainly occupy our minds. And it's not just because they are so handsome.

—No, exactly. That would have worn off a long time ago. It's because they are . . .

—Mysterious?

There was a long pause, then Tim said,

—It's nice then. It's good they are here, if they brought us

139

together. If we are talking again.

—Yes. And they are changing the others too. Javier . . . well, you know. And Jamie . . .

—What about Jamie?

—Jamie's not going out any more. Have you noticed? He used to be out every Friday, Saturday, even weekdays, in the bars, the park, or meeting people on the net. He's not been out for a week at least, two I think. Not as much, anyway.

—Really? I hadn't noticed.

—Maybe he's got a boyfriend.

—Nah! Jamie? A boyfriend?

—I am telling you. Everything is changing around here!

PART IV

And so it were: everything were changing. A few nights after Lukáš attacked me, I were sat with Jamie in the kitchen. And Tim had been right: he had a boyfriend! It were late, maybe ten, with the last of the daylight flowing into the room—golden, dusty rays shooting over the fruit bowl, the sink, the table, and onto the American's ripped body. He spoke of nothing but his new flame, Maurizio, whom he'd met not in a bar, but at work. At first I thought it were just another trick, another of his casual fucks, but I soon realized that it were much more.

The museum was preparing an exhibition about Venice at the time of Casanova, and had flown in two models, a boy and a girl, for a series of shots.

Jamie never saw the girl (she was probably there, but he just ignored her), but fell in love with Maurizio, Spanish-Italian-Lebanese mix. He were cute as pie and boyishly handsome, but completely different from Jamie. Dark and a little short, with a thin frame and that Mediterranean elegance; that look, more than a boy, less than a man, but all of the above; and with two rows of perfect teeth and . . . just exactly the type Jamie would fall for, if he ever did.

And then, well, he did! Our Jamie, who would never, ever settle down, began a real love affair.

I am telling you, head over heels!

Jamie—inspired, he said, entirely by the Slovaks and their sweet relationship, which had instilled in him a longing for a more steady partner—had asked the model out to dinner, after the shoot was over, and Maurizio had agreed. So Jamie had a date with him a week later. That's what we talked about that day.

—In a week! A whole week! That's quite a time horizon for you, old chum.

Jamie had a soft drink in his hand and was leaning against the refrigerator.

—I know. I must be *really* in love. *It were amazing, lad, the bugger's amazing!* he said jokingly, sounding like Inspector

Dalziel.

—Don't mock me! I am trying to do my best.

—Your best?

—Yes. I am trying to speak properly with them. Lest they learn all the wrong English from me.

—So I shouldn't talk to them at all you mean, being American.

—You better not. But not because of your American accent . . .

—Waddaya mean?

—You know all too well what I mean, Jamie. Hands off the Slovaks!

—Oh, that. Sorry—no danger there. I'm in love.

—Ah yes, I forgot.

I grinned. He gave me a broad smile. Then, exactly then, I knew he was dead serious. He was in love.

—How did you meet?

—Meet? Oh, he swept me off my feet!

The moment he'd said it, he looked at my wheelchair. Many people do, when feet and dancing and running and jumping are mentioned.

—It's fine. I'd like to be swept off my feet. I once was!

There you go, Mr Dedalus. I admitted it. You did sweep me. If only for . . . ah, forget it. I am tired of talking to you.

Jamie was wearing only jeans and nothing on top, like so often. I realized Claudio had been imitating him, that kicking about the house in a state of erotic undress, to make Tim and Tim blush—they did it on purpose! He looked tanned and relaxed, suave and rather vulnerable. The light danced on his stomach muscles, yet somehow, he didn't look quite as chiselled as he used to. There was a glow about him, a soft and emollient glow. I asked him again how he'd met his new flame.

He looked out the bay window for a while without answering, as if he were reliving in his mind those moments he was about to recount. When he spoke, his cheeks began to shine. His right hand held the can, but the left played with the hair just below his navel, pulling it gently, absentmindedly. I really tried not to look.

—Oh he is sweet!—all in his American accent, and very emotional—I mean he is sweet! Sweet, sweet, sweet! Not just handsome—he's got that . . . that something! He is charming!

From the moment I saw him, I knew ... I waited for him outside the museum. We'd made the barest of eye contacts, because he was working—there were other people there, of course, and he was nervous, and he didn't know who I was! But outside, I waited at the corner, and I saw him walking towards me. He did something with his phone—checking e-mail, or Facebook or something. I stopped in the recess there, you know, across from the church, and he—when he came up, he just grabbed my arm and pulled me down the alley! He wouldn't let go. He—there was just a quick glance, nothing more, and he recognized me, smiled, and he just ... he just grabbed me! *He* grabbed *me!*

His hair-twisting accelerated; now he was drawing circles, pulling, pushing into his navel, tracing the line down to his crotch, and up again, and over his pecs. When he drank, a drop ran over his chin onto his chest. He looked down on himself, held the flat of the palm against his washboard, and for a moment, he was lost to me. Because of how the light fell in, and how the fine hairs shimmered, I thought at first he was admiring his own physique, but he was not. He rubbed his pecs a little, and a smile came over his face. It was the memory of the meeting that had him so entranced, not self-adulation. His eyes were looking nowhere. It was another person which did this to him. For the first time ever, I saw him helpless, weak, mesmerized by something other than his own virility and beauty.

—So ... there were a couple of trash cans—I mean wheelie bins—which blocked the view from the street. It was just after six, and traffic was heavy. We slipped behind them. I thought for a moment he was crazy. But before I knew it his mouth was on mine and he was kissing me! He was—he really just went for it! He kissed me!

—He just kissed you like that? You hadn't talked to him at all?

—Yes. No! No preliminaries, no chit-chat, he just ... he just *took* me. He ...

—Ravished you, did he? And you let him?

—I let him. Ravished, yes. It really ... I was rattled. I ... I don't know, we kissed for some time, a few minutes. I remember how sweet his mouth tasted, so fucking sweet. Not like after someone's chewed gum, not food-sweet—I mean naturally sweet. What's

143

the word . . . ah fuck it. Some people taste sour, some people have a very strong bodily, fleshy taste, some taste just like sex, but his mouth was . . . alkaline. Soft. Pleasant. I don't know how to describe it. Like . . . like a bed of flowers, like an evening breeze, like, that feeling of happiness you have when . . . like a soft warm towel after a shower. I am just bad with words, but you know what . . . just sweet. And he smelled sweet too. Fresh, sweet, soft skin and . . .

—I remember that, and the sound of the traffic, and somebody . . . Then he said, like, 'I saw you looking at me,' and I said, 'and you were checking me out!' Then he said he liked me, and wanted to see me again, and . . . he asked if I was free, after all his work was done. I thought he'd be here only for a day, or so, but he said he would stay, he said, for a few weeks, and . . . then he kissed me again, hot and long and wet, and with . . . so hard, so strong, so . . . he pressed me towards him, he held me here, and here, around the waist, and he kissed me like he wanted to remove all doubts!

—What doubts?

—That . . . I don't know! I don't know! I mean . . . there are always doubts, there is always something lingering in the back of one's mind, you see, even with a first kiss, when you pick up a guy in a bar and . . . you have thoughts. You know? You think while you kiss. Is he gonna be a top or a bottom? Is he gonna want to come home with me? Or something. But with him, with Maurizio, I mean . . . I just couldn't think, when he kissed me. One is always careful, and doubtful, and at least a little hesitant, when you meet someone, but his kiss . . . it was like a statement. A bold, loud, proud, wild statement! He took away all doubt—doubt that he was maybe just fooling around, or playing with me, that I was just sex behind the wheelie bins. He kissed like he was saying, 'you're mine now, you know?' and my mind went blank. I swear! His hands were all over me, and I touched him. He's not a tall model, not perfect. I mean he's perfect for me, but he's not . . . whatever! He is so fucking cute! When we broke the kiss at last, he said he really liked me, he *wanted* me.

—Is this just the Latin fire—I wonder, you know. He is half Spanish, and half—I forgot. Lebanese? He told me . . . yes, Lebanese. But he is from down there, from the sun, and sometimes they are

144

a bit over the top, too . . . driven, too much energy. He grabbed my bum, and my cock—of course I was hard, hard as hell, I couldn't think straight, he just, he came over me like a fire. Like a . . . a . . . a revelation! He also put his hand into my pants—I mean, he was about to, just as a door opened and a woman emerged with a dog on a leash. We separated of course—I mean, clearly, we couldn't make out there. We waited until the lady passed. We were both flustered, his face was glowing, radiating brilliantly, and he smiled. He had a big fat smile on his face. He looked so fucking hot! He was like—it was like he had found something, you know, like this was really important, and I . . .

—And you? Did you feel that way? Do you—now?

—Feel what way?

—Feel as if . . .

—I don't know. He is really, really sexy. I couldn't sleep last night. I just lay awake, thinking about him. And he seems to like me a lot. It's very different from . . . the others. It's . . . oh fuck! Oh fuck!

And with that I knew the truth. I knew the end of our wild Jamie had come. Suddenly he took my hand. I noticed his eyes—open wider than usual. Surprised.

—You think I am in love? Is that what love is like? Oh fuck! Am I in love? You think?

—Well, you sound like it!

—Oh wow. You see, when the woman was out of sight, he looked at his phone and said he had to go. And then he held me with both hands on my forearm, here and here, like, you know, you see? Here. And he said, 'but I want to see you again! You understand?' He said it like this—Jamie reached towards me, bowed down and grabbed my arms hard—he looked at me and said almost pleadingly, 'I want to see you again! I must see you again . . . ' That was it. That was all that happened—we didn't do anything else.

—And now you have a date?

—Yes, now we have date. I can't remember the last time I had a date. Hell—I can't remember the last time I didn't sleep with someone I met and liked immediately. It's a strange feeling. I want him more than anything. I really . . . I didn't get any sleep. I just

145

keep thinking about him.

—Oh, we always want what we can't have. He's left you hanging . . .

—Yes, but . . . I like it. It's such a warm feeling, looking forward to it. Knowing that he is out there, waiting, like I am waiting. I don't want to do anything else.

—What else?

—I mean wait, I just want to wait! I don't want to go to the gym, I don't want to read, or go to work, I don't . . . I certainly don't want to go out in the evening. I just want . . . I can't concentrate on anything else.

—But you stopped going out before you met him. I noticed.

He nodded.

—It's like I was . . . like . . . like I was preparing to meet him. We are going to be fine. We are going to be like Lukáš and Claudio. We are going to be . . . lovers! There, I said it. I know it's going to happen.

He righted himself and let his hand glide through his hair, and suddenly he realized that he was naked in front of me, and standing so close. And he was ashamed. He looked about the room, saw his T-shirt over a chair, and went to fetch it. He dressed, and when he was done, looked at me sheepishly, as if he couldn't be naked any more in front of other people. All the signs were there! So bloody obvious.

—He's working somewhere now, in a studio. I don't see him; he's not at the museum. So I am just waiting. The thing is . . .

—Yes?

—The thing is we haven't made an appointment. We haven't . . . said where we would meet. It's very vague, but I can feel it's real.

—Real?

—Yes, that he's really got the . . . that he really likes me, you know! Oh I feel . . . oh fuck. I feel so stupid!

I looked up into Jamie's eyes when he let go of me, and could see they were moist.

But then, quite unlike his wont, he didn't go on telling me in detail what the boy looked like and what he intended to do with him once he had him in his room. My Jamie, my boastful, proud hunk, who night after night had related all the juicy details of his

146

sexcapades—who'd fucked whom in what position, and how the cock had felt up his arse—ass, in his case—and how the guy—or guys—had eaten his cum, or shot on his back, or ... all the pornographic details of his nights—my Jamie said nothing. Unlike so many times before, there was nothing more to say. Instead he stared out the window into the night in a kind of love-drunk stupor. So clear, yes, so certain: he were in love with him from the first, that cute lad Maurizio.

We didn't need to go on. He wiped his eyes, and then smiled at me.

—Oh fuck, I am so excited.

I squeezed his hand. He was fighting back tears.

Suddenly he jerked.

—So, what about our mystery boys? The Communist bromance?

Yes, the bromance.

—It's not Communist any longer, you know.

—I know.

I told him what I had observed some time ago, about Lukáš and Claudio smelling each other, and of their kiss, and then we relived the moment Javier kissed Claudio, and Jamie said how shocked he had been! Jamie admitted he would never have dared—not with someone he knew! Kiss a stranger maybe, for fun, but not like that! We agreed that Javier had surprised us. Yet strangely, I remember now, I didn't tell him about Lukáš on the landing, how he had cornered me. Maybe because it made me feel so helpless. That I could be so assaulted in my own home; or maybe I didn't tell because it didn't make sense still, back then, what he had said. Or because it would have taken so long to tell, or because it felt like Lukáš had confided in me, in me alone, his view of the world.

I should have told Jamie of course. I would have ... well, maybe it would have changed nothing.

—They *must* be gay then, he pronounced when he heard about the kiss on the floor.

—He said they were broken. He said ... he said they'd had enough violence in their lives.

—Meaning?

—I don't know. Maybe they'd fought over a girl and almost

147

killed each other. Maybe something altogether . . .

—No, no, they are gay all right. At least Claudio! I'll show you, I'll . . .

And he stopped again. After a pause, he grinned.

—So yeah, I am thinking, Claudio, maybe he's caught in the wrong body—so they love each other as man and woman, but they can't do anything about it, because Lukáš is a homophobic prick. Problem solved, there you have it! He's an Orlando! Oh, fuck, they are too strange. Weird!

He came back to my side and I punched him in the shoulder.

—Ouch. Well, do we know?

—We *do* know, I said.

—*How* do you know? Oh, you have spied on them?

—They took off their clothes to do the laundry. And their jeans. There were bulges.

Jamie grinned.

—Bulges . . . or BULGES?

—There were bulges. Nice and well proportioned. They were doing the dishes, not watching porn.

—I bet they do though.

—Do what?

—Watch porn and wank together. Even if they are not gay. I am sure they jerk off together.

Somehow I doubted that, but I said nothing. It seemed, for some strange reason, to be wrong to cast aspersions after what Lukáš had told me. It seemed petty.

—Or, they could be vampires! They could be immortal—bound together, immortal lovers by some ancient Romanian, Slovakian, Ukrainian curse. They drink each other's blood, but they can't have sex! If they have sex, they evaporate—no, they turn to dust. To dust—pfffffff, like that: they crumble!

—Oh for god's sake. Jamie!

—Vampires are very popular! They could be vampires! I mean they could, couldn't they?

—They are *not* vampires.

—Yeah, but wouldn't it be cool?

—No it wouldn't.

—It's not really a metaphor, you know, it's too obvious.

148

—It is. But they are *not* vampires. And they are *not* gay.

—Well I am convinced Claudio is! Although . . .

—Although what?

—Well . . . he's not . . . I mean, he's never . . .

—Oh, I get it. None of them fancies you, so they can't be—is that it? I already thought of that. You'd be the best test.

Jamie nodded.

It sounds pretentious, but it was true. He wasn't a man's man. He either fucked them or they hated him. Or both! There was always some tension between Jamie and *any* other male, regardless of orientation.

—Absolutely nothing, no reaction at all with Claudio and Lukáš!

—Just remarkably friendly. And cute as hell! They are so fucking cute together. What is it this summer? Why now? Where are all these cute guys coming from? Conspiring to . . . You know Javier, he is . . .

—Conspiring to change our lives! I know! There'll be trouble.

They've got no testosterone, I thought, but did not say it loud. Just what Lukáš had said. Lack of aggression, of manliness. So Jamie isn't a threat, in any sense. Not even to their pride.

—You like Claudio better, of course.

—Of course!

—Because of the muscles?

—Of course!

—You are very easy to read, Jamie.

—That's my secret!

The kettle boiled at long last and I poured the hot water into the pot. We sat in silence at the table, Jamie apparently deep in thought—or just dreaming of his Maurizio again.

Yet suddenly he blurted out,

—They could be really straight, and very good friends, you know. It could be true. Maybe it's like in the old days.

He sounded sardonic and suddenly very factual.

—What do you mean, 'in the old days?'

—Well, before homosexual became an acceptable lifestyle . . . before there was such an identity as 'gay'

—In some cultures!

149

— ... in *some* cultures, yes, before a man could even be considered permanently homosexual instead of just hormonally and temporally arse-bound ...

—Are we talking nineteenth century?

— ... and early twentieth, yes, there were a lot of male friendships that went very deep, and talked openly of love for each other. Without being physical, that's what I am trying to say. I am reading about it. Late nineteenth century is full of touchy-feely male bonding. Nice chums, all that stuff.

He gave a sly grin. I poured the tea.

—Literature is full of examples of male bonding that doesn't involve bum fun.

—Because they couldn't write about the fun part?

—Or because it wasn't there! Sex does cheapen everything.

—Bummer!

—What?

—To hear that, from you!

—What? What? There are ways to bond, between men, that doesn't ... and just because I am drop-dead gorgeous and sleep with lots of drop-dead gorgeous boys doesn't mean I don't know what's important in life! I am not shallow! I *love* sex—I am not addicted to it. I know I need to settle down with a cutie before I get dry and wrinkly.

—Is Maurizio going to be your cutie?

He didn't answer. We blew on our steaming teas, but he was so absent-minded, he put the cup to his lips too soon.

—Oh your fucking tea! I fucking burned myself ... again!

We both laughed, and sat and looked at each other. I noticed all the changes in him then already. He was so calm, so relaxed.

After a while, he said,

—Or they could really just be two fags in the closet. They grew up in a small village. They don't know how to be gay.

—They've lived together and travelled all over the world! They've been to San Francisco for fuck's sake! Don't you think they would have learned how to be gay by now? In the age of social media and mobile apps? Surely, it's easier than ever!

—And the rest still in the dark ages! Maybe their homes were very religious.

150

—They don't seem religious to me. Not even repressed. And remember: they've been everywhere! They've been to Madrid, Rome, London, Paris, to the States even. And South Africa. And Finland. And the fucking North Pole.

—Iceland. They've been to Iceland.

—There you go!

Jamie thought for a while.

—And what about that rich uncle? What's that all about? Who's ever heard of a rich uncle in Bratislava! Why didn't he figure when they were younger? You heard them talk about gathering firewood, mushrooms, about collapsing roofs and desolation, about—what did he say?—roaming bands of thieves; about thugs, about Mafia-like criminals controlling their town and how they hunted for rabbits together in the forest, even though it wasn't allowed. They do the same thing as the Germans, have you noticed? They say '*it is* not allowed' instead of 'you are not allowed'—IT IS VERBOTEN TO HUNTEN THE RABITTEN! IT IS VERBOTEN, YA!

Jamie jerked with laughter, spilling half his tea on his lap, then screamed in agony.

—Oh for fuck's sake! This fucking English tea . . . ! This never happens in America!

I chuckled.

—No, it doesn't. You only freeze your brain with all the ice-cubes!

—Speaking of ice cubes . . .

Jamie got up, fetched three from the ice box and dropped them into the tea.

—There. Now it's a sensible beverage.

We smiled at each other—a bit exhausted maybe from the banter. I think we had gone through the same scene far too many times. He always burned his mouth with tea!

—Why don't I just make some tea, fill it in a bottle, and put it in the fridge for you? That way you can have cold tea with me.

He looked offended at me—and so unbearably handsome again. His cheeks were still aglow, and his eyes . . .

—Don't do that!

—Why?

151

—It would be half the fun. Besides, I like our nightly meetings. I like the sound of the kettle boiling, the steam, the . . .

—Scorched lips?

—Well, it's more for show.

—You don't have to put on a show for me, Jamie.

—Well . . .

He reached for his T-shirt and tore it off in one big energetic move. His beautiful young torso, the golden tuft of hair between his perfect pecs, the slightly darker treasure trail disappearing into his low-cut jeans.

—I am sure you don't mind a little show.

I looked away.

—One last time!

—You are too generous, I said, oddly surprised at how miffed I sounded. Why one *last* time?

—Because if Maurizio and I . . .

He didn't finish, but reached for his shirt again.

—Well, if you don't want me to!

—No, no . . . leave it off. I do appreciate a bit of charity. One last time.

He saw me blush, and put the cup down. Then he got up. He said again,

—This may be the last time. Our little secret, momma. The very last time.

I nodded. I quite understood.

He did his well-scripted dance for me. Not too erotic, not too obvious, nothing sexual. Not like charity for an old man who's got nothing left in life to look forward to. He made it look natural. As if he were just stretching his limbs, inadvertently giving me a bit of a hard-on. But my mind wasn't on him that night. We'd done this a hundred times. It's just a tease; after all, he likes to be admired.

It's a different generation of gays now. When I were a lad, we were still ashamed of who we were. Everything happened in the dark, in toilets, in motorway service stops.

The next generation had to face AIDS; they were ashamed to be alive after all their friends had died.

Now they've run out of things to be ashamed of! They've

become completely shameless.

Perfectly transparent society. It's the age of online profiles, fake or real; the age of Facebook. Everyone's out on Facebook. No more privacy, and yet, you can hide behind any *persona* you invent for yourself. Just turn on the telly and watch reality shows!

I wonder what they would make of our little menagerie. With me in my wheelchair, watching Jamie play with his nipples. So seductive. He was getting hard. And yet knowing about Maurizio, I felt awkward. It felt wrong. I reached for the shirt and tossed it in his lap.

—It's fine, Jamie. Keep it for your boyfriend.

He stopped abruptly and stared at me, then, very slowly, and very quietly, while he sat down, a pleased smile came over his face. He liked the idea of having a boyfriend.

He drank his tea.

—I noticed you lost your whippet!

—My whippet?

—Yes. No more 'lads' and 'bugger' and 'I were,' 'he were,' and . . .

—Well, I am trying, *tha knows.*

—Ha. Because of the Slovaks?

—Partly. Don't want to teach them wrong. But also . . .

—Of course, Jamie said, abruptly back to the subject. They could just be so absorbed in each other that they ignore me! Some immense boyhood crush.

—That's all this is about for you, Jamie, isn't it? Why don't they like me? Why aren't they paying attention to me! I said jokingly.

He grinned.

—Have you finally found your match? Men who don't want to fuck or kill you?

He looked at me, and for a moment I thought he would cheerfully agree to my tease. But he was taking this one step further. He laughed, and sounded elated—emboldened. Maybe 'cos I'd acknowledged that Maurizio was his 'boyfriend.' People take such pride in being 'a couple,' and so much strength from it.

—I bet you fifty quid we can make them gay in a month.

—We?

—Okay, I. Fifty quid!

153

—Jamie, don't!

He reached under his T-shirt and rubbed his abs again. As if that would make the taunt sound more honest, more believable. But it was just a young lad proud of his body.

—Don't do this Jamie, please. Don't go there. Leave them alone.

—Why? If they *are* straight, they'll be immune and you'll get fifty pounds beer money. If they are gay, it's time they woke up and shagged each other like normal guys!

I chuckled. The self-image of young gay men never ceases to amaze me. Being gay has become so commonplace in some countries, it's almost beyond belief. Especially for someone like me, who remembers Stonewall, and being arrested in Princes Street Gardens for looking twice at a bobby in civvies.

What happened to all the dark alleys of my youth? What happened to guilt? I thought of an answer then, but Jamie was out the door and in his room before I could speak. He'd kissed me goodnight, and off he went. He had forgotten to help me up the stairs as he had promised.

Just one day after, trouble started. I were in the laundry room sorting out the whites when the front door of the house slammed shut with a bang so loud the walls shook and the glasses and plates in the kitchen cupboards jangled so wildly I could hear them all the way down there. One of them shouted in Slovak, two pairs of feet stomped up the stairs above me, another door slammed, there was more yelling, and one pair of feet came down again, and found me with the empty laundry basket on my lap.

—He locking me out! said Claudio, his face red and blotchy. He looked as if he had been crying.

—What are you two fighting about?

—Oh, I don't want to talk. I can't say!

He walked into the kitchen, grabbed the milk carton from the refrigerator and drank, a trickle of liquid running from the edges of his mouth onto his chest.

I cleared my throat.

He realized he should have used a glass, as he had on every occasion so far. If he drank from the carton of milk like that, the milk everybody used, he was clearly upset. He put the milk back after wiping the plastic rim, said sorry, and sat down at the table.

I waited quietly until he had calmed down. But he didn't. Instead, I saw the tears come. I saw his torso jerk, and his hand hit the table surface, and then he sobbed. I wheeled myself to the counter, took the kitchen roll and handed it to him.

—It's so stupid! I am so angry!

I considered comforting him, but when have words ever comforted anyone, really? If my silent presence couldn't do it, why should my babbling?

He took his time. The front door opened again and someone came in, said hello without looking—I didn't recognize the voice, one of Javier's friends maybe—and made his way up the stairs.

When the footsteps had faded, Claudio said,

—We separated! In school. After one month 'observation,' they put us in different levels.

—You mean you *have been* separated.

Hardly a reason to come home in tears, I thought. He didn't continue, as if that fact were enough of an explanation. I looked with wide eyes, indicating that I didn't understand.

—Yes, we separate . . . ! I made scene. I ask the teacher to put us together. She explained that Lukáš was no as good English, and made too many mistakes on a test, and . . . that I was better and should go in higher level. I told her I didn't want to take higher level, I wanted to be in his level, and she—she insisted I will not learn anything with the *Beginners II*, and that I must go in the higher level . . . and . . . and . . . She want to put me *Intermediate!*

Tears made their way down his cheeks again. I was surprised at the way he showed his emotions over such a trifle.

—She wouldn't allow me to go in the lower level. And I becomed angry.

—Was that . . . 'became,' not 'becomed' . . .

He interrupted,

—It was in front of the whole class! So Lukáš got very embarrassed because I making scene, and everybody was looking us, because I said something, I think I say, 'you can't separate me from him, I want to be with him,' or so, but I didn't mean it that way. I only wanted to say that we should be together in the same level. I want to be in same class, that's all.

155

—But you'll still be in the same school!

—Yes. But not together.

A sudden sound crashed in from outside, like two cars colliding, but far, far away. A radio played somewhere with the news on BBC Radio Scotland coming on. We listened to the gong, and the announcer.

There was a curious lapse in time, and when he spoke again he quite caught me by surprise.

—We've never been separated, you see. You know?

He looked at me, his eyes red.

It seemed the most ridiculous thing to fight and get excited over.

I rolled closer to him and reached for his arm. He let me take it. I held his hand, in the fatherly manner I am allowed to assume mostly because of the wheelchair and my wrinkles. Yes, or *motherly*. Take your soddin' pick.

—Claudio, I said with a voice I wanted to sound calm and composed, but which came out giddy and nervous. Claudio, are you sure there isn't more between the two of you? Something you are denying and . . .

He withdrew his hand and stood up so forcefully the stool fell over.

—I know what you mean but it's not, stop trying make us gay! Just because *you* are all, does not mean everybody is! What we have, between us . . . is complicated. Many years ago, I did something bad. Very bad. And Lukáš, he help me, okay? He standing by me.

He ran out of the kitchen, made left for the stairs, then maybe remembering that he was still locked out of the room, turned towards the front door. I rolled after him to see what he was doing. He turned around again and said,

—I kissed Javier, but it was only for fun! It was only fun! I am . . . I was . . .

He didn't finish. He hesitated a second. Behind him, the door opened and Tim's sister walked in. Claudio bumped into her, and without a word of apology bowed and slipped under her arm and out the door. It fell shut as she came walking towards me.

—What's with handsome? Lovers' tiff?

—Something like it.

—I swear, you gay men, it's worse than womenfolk!

She kissed me on the cheek.

—So emotional! I brought some chicken liver.

I made the sound I usually make at the mention of liver.

—You will eat it! You need iron, remember what the doctor said.

I was unable to sleep that night. Claudio still hadn't come back. By eleven, I had undressed and climbed into bed without help, but I was tossing and turning, fearing the worst. So I climbed back into the soddin' chair and wrapped myself as best I could into a blanket. The bally liver lay heavy in my stomach!

Edinburgh is not crime central, but it is full of dodgy characters. If you go to the wrong pub, especially as a foreigner, you can easily end up in unpleasant company.

I wanted to send Jamie after him. Claudio was sure to be in one of the pubs between here and the school. But I couldn't find Jamie anywhere to help me search, so I wheeled mesen about the house and wallowed in my mad thoughts. Violence in their past. Claudio had done summat bad. Killed someone? They were covering for a crime? What could it be? Or Claudio, the stronger one, had tried to force himself on a much younger Lukáš? Tried to . . . but he forgave him? In love—doomed? Maybe some deep-seated religious scruple? Father, abusive father? Both abused by the same older man . . . ? The poor lads! The inner torment . . .

It were close to midnight when I took the stairlift down. With the usual bump it stopped at the second floor. The same instant the door to Claudio and Lukáš's room opened. I expected Lukáš to step out, and readied myself to invite him for a drink and a talk, to sort him out, or ask him to go looking for Claudio. I didn't see who it was at first—too dark.

The figure closed the door, and turned to me. It were Jamie!

—Oh no! I said.

—Oh yes! said he, grinning cheekily.

—Oh no, Jamie you haven't?

—Oh yes, my dearest, I have!

157

—Both, or Lukáš? Is Claudio in there with him?

—Nope.

—Only Lukáš?

—Yup.

—And you . . . you've taken advantage of him!

—Oh don't that sound grand! Taken advantage of the poor boy! You sound like a Victorian novel!

He smirked, such a broad grin—but for a few seconds too long. It fell apart while I looked on; he were bluffing, I could tell. And he saw that I saw.

—You can keep your fifty quid for now. We were just talking.

—About what?

Jamie looked at the closed door, then came over to pick me up and carry me down the stairs into the kitchen. I have little physical pleasure in my old days, but being carried by a strong, muscular young man as beautiful as Jamie must be the pinnacle.

—Shall I put the kettle on?

—Something stronger today.

He poured us both a glass of wine, and sat down, then almost immediately got up again and filled the kettle.

—I still like to hear it boil. We don't have to drink it.

He looked very pleased, but also a little disturbed.

—I knocked at their door around nine, thinking they were both in. Just dropping in for a chat. But I found only the ugly one.

—He is not ugly.

—All right, plain. Plainer. He's cute in a way, with all that beard stubble. Very rough. Mountain climber. Too skinny though. It's amazing he climbs with such thin arms.

—I think he runs a lot too. I always thought he was rather aristocratic looking.

—Might be, anyway. Aristocratic? No! He's a rough type.

—Maybe it's the beard.

—Maybe. Anyway, he was upset about something, so I stayed and we talked.

—Did he tell you? About the school?

—Everything.

—And?

—What and? I still think they are weird.

158

—What did he say?

—Lukáš? He wished Claudio was back. He was worried. He has forgiven him, for all intents and purposes.

I don't know where Jamie picked up that phrase, but he uses it a lot.

—Do you think we should go looking for him?

—Nah, he'll be all right. What can happen to him?

I gave Jamie a stern look. Last year an Italian lodger had got into a fight outside a pub and been hospitalized for three weeks. People do commit suicide after public embarrassment. And he was a foreigner, in a strange town. It's not unheard . . .

—I guess you are right!

—What did he say about the scene at the school?

—Oh yes, the weirdest thing . . .

—What? Do I have to drag everything out of you? Jamie. Speak!

—Well, he told me how embarrassed he was when Claudio had protested so much in front of the teacher, and how he didn't want people think they were a couple, because everybody would think they were gay—I mean, he's got this real . . . this . . . Well, when he is here, with us, he is all gay-friendly and all, but the way it came out, he made himself sound as if he didn't want anybody to know how close Claudio and he were. Like he really hated being thought of as gay. Totally different from the way he acts normally, like if he doesn't mind being seen touching Claudio, you know? Mostly, I think, because he had his eye on a girl in the class, he kept going on and on about her, and she was the first who looked as if she had caught on.

—That's not weird.

—What's weird?

—Oh for god's sake Jamie, you said he said a weird thing. What weird thing? If Lukáš is straight, not wanting people to think you are gay is hardly weird.

—He said—Jamie looked up and very seriously into my eyes— he said, 'I know he loves me, but . . . he can't.'

—But what?

—But nothing. Only that. 'He can't!' Oh, and 'I am not worth it.'

—What does it mean?

—Don't ask me. Weird!

159

—So Lukáš knows Claudio is in love with him? He is trying to keep Claudio 'straight?' He's done something bad, so he is not worth being loved? I thought Claudio's the one as did summat evil? What evil? Seriously—can you imagine any of them involved in something . . . evil?

I stared at Jamie. He shrugged his bulky shoulders, grinned sheepishly, his eyes squinting. Were those crow's feet?

We drank from our wine, listened to the night, the kettle rumbling noisily.

—Of course he is in love with him, said a voice from the door.

It were Claudio, his hair a mess, his clothes in disarray, the boy himself very clearly worse for wear, and pissed as a rat's arse.

—Claudio!

I wanted to jump up and hug him. My upper body jerked, but the rest stayed glued to the chair.

—Where have you been?

—Drinking. Out in a pub crawl. That's what you call it.

—Almost. You are very drunk.

—Who gives a toss!

—You learned a new word then, have you? I said. Come and sit down.

—'Toss,' I knew already. As in 'tosser,' like in Lukáš, the tosser. Fuckin'ell!

—Ha, you learned to swear too!

—Now, now, I said, trying to calm him.

He were well pissed, but his English seemed to have improved considerably in the process.

He went over to the other side of the table, Jamie did, and pulled up a chair for Claudio, then led him over and sat him down. Claudio let it be done. Suddenly his hand was on Jamie's bum, squeezing hard, then slapping him.

—You know you are fucking hot, Jamie!

Their eyes met, but Claudio was too drunk to signal anything meaningful. Jamie turned to me and winked. I shook my head. I hoped he wouldn't take advantage of the situation. He came back over to my side and said softly,

—Don't worry, I never bother with the drunks. Not much use

in bed, are they?

—If I weren't so fucking straight, I would make a pass at you, said Claudio, his speech slurred. I would fuck you! But I am straight.

—Are you? Jamie retorted very calmly. Are you really?

Claudio looked up. He reached for the wine bottle on the table. Jamie put it out of reach, stood up and poured him a class of tap water.

Claudio took a sip.

—Wah, water! Dissa-gusting!

He put the glass back on the table.

—So, out with the truth, said Jamie. Out with it now!

I wished he would shut up and get the lad to bed instead. What good could come from some drunken confessions in the middle of the night? Suddenly Claudio blurted out,

—Of course, you bloody moron!

It seemed he had learned more English in a night in the pubs than in his entire life up to now.

—You don't know a half of it!

—*The* half, I mumbled.

—Of course I am in love with him! Have been since I was fifteen! Of course I am. I love the gay—the guy I mean. We are best friends! But he isn't interested in me ... in that way. And I ... oh I am not going to ...

He looked at me, at Jamie, then at me again, making sure we understood whatever there was to understand. But then he muddled the waters again.

—But that's it. I just love him. I don't want to fuck him! It's not about sex.

I desperately thought of something to say. The obvious, 'get over it, find a man who will requite your love, accept that you are gay'—something—but I remembered in a flash that they were together: they *were* in love. It was too bloody obvious! They were just fighting it. His love wasn't unrequited—it was just not physical. But this couldn't be healthy for Claudio. He had been tormented for twelve years, sacrificing his own urges for ... what urges?

—It's not what you think, he said suddenly, sounding sober

again. I am not a desperate . . . how you say, pedantic gay man . . .

—Pathetic, I offered.

— . . . yes, pathetic gay man in love with a straight man for all his life. I don't need sex with him, I'm not gay! It's not about sex! We don't want . . . sex from each other. That's why . . . we talk it over, you know, some time 'go. We agree that we liking each other, and that we staying together—especially after . . . that we didn't want to get girlfriends. Women are so complicated! It so much easier living with a man. Women ruin everything. Girls ruin everything, they swallow you alive! They suck you up. We made us a promise, that we would give each other all the freedom we want, and if we meeting love-of-life girl, we go separate way, but that we want to be together for now. We love each other, only you can't say that without sounding like a fucking faggot—I begging pardon. I am . . . so sorry. I drink too much. I never say that word. I am so sorry. Please.

I wanted to be offended, tried hard, indeed, but couldn't. It was plausible, possible at least, what he said, but it sounded all so . . . painful.

—What's that about . . . done something bad, in the past. What did you mean?

—He even give up marrying for me twice.

I weren't sure then if that were an answer to my question.

—He did what? said Jamie, coming alive at the revelation.

—Marriage. He giving up marriage!

—Is that what you mean, about doing something bad? You made him give up marriage?

He didn't look at me.

—He supposing to marry a girl in where we come from, in Slovakia, when we were twenty-two. She was from same village. But in the last minute, he back off. He told her he want stay with me instead, and not marriage and make baby.

—He told his fiancée he'd rather stay with his non-gay friend than marry her?

—Yes. I know, everybody laugh! We cannot tell our friends, because everybody think we are *homo*. He so angry for a while, at me. We was so angry. Like with the school. When I make scene. But . . . I need him.

He looked up. His eyes narrowed. He lifted his arm, slowly, then brushed over his face, as if to wipe away not tears, but the whole memory.

—Many people making fun of us then. So we stay away. We find job in Bratislava for some time, and we hang out with gay people, because easier—not so many question. We fit in better, you know—maybe you can see? Maybe one day just give up, and just say we gay. People always needing category! Always need a label, stupid, for everything. It's all about label! We are just friend, you know, buddies, and much easier than being gay and sex, or with girls—but everybody want to make us . . . something.

He pressed his head between his palms. Jamie gave me a strained look.

Claudio emitted an odd noise, like belching, or sniffing—we couldn't be sure.

—Why not can leave us alone, like we are? We are so simple, our relationship. We are so . . . simply!

—He must love you. Lukáš *must* love you. It's not just friendship—it's love!

—He does, he does. And I loving him.

He looked towards the ceiling and shouted at the top of his lungs,

—I love you man! You fucking tosser, man!

Then he raised his hands, pleadingly, before collapsing.

Jamie turned to me. Claudio put his hands on the table and his head fell on them. For a moment he was out of it. He smelled of beer and whisky and cigarettes.

I pleaded silently with Jamie and he immediately understood.

—Put him on the sofa in our room, I said. Don't disturb Lukáš. Just put him on the sofa.

Jamie walked ahead of me, the figure of the drunken lad in his arms, and ascended the stairs. I took the lift behind him. He was almost past their room, when the door opened and Lukáš stepped out.

—Oh my god, you've got him. Is he hurt? Did anything happens?

He helped Jamie carry the seemingly unconscious boy inside.

—He's only gone and drunk himself into a stupor.

They put him to bed, and Jamie went to the bathroom to fetch a pail and a glass of water. He lifted the pail up as he passed me.

—Experience! he announced. Just then, we heard Claudio retch, and Jamie rushed in.

A minute later he came out.

—Too late? I said.

—No, caught it in time. But he'll be out of it for a while.

—He smelling awful, said Lukáš. Where he go?

—He's been to the pubs. Drinking himself senseless!

—And why? All because of this morning at school?

—No, bro, said Jamie, punching Lukáš on the shoulder very hard.

I wanted to signal him not to say anything, but he didn't pay any heed to the cripple on the stairlift. I waved a hand. I regretted not telling Jamie about . . .

—All because you—he punched him again, and Lukáš flinched—all because you don't love him the way you should, you fucking coward. What's wrong about a little man-love?

Lukáš turned to face Jamie, who was suddenly dancing around him like a boxer in the ring.

—What do you mean?

—I mean, it takes courage to love!

—What? I do love him. He's my friend he's . . .

—I mean physical love.

—Physical love?

—Yeah, sex man. It's part of the package! Just fucking fuck him! Kiss him. Hold him! He's so obviously into you!

—But I am not . . .

—I know you are not 'gay'. But it doesn't matter, does it? You love him! And he loves you. So kiss him. Be physical. Have sex! Cuddle for fuck's sake! You morons! Cuddling doesn't count!

—But I am not . . .

—I know you are not gay. That doesn't mean you can't love him. Make up your fucking mind! You two are together. Forget the fucking labels!

—But I . . . You don't understand!

—Oh fuck you, I am going to bed! Just make up your mind! You are turning this whole house upside-down with your fucking bromance!

164

Lukáš said something in Slovak and then disappeared into the room, slamming the door.

—Fucking nutcase. Need me to carry you?

Jamie didn't wait for an answer, grabbed me, and brought me into my room.

For a moment, he stood there helplessly. I held onto his shoulders, relishing the firm muscle, even though my mind were on a million other things. Did we really have a right to interfere? Should we just back off? Was that the bad thing Claudio had done, keeping his friend from marrying?

Tim was awake reading and moved to get up to help me undress.

—I got it, said Jamie.

It was the first time he offered, and I let him do it. He lifted me out of the chair, took my trousers off, helped me into the nightshirt and carried me to the bed. Tim watched us, silently.

Then Jamie stood there, puffing, and looking altogether marvellous. Lucky Maurizio!

—I don't know how you manage, Tim. That fat old cow is fucking heavy!

I said nothing, but listened to Tim snort. It were just Jamie's way to overcome the awkwardness. It were his way of acknowledging that he was intruding. He looked at us—two old men in a bed—for a moment, then turned and made for the door.

—Thank you, I said feebly.

—'S'aaawright! he bellowed back very happily, but before the door shut, he came back and stood before our bed, legs apart, arms, his strong arms, folded, then opening, then folded again, silently—and embarrassed—for a moment. Then he said,

—I want to have a relationship like you guys! Complete intimacy, so intimate that sex doesn't matter any more. Men together—just as friends. Sex always gets in the way of everything! It's all fucking hormones! I can't wait to get old.

He gave an exasperated sigh, smiled quickly and awkwardly; then turned and ran off. The sound of his naked feet on the wooden floor echoed in the room—or only in my head—long after he was gone.

So confusion reigned, Mr Dedalus—absolute confusion. Queer or not queer? One queer, one not? Both not? Denial? What the soddin' fuck was going on between the two? I needed help. I needed to talk to other people about it.

We go to The Anchor and Bride sometimes, Mary and I, often on Thursdays, but that week I went alone, Rolling Down the Hill! Down to Leith! It is more my kind of place anyway, and certainly not Tim's, and I don't take the lodgers there either. It's my secret that I go there; not even Tim knows. I tell him I go to physio, or to the AIDS charity to bring them some stuff. Our tiny little secret. It's really the only thing I keep from my old man.

I like it there, truly, more than anything, that cocoon of utter weirdness. It's not your usual pub. I need to be in a particular mindset though to go there; my usual sleepless nights are not enough ... it needs a mixture of melancholy, horniness, desperation, an urge to talk, or a curiosity, and a thirst too—for nothing happens at the Anchor without a lot of booze.

I like it; I like the people there. I like strange characters— it's the normal ones, people who lead normal lives, people who constantly find fault with the lifestyles of others—those give me the creeps.

The proselytizing normality-freaks, oh gaw, ah kin nae stand them! I could not make sense any more of the Slovaks, and my sense for foreboding grew stronger by the day. So I called my disabled taxi and headed for Leith. I needed a consultation; listen to the real experts.

Down in Leith, hidden not by its location—it is right on the main street—but by its shabbiness and grey façade, its almost hilarious unsightliness, it stands like a leftover; like an object from some scurrilous parallel world in which nothing is bloody *normal.* So when I roll in in my wheelchair, it all fits. That, Mr Dedalus, is where the disabled people meet, and the outlaws and outcasts of this place. If it only were that simple.

It has a strange selection of patrons, a curious mix that reminds one of a nineteenth century novel more than real life. Indeed, you find on any day there a group of sailors from all over the world; a few whores, transvestites and transsexuals in any number; a gaggle of queers; a known drug-dealer; a Syrian tea merchant who comes here to escape his wife who beats him savagely; two or three machos and some homos, indistinguishable; and all that in various stages of drunkenness and willingness to be fondled and snogged, interspersed with the people from the neighbourhood: bricklayers, corner shop merchants, postmen, women from the clinic, lawyers, and Bill the mechanic, and off-duty policemen, who seem to fulfil a need to mingle with the shady characters they usually harass.

It is there, in this Arcadia of the senses, in this underbelly of the organic-orgasmic wannabe capital, that life really blooms; here are the naughties and the nifties, the transparent people (not hollow, transparent), the real people; here are the lewd and the lawless, the men and women from whom the mention of patio furniture or a dog for the kids would evince only a sneering whimper; people who honestly don't do tax returns, and always lose their HealthNet card; people who have a million ailments when they go to the doctor, but can't pronounce even the name of their fungus ointment, or remember the name on the package, and that includes the lawyer, whose name is Indian, and who's mostly doing eviction cases now. Yet all of them, not forgetting the policemen, have strong opinions on the price of oil, the fisheries, the weather (this year, the wind so much warmer when it came, as it did, from the south), and the demolition of the old fort for a new high-rise condominium.

I made a quick calculation: it would take Francis, who's worked on ships ever since he was twelve, a total of four point seven lifetimes to afford a flat there, and in the meantime, he'd have nothing to live on, except the pints he scrounges, and the free meals, and what he can get in the canteen. He's had lovers of all three sexes!

So at the big table by the corner, where they've made way for me chair, and told me I should try the onion diet—in this round, on that Thursday, we are assembled.

We are the creatures of the underworld, the outcasts of Leith. And I feel that they—only they—will be able to give me an answer, so I tell them about my boys. Only here, in this motley mass of miscreants and misfits can I talk freely, and receive, by steady, soft-spoken, almost reverent accord, their opinions, always

167

strong, always truly held, and with conviction, until another pint or a better man with a louder voice comes along, and the house of illogic we built comes crumbling down.

But it is joy to listen to these colourful voices, these masters of disguise, and it relieves me of my sleeplessness, and the dull pain in my legs that always assaults me when I think a lot (even though technically my legs are completely numb!). It is as if the stone in my lap, a giant boulder that presses down, my *thinking* bolder, Mr Dedalus, were lifted. Here, at The Anchor and Bride, it doesn't exist. I am free to ask them—first the queers, then the machos, and soon everybody chimes in.

—I reckon they are well queer then, if they do this! Well queer!

That is the voice of a whore by the window, hugging her knee, looking down at me explaining to the queers what I think is going off. But her judgement could be clouded by my partiality.

—I mean, real men don't . . .

There is no offence taken in such a twilit place, even for words like 'real' or 'normal.' Political correctness has no home here, and neither does protest, for in here queers really aren't real men— real clients, that is; or men who beat her—the one in fact who gave her the black eye?

—Not necessarily, must come the inevitable objection.

I scratch my neck; I start to listen. They have taken the conversation from me and go with it, and one by one they report back. It's a young man talking with a large pimple on his cheek. He can't be older than seventeen, but drinks like a fish and smokes like a chimney, and curses too. He's sucked cock for money since he was twelve, and been on all kinds of drugs. He lives with a boy from Croatia just above the Halal butcher. Then he says something that rattles me.

—They could have some . . . shared calamity. Some calamity. Something in their past. A calamity.

He pronounces the word 'galamee-ee.' Somehow I get the impression he's got it off the telly and his understanding of it may be slightly skewed. Whereas I think of earthquakes and storm damage, he might think of emergency wards, and severed limbs. But his eyes light up when he sees that he's given me ideas. I think of Mary and her traumatic woman. I think of the evil deed

168

somewhere in their past.

—They still sound like lover-boys to me, says the whore again. She has made up her mind. Men who don't fuck her, look at her, give her black eyes, don't count, and must be queer.

—Maybe they belong to some church?

All eyes on the woman next to her. I don't know her profession, but she wears the same make-up. Could be a tranny. Not looking too closely.

—Or some weird sect, you know?

—You said he was always looking out for his mate! And you said they touched, in the kitchen, and you chanced upon them—the one with the head on the belly of the other. Give us a break! Queers they are, there's nae question aboot it!

I think about the religion for a moment, but there wasn't any hint of that at all. They'd slept in on Sunday, they'd never mentioned any interest in churches. There were no rituals, no strange noises. And they'd never talked of god or any such rubbish.

—So we are back to queers in the closet? I say, smiling at the whore.

—Aye Tim, ye auld fairy, she says. Just as you want them ta be. That's what ye here for, isn't it? So you know where ye stand, before you sink yir teeth into them!

I smile politely while she laughs; no one else has heard her last sentence. But now she repeats what she thinks, by nodding to everyone in the round.

—Fairies they are, nae doubt aboot it! Fairies!

Her insistence should garner support, I am thinking, and all the lovers of men should now bring their own reasons why my two lodgers suck dick; but it does the opposite. Maybe because she's a woman; maybe because she is a whore, but all of a sudden, nobody agrees with her. She is being dismissed, with nods, looks, a palm hitting the table, two pints being drained too fast, shaking heads, laughter even.

—Fat chance! No way are they gay. If they were, they wouldn't deny it, not in a place like Tim&Tim's! Your B&B's like fag central of Edinburgh. Why should they deny it there? Usually us queers is happy to find support and a home, we wouldn't be lying to a landlady like Tim here—a true lady.

He gives a curt bow. I've never seen him in here before, but apparently he is a regular. Not bad looking either.

Laughter, and a song comes on we all like, and for a while, we forget the Slovaks and live somewhere in the past, when we were all young, or younger, and didn't smell so bad.

There is a stench now, a mixture of alcohol, cigarettes, someone's dinner, bad teeth; an assault from all around me that makes me regret my decision to come here. I see the Polish girl with a broom and a bucket rushing towards the toilets—so that's what happened.

I want to be at home at my window, looking for Mrs Erskine, drinking alone with Mr Dedalus. These people aren't helping. They are nice, they are friendly, they pretend to care. But I'll have to solve this on my own. Shite and onions! I will solve it!

To avoid the stench, the group returns, after an excursion to last night's news about a scandal involving the Princes Street Gardens and a SIP MP, to my lodgers. Abruptly—he hasn't moved all evening—in his corner, hairy homo number one has something to say. He's tall and well-built, over forty, with a thick neck and a gold chain, thin lips and deep-set eyes, here almost every day to shag the sailors who want shagging: the queer shipmates, and there is plenty of them, potato-peeling perverts who want their arses ripped open by a real stud. For a certain type of man, in a certain type of pub, with a certain type of libido, gay sex is all about raping hairless young boys who can't spell their name; but that might be more my porn life than Leith, and hairy homo might be no Querelle, and really gentle in bed. He too has done it forever, and his hunger is unquenchable. He makes them think he likes women, he shows them pictures of his children (cut out from a mail-order fashion catalogue, everybody can tell), he tells them his wife died in a car accident; the details resembling any last episode of *Taggart*, including a bonnie WPC; he lets them buy him drinks, although they can ill afford it, probably he's never paid for a pint himself, but they succumb to him, his laughter, his bushy hair, his sideburns, the thin lips, and of course the tight jeans he's worn since he was twenty-three. Around the groin they are so snug, you can see each nut in relief, and of course . . . what

170

they really want: the fat shaft.

When they are drunk enough, or mellow enough, or horny enough, he takes them home, and they are happy on land, and never want to go back. He's got the biggest cock in Leith, some say, and uses it well. I reckon every harbour has a stud like him, in the twilight of virility, where chest hair has a special allure, and tattoos all a secret meaning. Of course, on the wall, in his room, are pictures of pin-up girls, with enormous breasts; but he does not dream of them.

—Why don ye introduce us to one of them—or betta both! says hairy homo number one, with his deep voice.

This is the same man who gives gay people snash in the street in the daytime—especially the effeminate ones. I think by 'us' he means himself and his trouser snake—his favourite, if childish, word, but allegedly, it is curved, and takes long to get from snake-like to rock-hard, which it then stays for hours, to the delight of so many young sailors.

—Mah trouser snake would find out right away if them's queer or wha'!

I wonder if he does it for money, or just for the fun of it. I wonder if he thinks of himself as gay at all. Probably not. I wonder what that look means one of the younger guys is throwing him now. Memories of the snake in his burrow. Here's a metaphor, Mr Dedalus. Just like when we stopped over in Curaçao, on our cruise around the world, remember, and you wanted to play again, Mr Dedalus. How prude I was for a boy of nineteen, twenty—how lewd the owner of the snake seems in comparison. I was brought up all wrong!

—So, aye, bring 'em 'ere. Lessava look ayya boys. And if they are not—he rubs his groin now demonstratively—I shouldnae wonder if mah snake here couldnae tarn them aroond!

We are overheard by one of the lesser locals—Bill the mechanic, who comes here for his own reasons. He's got nothing to do with homos, and for a long time I thought he didn't approve; but he never heckled, never complained, and in a way, he seems to feel as much at home amongst the rabble as I do. He's always dirty, always looking at the soot under his fingernails, and a very slow drinker—of Irish cider at that, high treason in our book.

171

The pub serves haggis on Wednesdays, that's when you meet him for sure. Do you remember haggis, Mr Dedalus? You were so appalled! Claudio didn't like it much either. I think it reminded him of home.

—What's that about two queer boys from Hungary?

—Slovakia.

—So? Whassit aboot?

—Well, we aren't sure if they are.

—If they're wha? Queer? Well . . . that shounae be hard ta find oot. Do they play with each other? Har har! Do they?

—Haud yer wheesht! Just bring 'em and lessava look! says hairy homo, insisting on his crude strategy.

—Aye, less see da boys, says another voice I don't recognize. I turn around. There's a sailor behind me, young, Mediterranean looking, with a Glasgow accent and a cute smile. He gives a brief nod, by means of introduction, then says,

—Are they cute?

—That's the thing, I say, trying to sound educated like Tim, who I wish were here with me to witness the scene. That's just the thing. I've been observing them . . .

—Abservin, have ye?

—Yes, observing them, closely.

—Ya derty old faggot!

Again, here, in this place, that's not an insult.

—Ya bin watching them in da shower! I betya 'ave!

There is laughter, a hand on my back, slapping me. Maybe that's why I like it here—everyone's fucked, and a cripple's at least got *gevermint* money to live on.

—I bet they done something bad, says the quiet whore and everybody is staring at her. She blushes. Things that make a whore blush, I am thinking.

—Say that again?

I heard what she said, but I need her to repeat it. It amazes me that she would suggest exactly what they themselves had said to me, that they had done summat bad.

—They done something bad, 'aven't they?

—What sort of bad?

Hairy homo grabs my arm, and his eyes come alight. His face is

172

right in front of mine, and it's glowing with excitement.

—Maybe, maybe … maybe they've killed someone. Aye, aye, thassit—maybe they are killers on the run.

Nodding, yelling, everyone in this dump watching too much television.

—Don't be daft.

The blushing whore gathers her wits.

—It might be killing … no, maybe not killed someone. But they might 'ave, you know, stolen something, or … something. They may be running from the law, really. Gambling debts. Maybe they are running from the Mafia.

—And running from the police or the Mafia makes them act like lovers? I say, too loud.

The word 'lovers,' I realize, too late, has no place here. The whore and the tranny both stare at me, then both shrug their shoulders and look away.

Someone in a recess responds with a dark cough.

—Did ye see that new show, *Bourniston*, on telly?

There are some attempts made to digress, but an hour later, we are still talking about the Slovaks. The lawyer has laid out his ideas of how to find out if people are queer, and they are all ludicrous. He also wants to know if I want them gone—he could help me there.

—Brilliant. Are they paying the rent then?

—They are.

—You've got bias, you know—all gay people have it. You always want other people to be gay, more like you. We all have bias, we all want others to be more like us, so we can feel more at home in our skin. But gay people, you are insufferable, because … you are like religious people. You want everybody to go to the same church. You know religion is so popular not because there's a god, but because people like to belong—belong to a club where everybody believes the same irrational tosh. Like vampires or rock concerts, or Harry fucking Potter.. It makes them feel superior.

—Are ya sayin' Harry Potter is queer? I'll bash yir heid in! the dark voice rings again.

—And you queers … No, I'm not saying that. I am saying queers are the same, that you too feel united, want to feel one. We

173

all do. Like a church. Just like a church!

—Wa' kirk's that then ye tosser? The kirk of the shitty dodger?

Hairy homo's joke doesn't go down well, and he's already moved on to other things. Two strangers have arrived, in actual sailor uniforms. They are sitting at the bar and are looking uncomfortable. The trouser snake has found his prey.

—Do they sleep in the same bed?

The tranny is applying lipstick.

—No, but . . .

—Aye ma auntie! Yir just gessn!

And finally, something sensible, from the barmaid, who's just hooked up another keg to serve the newcomers.

—Shut yer geggie, Marvin. Da point is, have ye ever see them snog?

—Yeah, that's it. If they don't snog, they ain't queer. Not just fakin'' it. Real snoggin' I mean. When nobody's watchin''.

Bill the Mechanic thinks we should just take them to a gay bar and observe them; I tell him we have, and we aren't any smarter now, and no, they don't snog, not for long, not that way; although, I retort, as an excuse, a bit desperately,

—But they might just be shy.

Then the transvestite with the red wig gets creative.

—Why don't you go camping, put them in a tent, like in that film . . . see if they get it on!

Great laughter from the queers, only the rest of the pub doesn't know the film she is referring too.

—Bring them here, says hairy homo again, and we'll check them out.

He doesn't give up. The whores are moving up to the sailors, and they are not rebuffed. I can see hairy homo's annoyance.

—It can't be that hard to find out if a man's in for a bit of cock. Like him here, (she means the tempter of sailors and his trouser snake) we knows he's queer since he's a little boy.

—I punch your teeth oot, ye cow!

—Steady, steady.

There are always brawls being cooked up in this pub—but they seldom take place; too many strange genders, too much make-up, too much hurt already. Maybe, too little to lose.

174

—You gotta be careful, they might turn the tables on you. Some people do that. They burst into your life wanting to be discovered, and loved, and in the end all you do is discover yourself. And you change. Some people are sent your way so that you can change; they have no other purpose. Some people cross paths with you for mysterious reasons—you won't know until it happens!

I turn around to see who said that, but there is nobody there; then the door swings shut. It seems like the most profound statement ever, and I hold on to it. Some people come your way for a special reason.

In the toilet, two pints later, I play with the snake a little. Hairy homo didn't score with the sailors.

—Go on, 'ave a go! Can't be fun sittin' in that wheelchair all day. Come on, touch it! Here—touch it!

Oh, Mr Dedalus, I shall abdicate, I shall—I will! I feel it!—leave you to your long home, your dark grave, your decomposting-composition-compositioning. Today, an exception. How humiliated, back from that pub, how humanly humiliated, how ... Not drunk in weeks, but today—here, John Barleycock, I kneel before you, shove it in my mouth, let me drown on it, tha gives the best juices north of Hadrian's Wall! Juices, my sluices. And you know why? You know why? Can you guess why? All that talk about the bloody Slovaks, but that's not what's breaking my heart, no!

I roam the streets of Edinburgh, my wheels on fire, I sit alone down on the heath, and cut my wrists with wire. I want to fly, to soar, to walk, to be alive again, to frolic, mollick, torture-lick, in bars, in parks, in gutters even—a whore! I want to be a whore again!

How dare he, Jamie, fall in love and leave me, tha knows what a sensitive creature I am. Tha knows I can't exists in this world without love. Loved by my husband. The joke! The pity! What pity? A life of pity! Has nae given me anything but pity over the years, lenient, circumspect pity. What is he on about? What does he want from me? Why did he not put me out to die, leave me on the mountain to decompostate-decomposate!

I want to be with you, old mucker, Mr Dedalus. Ya hear me?

175

I want to join you in your fucking grave. I am done with Slovaks I cannae decipher and with washing their fucking undies. I am done with cleaning up after people and helping them. Who's ever helped me? Tim, yes, pitied me to death, suffocaterated—pillow-with suffocated me, with his gentle nettling, with his suffonettling, with this love! Shite and onions! With his twenty-four-fucking hours consideration.

Couldnae find a better man in all of bloody Scotland. Couldnae hart a fly. And yet his kindness, his daily kindness, his . . . doesn't the bugger ever get tired of pushing my chair, changing my underwear, undressing me, dressing me, doesn't he realize that my life is over?

My life has been over for thirty years! I live in a fucking wheelchair! Wheels on fire I vegetate. I am a vegetable on fucking wheels! And I was so young, and so handsome, and so cut out to be . . . something! I was a queen destined to be, a great man! I had it all planned. Saying no to you, and falling in love with a handsome film producer. A TV man. An actor. Some-bloody-body to take me away from fucking Yorkshire and take me!

I could have gone places! Not just once around the world with an old Irish pervert. I could have done so much more. So much more. For example, if you care to listen, Mr Tallisker, I shall enumerate my possibilities, for example, fuck, hell, I could have been . . . a comedian! I am funny! I could have presented that antiques show! I have a sense of . . . a sense of . . . something, summat sense-full, and meaning-filled.

Oh, look! There's Mrs Erskine. Fuck I would like to be in 'er skin tonight. I am going to have such a hangover!

Comedian, yes. I should have been a stand-up comedian, not a sit-down failure!

The Fringe started around that time. We all went to see a show by an Australian who delighted in insulting people. Perfect copy of reality TV; now there's reality theatre. Indian bloke laughed and laughed, because he didn't get it. And the masses sat on fat arses are delighted. And it's all delightful, only it's complete bollocks, Mr Dedalus. Slovaks didn't understand a thing. Had to leave early. Dumbest show at the Fringe, and Tim got us tickets for it, as he thought the Slovaks could learn something about British tolerance. How much more advanced our Scottish society was, guessing hearing about gays in public would draw them out of their shells. Weren't that easy, was it? Because it were a daft comedian in the first place. All canned laughter and PC gobshite.

Why do so many people like to be insulted by bad things: bad theatre, bad movies, bad TV—empty, mindless programmes? Haven't they got brains? Is it like in the Middle Ages, is it that? The transparent society, no more privacy. Every joke at somebody else's expense. The god-freaks, the homos, the Muslims, the turbans, the Indians with the funny accents—ah yes, *no please to not mistake me for an Indian, my mother is Punjabi.* People love a spectacle, a beheading, a torture, a ridicule. Germans got it right with their *schadenfreude*: people love to watch others in embarrassing situations. People are vile to the core, Mr Dedalus; vile and irresponsible creatures, and only after their own delight ... People are shallow and want to be entertained, preferably without thinking at all. No better than monkeys watching a fight. Oh what monkeys!

I worked for thirty years in programming, and I know where reality TV comes from: privatization. Giving greedy private media conglomerates their own channels. Of course, they keep down production cost. There's no money to be made if you spend it all on lavish productions. So the Murdochs of this world move in and everything goes down another notch, and the mob gets their mindless entertainment, and the monkeys cheer. Clapping stupidly with their cymbals attached, permanently! Hand-palm-cymbal, clap-clap-clap. Live in percussion. Haha, now let's make fun of the cripples! Oh wait, there's one: a lad in a wheelchair. And he's fat! Two in one, poke fun at the weight and the missing legs. Now let's hear him talk—oh, he's got a funny accent too. It's three jokes for the price of one! You are something else, my fat friend!

I worked in television for thirty years, I have seen, Mr Dedalus, the slippery slope. First the budget goes, then the quality, then the talent leaves, or sells out, or withers. That's what we have been doing in Britain for the last twenty, thirty years—whittling away our withering, withered talent; withering on our withering-wuthering, dithering-duthering heights. At least the Americans

177

never had any; they've always subsisted on junk. But we—oh, we had talent! Britain's got fucking talent. I mean, look at the fucking Beatles! Now we have Sussex and Essex—summat; and Euro trash everywhere. The Finn with this earth song is fun, but he won't win. It'll be the mindless voting again, the young girls. Nothing more mindless than teenage girls. But they've got the busiest clicking fucking fingers on fucking Facebook. It's no wonder so many Poles come to Britain. Same lack of talent, style, substance—sustenance. Oh don't hit me, I know I am whining, Mr Dedalus, but I am so distraught! Tha knows how I gets when the shit hits the mirror. Smear it, smear it broad. Shite and onions! One of these days, I'll jump!

Entertainment is supposed to be about art, about *ability*, about people who have exceptional minds, about magic and illusion, about the higher feelings, about seducing people with the power of well-chosen words, not calling them racist pigs to their faces and spitting on them, and taking off your clothes, and nothing but sex, sex, sex and running feet and shagging limbs and soddin' six-packs! Times are a-changing but ne'er for the better. But that's what every generation says before it gets used to the shite thrown at it. Every generation grows up with different tools. We aren't equipped to understand this new world around us. The shallow people are taking over everything! Click here if you like this loving picture. What's it of? Never mind—don't think, don't even think if you really do, just click, you cheering monkey!

Some of them are quite cute though. And the ugly ones use it to make up a life they'll never lead: it's the first virtual reality.

They say it's summat new, but it's not: we've made our own virtual realities for decades. Mine's an altered state already, with Dr Macallan—blimey, when did he get his PhD? Welcome to the club of heavy drinkers. May I introduce Jack Grapefart and John Swish—Swish-a doodle. Coodle. Cuddle. I need someone to cuddle. Someone who doesn't pity me!

But that is the point, Mr Dedalus. Really, I thought, when I sat in that tent, listening to a bad comedian trying to get laughs by making fun of obviously planted Muslims and queers and thickheads—the louder the laugh, the dumber the guy, the more the monkeys cheer.

I retreated, I went back to you, Mr Dedalus, as I always do with the right amount of alcohol or desperation—and then I realized that I hadn't spoken to you in days. I am indeed neglecting you.

Claudio and Lukáš occupied my mind now constantly, and I worried miserably about Jamie leaving me, and at the same time hoping that he and Maurizio would be happy together, and neither Dr Macallan nor you were of much help. The doctor's not helping any more; there is no cure for my misery. Maybe I could finally rid myself of you, I thought, just as the comedian started poking fun at disabled people, looking at me in my wheelchair first, but then attacking a guy with a crutch. That's when I knew they were planted, the people he attacked; and I saw right through the dumb show, because with my bald head and my grin, and my oh-so-obvious wheelchair, he should well have gone for me.

I hated myself for being there and having to endure that infantile theatre. I hated myself for being alive. I hated the chair, and Tim's compassion, and the man—if it were a man, who knows—who ran me down and put me in this bally contraption.

I could have been so bloody much more! I could have made so much of my life! So much! There wouldn't have been any self-pity, any drinking: there would have been a life, period, and not just an *existence*.

Oh shut up, Dedalus—shut up, shut up, shut up! I know it's all my own doing. I know it's I as has given up. So long ago. A bloody lifetime ago. Gave up too soon, too easily!

So, recovered, sober, back in the saddle again, as Jamie says cowboy-style. I recall this:

After that infernal show, we all went to a Moroccan restaurant, except Jamie, who raced to fetch his Maurizio. It were the night of their first date. What was it then? A Friday? I thought the show was on a Saturday? Must have been a Sunday. Anyroad, by chance the two love-birds ended up sitting across the room feeding each other couscous and looking very dishy and sappily romantic. I ate listlessly, stealing envious glances. I felt embarrassed. It were such a clear romance, such a love affair, one felt one ought not to disturb them. One felt one had no right to intrude.

But of course, I was happy for Jamie, and yet insanely jealous. I

179

knew that this Spanish-Italian-Lebanese model would be the one to take my Jamie away from me. I knew it—I knew the moment I saw him. I knew even before, when Jamie first talked of him. He was handsome, tanned, full of life; not as stunning as Jamie had made him out, but still a marvel of youth. A bit on the short side. But more, much more, he was in love with Jamie. He behaved like a little girl; they both did. He giggled! He cooed. He batted his eyelids; he crossed and opened his legs. And he giggled again! All the toolbox of a girl in the svelte body of a dark-limbed Italian god.

They were out on a real date, and they were quickly falling for each other. Anybody with eyes could see that. I had the lamb stew and Tim the shashlik, and we shared some salad. I don't remember who else were there, to be frank. One of Tim's friends, I think, but I can't remember. I had only eyes for Jamie, watching him flirt. How men can flirt! How they push out their pecs, and show off their biceps—Maurizio touching it, making sure the shirt sleeve was rolled up high enough, showing off the tattoo band. Oh, men can flirt! They are worse than women. Or rather better at it. And how openly they do it now. In my days it were smoky bars and backrooms, parks and toilets. Now Maurizio was drawing hearts into Jamie's palm—now he was kissing him. Right there. Right in the open.

We had coffee afterwards, and we smoked a cigar together in the yard—one of them thin affairs Tim got as a present from Mary last Christmas. She'd ordered them off the telly, of course, by mistake.

And then we saw them, sat on the stone steps leading up towards the Castle Road, just as Tim was about to hail a taxi. She had her arms around him—she was kissing him good night. We saw that it weren't a romantic kiss she intended; it were more playful, but nonetheless, Lukáš reached around her waist and pulled her closer, and then, Tim and me looking on, mouths open, beholding the final confirmation, the final slap in the face, the dismantling of all our theories, we watched Lukáš and Aleysha kiss.

A taxi stopped. Tim helped me into my seat, shoved the folded chair in, and sat down beside me. The driver wanted instructions, but we told him to wait.

—Start the metre, Tim said, if you must. Yes, start the metre, but don't drive. Wait!

We waited. We observed. Tim wanted to know, I think, even when I had seen enough. He wanted to be absolutely sure that this was a straight couple making out, that this was our Lukáš, who'd been so tender with Claudio—who'd told us again and again he liked women, and whom we simply could not believe wholeheartedly—and our Aleysha. Aleysha with the boy-child. Aleysha from Uganda. And it was him. And it was her. And they were still kissing.

—Well, gentlemen? asked the driver at last, and Tim gave directions.

We didn't speak a word until we were home.

I made tea. I thought of Claudio up in his room—even though, thinking back, I can't be sure he were home. We drank our tea in silence, and only when we had undressed, when we lay again next to each other in the big bed, Tim said,

—Well, there you have it. There can be no more doubt.

—It doesn't explain anything. What do you mean?

—Well, quite obviously . . . or he's bisexual.

—Obviously what? He may just try to turn himself around. He may still be fighting his true nature. He may still . . .

—Tim! Tim! Give it up!

Suddenly my husband was forceful: he turned on the light again on his side, and sat up. He touched my arm and said,

—Tim! Stop it.

There should have been an argument; I felt it. There should have been resistance, but I had no energy.

So be it. Sod this for a game of soldiers! Just let me get to sleep.

PART V

After catching him with Aleysha, should it have come as a surprise that I saw Lukáš emerge from her room next Sunday morning stealing home at the crack—home, of course, by the very fact that Claudio were his home to return to. Should I have been surprised?

I'd risen with the sun at five, sleepless as ever, and taken a cloth to the balustrade when I heard the bed squeak, interspersed with short piercing cries. Then the baby went off just like expected, and seconds later Lukáš dashed out of the room, his cock still hard in his undies, rest of his clothes clutched to his stomach, stumbling right into me and getting his big toe caught in the wheel. He winced, and cringed, and held onto my chair. The trail of hair from his navel was all I saw, and a tiny mole on his pale flesh. He'd lost most of his tan by then.

Inside we heard Aleysha take up the baby, sing to it, then the tearing of plastic. And finally the end of the wailing. We waited for it, motionlessly on the landing, Lukáš's face in pain, now clutching his injured foot, as if our continued existence somehow depended on the baby to stop crying and have its nappies changed. I was still staring at his treasure trail and almost reached out to touch it.

I wanted to say something witty, and then something motherly, or something endearing. I wanted to let him know that it was fine with me. The cat got my tongue, but, as I watched him writhe, and when he calmed down and looked at me, now trying to cover enough of his naked chest as possible with his hands and instantly forgetting the toe altogether, Lukáš seemed serious and honest. Not at all like a young man caught with his trousers down, but as if what had happened in there between them were clearly more than a fling. He pulled himself together. He stood upright, and when he slipped into his sweater at last, said very earnestly, stressing each syllable,

—She is very nice girl!

I nodded.

—Will you help me down?

I don't need help with the lift, I can get on and off myself without problems. But I did want to talk to him alone, and not here, on the stairs again. He pushed me onto the platform and walked next to me as the lift descended, finishing getting dressed with whatever he had grabbed. When we arrived downstairs, he had a baffled look on his face: he was holding a woman's blouse.

His cock was still a little hard, but the bulge shrunk now, while I tried not to look at it. We settled in the kitchen. I put the kettle on.

—I am missing a socking.

—You can miss a sock, or a stocking. I assume it's a sock, I said, looking straight at him. Was it an aristocratic face or the face of an adventurer? Maybe both—in any case, it turned a canny red.

—Why so many English words have 'ock?'—sock, cock, suck, sick, tick, lick, look, talk, pack, always *ack ack ack*. Like Martians in the film.

—I don't know. You'll have to ask Tim. He's the linguist.

He looked away from me, onto the floor. His hands changed position. He was fumbling; he couldn't sit still.

—Are you embarrassed? I asked.

—Embarrassed? What mean?

He pretended not to know the word.

—You know exactly what I mean.

—I am not embarrassed.

—That I caught you with Aleysha!

—What? We are both adult. I can sleeping with whatever I want.

—With *who*ever, I corrected him. Or is it *whom*ever?

—What?

—Never mind. Of course you are adults. Of course it's nobody's business. I am sorry. What am I like!

I wheeled closer, and for a moment it seemed like I were scolding a child. He expected a scolding. He weren't embarrassed to have come from Aleysha—he were embarrassed that I caught him sneaking back to Claudio. Or so I imagined.

His head hung low; his hands were ready to be raised in a protective gesture. He'd been found out. Whatever had been going on between Aleysha and him, he hadn't wanted it known. If I wanted to get something out of him, now was the time—he was vulnerable.

It were five minutes past seven. We heard the door open and footsteps—Jamie and Maurizio back from a run or a nightclub. They didn't step into the kitchen. We waited patiently, turning our heads, following the sounds down the corridor, up the stairs and into their room. I don't know why we both had the impression that our conversation would be important. We could easily shrug it off. He could go back to his room and hug his friend awake, and I could continue with my chores. But I had asked him down to the kitchen. He was certainly expecting a talking to. Yet suddenly I did not know what to ask him, and I certainly didn't want to be angry.

What I *did* want to know, I felt I had no right to ask. I couldn't just blurt out, 'Well that's it then. So what about Claudio, eh? What about your friend? You jerk!' After all, I still didn't know the first thing about their relationship. I were still in the dark after all these weeks.

Instead I said,

—Was this the first time with Aleysha?

He shook his head.

—You do know that the father of the baby is about. You do . . .

He said quickly,

—Yes, but he is gay. She tell me.

—Yes, he is. But he does look after them. You have to share her with him . . . in a way. He is not a bad man. He hasn't deserted her.

—What mean 'deserted?'

—Left her. He hasn't left her. And it's 'what does this mean.' Not 'what mean this.'

He blushed some more, and his fingers were dancing on the table. He was nervous.

While I observed him, I realized my argument wasn't very convincing, or even necessary. If Lukáš was after a relationship with Aleysha, things would settle differently. I caught him looking at the clock again and again.

—Do you need to go back? I said, just as the sound of water boiling started to fill the room.

—No, no.

—But you don't want Claudio to find out?

It came to me—that was what I wanted to know, what I had

184

wanted to ask: whether Claudio knew! If Aleysha were a betrayal of sorts.

The last thing I had seen was Claudio submissive, ending his gay escapade as if by order, and coming home with his friend. Now the friend was dallying with a woman. But of course I knew already, when he glanced at the clock again.

—You are afraid Claudio will wake up and find you gone. You don't want him to know!

He just stared at me a little, then nodded very slowly.

—Has Claudio done that? Has he ever had an affair with a girl ... while you two were together?

I wanted to say, 'Has he ever betrayed you like you are betraying him now?' But of course, I couldn't say that. If he liked Aleysha, if he loved her—what betrayal was there? What nonsense, my narrow, gay, wishful perspective. I had no right.

Can love betray friendship? Even such a friendship as theirs?

Lukáš looked at me as if he hadn't understood the question at all.

—Or is it only you? Are only *you* allowed to have women on the side? I said, rather more acerbic.

—He can do what he want! We can both do what we want!

—I am not quite sure about that. What's that about marriage; Claudio making sure you didn't get married?

—What? Did he say that? It's not true. I broke it off. I was not ... ready.

I put my hands on his, to make him stop twitching, but he pulled away.

—Why did it bother you so much that he kissed Javier in the pub?

—It didn't.

—Oh Lukáš, it clearly did! It bothered you enough to attack— to corner me on the landing.

He didn't understand.

—The landing—the stairs. When you talked to me on the stairs? You were quite intense!

—Intense?

—Yes, you remember? You almost attacked me.

—I did not mean ...

185

—It's no matter. But tell me the truth. You aren't quite equals. He is clearly . . . I mean, you seem to have some power over him!

—Ah . . . ! He can do what he wants.

—Yes, but he doesn't do certain things . . . He always seems to ask for permission. What is this hold you have over him?

He gave me a puzzled look. I realized the 'having a hold' might be too difficult a phrase.

—You have power over Claudio, no? He listens to you! He does what you say!

He didn't answer. He wasn't thinking of an answer either, but went back to his fidgeting, tapping a rhythm on his thighs. And then he looked away.

—Lukáš, tell me! What is it that binds you two together? What is that bad thing you both did? Or he did? Or you did? You are the dominant part; you are the one who decides things. You are keeping him from . . . I don't know! He's your . . . What *is* he, exactly, to you?

The kettle boiled and spared him a reply.

I rolled back, took it off the fire, brought it over to the table. Lukáš turned to reach for the teabags, put three in the pot, watched as I poured in the water. It was a ceremony, a long and studied exercise in not talking. Even as the lid were back on, we watched the steam slowly rise from the hole and the spout— and somehow I am sure he were hoping that it would carry my question away.

—What kind of power do you have over Claudio? I said again.

Lukáš folded his hands. He was shutting me out.

—He can do what he want . . . only sometime . . .

—Yes?

—Sometimes, I must . . . I look out for him.

—Look out for him how?

—I did a bad thing, many years ago, and hurt him. Very bad. Very . . . I have to make sure he's okay. I have to look out for him. To make sure he . . .

— . . . he doesn't run off with anybody else? To make sure he doesn't find a man who'd love him back?

—Claudio isn't gay. I telling you.

—With a woman then? You make sure he doesn't leave you for

186

a girl—you want it both, then? You want your women—and him.

—No! No, it's not . . . when he meet girl, he go can marry! He can go be happy! Then I cannot protect . . .

—A man then. Protect him? You feel you need to protect him? Are you worried that he *might* be gay? I think he could easily have a relationship with a man.

—You are wrong. This hasn't anything to do with sex. We are not *like* you. Maybe he can, but I know he does not . . . he never have sex with man. Never! I know! We are not *like* you!

—You don't like gays, is that it? You hate . . . What do you think gays are like, Lukáš? What are you afraid of? Are you afraid you are gay yourself? Are you running from yourself?

I regretted my tone of voice, realizing how accusing I sounded, but I couldn't stop. Tim's warning was in my head: 'Stop it, stop it, let them be.' But I had to know. I had to know! Now or never!

—You understand all wrong! I don't like gay, because . . . because it is . . . dirty. I don't mean you and Tim, because you are old, but like Jamie . . . like Jamie . . . Jamie he make with everyone, always different . . . is dirty.

—You think gays are dirty?

He nodded.

—We are not like that. You sleep with everyone. I mean Jamie . . . and some gay we know before, many! You like dogs.

—We like dogs? Oh yes, absolutely, yes, we like dogs, but . . . oh I see!

—No I mean you *do it* like dogs. Gay sex, always, in the dark room, in the bars . . . it have no consequence. Is like dogs fucking in the street. Is disgusting, is . . . no worth! Is no worth! Your gay sex . . . is not real. Is fool around, like boy in school, like teenager . . . it never real.

I felt that at last I was onto something, that this was the key to the whole affair, but I had no clear grasp.

He found gay sex dirty. He had no respect for gays, certainly. He didn't want to be like that, but he knew inside, deep down, that he was!

I had an instinct, a certain feeling that this were it. Now I would help him find himself. Now I would help him see how beautiful love was. How wrong his prejudgments.

187

I poured out the tea, but he ignored his cup.

—You don't like Jamie?

He did not answer.

—He's got a boyfriend now. He is changing. He'll change.

I tried my tea—It was still too hot.

—Do you feel the need to protect Claudio from that? From the dirty . . . from dirty gays?

He put the cup to this lips, very slowly, but he didn't answer.

Some time passed. Spuggies fluttered outside, and there were a hammering noise. I knew I had to give him time, to let him work it out. If this were going to be his coming out . . . and if promiscuity were his hang-up, then he had to come out slowly.

Whatever we experience, whatever we learn in life, if we go too fast, it is as if we hadn't learned at all. That were my last glimmer of hope, that I might get him to say, 'Yes, you are right, we are gay, and being gay is wonderful, and let's have a happy ending and kiss and make up!' Forever hopelessly romantic am I, stupid sod. Oh, stupid, stupid sod! I ruined everything with my meddling. Everything! Interfering busybody.

—Lukáš, I said after a while, don't take this the wrong way. But have you never considered the possibility that Claudio might want more from you? That he might want physical love, as well as your friendship?

He looked puzzled.

—Claudio?

—Yes.

—But I tell you—we are not homosexual.

—Forget the labels for a while.

—No, *you* forget label. You forget put us in your . . . what you are! We are not what you are!

—You mean . . . dirty, promiscuous gays.

—Yes! And behave like . . . women, and make-up, like . . .

—But then why do you . . .

I stopped. Why did they seek the company of gays then? Why were they here, in this house, if gay things were so very disgusting?

His hands were shaking and he tried to steady them on the cup, grasping and releasing it over and over again. At last he caught my eye and I saw he was furious. He tried to stare me down and said again,

—Wrong! Wrong! You are wrong.

—I can see that, Lukáš. I can see you are not screaming queens, and neither is Claudio. But very few gay people are.

He looked away, and seemed to sulk.

—Most are *tunten.*

—No, Lukáš, they are not. What are *tunten*?

—Oh, is German. My German—we learn more German before English. I am sorry. Is queens, men who act like women.

—I see. Those are just the loudest and shrillest. Who make it onto the telly. They are not the majority. You mustn't judge gay lifestyles by looking at carnival celebrations. You don't judge straight people by looking at a swinger's club, do you? The majority of gay people are quiet, unassuming, normal fellows like you and Lukáš. They don't wear women's clothes, or make-up, they don't call each other 'sister,' or fuck in the streets like dogs. They have normal jobs; they are normal men. They lead normal lives, even married lives. Like Tim and me—do you call us queens?

He snorted and I waited for an answer, but none came. Well, maybe not the smartest question to ask, coming from *my* mouth. But if ever I were butch, it were during that summer of the Slovaks. Never once put on rouge, I swears!

He wiped his eyes, and then made a very serious face.

—But Claudio isn't gay. He isn't gay.

—And neither are you?

—No! he screamed, glaring at me for a while, then looking up to where, presumably, Aleysha were still nursing her little one, as an offer of proof.

—Are you perhaps afraid that Claudio might *turn* gay, if you let him? Is that it? What was the bad thing you did to him?

We were going in circles. No, I was going in circles.

To my surprise, he shook his head emphatically, and a smile came over his mouth, a smirk really, of desperation.

—Look! You don't understand! I know Claudio is no gay. I know, I know. I know him so long. We are good friends. It is not that.

—You kiss each other, Lukáš. You hug and touch each other like lovers. All your pictures, when you went north—they are all

189

pictures of you, together. To the world, you look like lovers.

—So what? We don't have sex.

—And Claudio?

—Claudio doesn't have sex with guys. Never had. Never will. You are wrong.

—What is it then? What's your secret?

He shook his head even more, and kept his embittered grin; but he gave no reply. In that moment, I was one-hundred percent sure that he was in the closet. That he was keeping Claudio from being gay ... and happy. In that moment, I despised him, and pitied him. How silly of me.

—You mustn't be afraid to come out, not any more. The world is different now, at least in the West. We have registered partnerships, gay marriage ... even if the sex disgusts you, you can find ways of ...

—Look!

He turned towards me, and said pleadingly, trying to get all his words right and the grammar with it.

—Stop try force us in label.

—I am not forcing a label ...

—You are. Don't you see? You just like straight people, same ... narrow mind. You only assume we gay because all you here are.

—*You* came to a gay bed and breakfast. *You* chose a gay B&B! What for? So you could be *yourself*. Subconsciously, you came here because you want to be free. Free and gay.

He kept shaking his head, harder and harder.

—I only want to help! I want to help you to be yourself. Coming out is painful, but ... If you love him, you don't have to be queens and promiscuous just because you love a man. You can get married, you can ...

—Aaah! Stop! You are mad! It not about that. I don't want to marry Claudio! We are not a gay couple. Shut up! Shut up!

I backed off. His wild eyes stared at me. His wild, moist, lost eyes.

—The whole marriage thing is stupid! I did not get married, because I don't believe marriage. Why anyway want gay people such stupid form of living? Of equality? Why want life base on your sexual possession? Why? Why? Because they are men,

190

and they want to possess. I am sure to be alone, or with friend is better—it mean be free! Free! Not be forced into something. All men want to possess, gay or straight! But I explain to you, Claudio and I—I am sorry my English is not good—we don't possess! We give freedom. We want free! We are friends! There is friendship—much bigger, much more beautiful than love and marriage. Friendship! Real friendship! Much more difficult too, to be friends, forever, not *own* a wife or *own* a man. It does not matter if it is gay or straight, if you fuck ass or … or … or … who you say?

—Cunt? And it's 'how do you say.'

—Yes! Cunt!

I swallowed, and then I had to laugh. He chuckled, almost forgetting that he was being mad at me, that he had his hand now raised in an almost threatening gesture.

—I sorry, my English … it is so difficult to explaining me to you, but you understand? You know? Everybody behave like man and woman is only way, I mean, husband and wife is only way, but it is ugly way! You look your parents: they never happy. Man and woman together for sex and children is never happy. It is stupid arrangement, so old. Only two people who friends, only friends is happy! Marry for sex, for money, for man want wife—it is possession, and greed, and shellfish …

—*Selfish* you mean.

—Yes, I say shellfish—selfish. Ah, I see. Live together as friends, and free, that is beautiful! We want be friends, Claudio and I, and people don't let us. All people say, we must marry now, make baby. I don't hate baby, I like, you can see—he pointed upstairs again—but people are crazy! I don't live my life for baby! I live for me! You say I am shellfish?

—Selfish, maybe.

—Yes. Maybe is. But then we going with gay people, because it is not so pressure! Because we can be more free. We like alternative, and gay, because less pressure. But now you go on and on and on—you want to turn us into gays, all the time. Why does everybody have be like you? Why does everybody want the rest of people be same? And all you want to making us gay! All the time you say us gay! And I say you, I say you …

—I 'tell' you.

—Yes I tell you, straight people too, when they are together, it only beautiful if they are friends. Not man and wife. They must be friends, then they last forever. Love is stupid, it is only chemical process in brain. Sex is not important, it is only animal instinct. We not need more baby. We needing friends. We needing respect each other. Friendship is real—because you need brain, and considerate! You need work, you need sacrifice! People pray to god of love, they adore love story, but love is nothing; love is shit! And sex even more shit! Only relief of chemical. Why you make your identity on who you have sex with? Why you defining your ... what you are, based on who in your bed? Where you stick your ... you know? Why? Why want legal bondage? Why marriage-bondage? Marriage is worst. Only stupid people want marriage. Why gay fight for marriage I don't know. I don't understand! We should fight for friendship instead, for real friendship.

—I understand, I know what you mean. You are right, except ... Calm down, please! Calm down.

He smiled quickly, but showed no sign of relaxing. His fingers moved constantly. He played with the cruets; he took the salt and poured some into the palm of his hand, then spilled more on the table; his right leg was quivering.

I reached out to him; I said again,

—Calm down! I understand. I know what you mean. I only wanted to help.

He started shaking his head, mumbling something in Slovak.

—Lukáš, please. It's fine. Your Claudio, if he is your friend, such a good friend, that no woman can come between you—and apparently no man—if that Claudio, if he wants physical contact with another man. Are you making him the scapegoat of your own cowardice? Because frankly, I am quite sure you *are* gay, despite everything! You are rejecting straight normality just like a closeted gay man. You are running away from yourself! Tim says I am a fool, but I am sure you are in the closet. Are you just using him to hide? And not let him be free, let him discover that he could be, that he *is* gay? You are manipulative, you are cruel! You mustn't interfere in his life like this. You can't control him! You must let Claudio find himself. You must let him be his own man!

192

He looked embarrassed at the table, his finger tracing an oddly-shaped long nick in the wood. I remembered how it had got there, how one of Jamie's one-nighters had played with a knife, then thrown it, and we ended up calling the police.

—I can see I am right! I can see I hit the spot! You are both gay and can't deal with it. You are hiding from each other like bloody cowards, and calling it a friendship. That's all your friendship is—a lie. All that ideal friendship talk ... you are just afraid to face the facts.

He looked up, but not at me—past me, at the wall. I got so angry, so bloody angry then. I had to draw him out, now, this was my chance. That he wouldn't see, that he just wouldn't respond to my ... manipulation. That he wouldn't let me help him come out, now and here.

I'd helped so many boys over the years. So many had come to our B&B in search of themselves, and I've helped them. Mother Tim, the psychologist. Helped them to find their true nature. I couldn't fail now. Not with this ... difficult case.

—How do you live with yourself, Lukáš? How do you live with yourself, keeping Claudio from being happy? When you look in the mirror in the morning, aye—when you look in the mirror, what do you see? A gay man, out and proud and in touch with his feelings, no! You see a coward pretending to be straight, kissing girls in the street, sneaking away from your lover to try and be 'normal,' and making Claudio your prisoner in the process. Tell me, tell me! What do you see, when you look in the mirror, eh? Tell me—WHAT DO YOU SEE?

God, I hate myself for this outburst! The moment the words came out, I knew I had it all wrong, and I had no right to confront him. I hadn't listened to a word he had said, only trying to press my own agenda. And I hadn't thought it out afore. It had come to me in a rush of emotion, and I regretted it immediately, but it were done, and I couldn't take it back.

I felt the blood rise in my face, I felt my arms twitch. I even felt my legs, heavy and as if they were on fire.

He just stared at me. No doubt he had only understood half. Then he opened his arms, shrugged, and let them hang down. His gaze went to the ceiling. He sighed. He looked vulnerable, all of a sudden, all the emotion, the excitement of our talk drained from him. His face lost all the blood, and his lips, his narrow pink lips were the only colour left. He turned to me, with a disconcertingly vacant stare. As if from one moment to this, he had become a different person. Even his voice changed. He sounded bland, younger maybe, and almost mechanical.

—When I look in the mirror, what I see . . . ? You want to know what I see? I see a monster! A horrible, ugly, monster. A man who has done something . . . horrible. Who can never forgive. In the mirror, I see . . . a monster!

—A monster? You mean I am right . . . you are gay? Being gay isn't horrible! You are not a monster! You are . . .

—NO!

He bellowed it out, louder and more assertive than I had ever heard him speak. It was a violent rebuttal, a denial from the bottom of his heart. He shouted loud and mad, and his head trembled.

He frightened me, and I thought I had gone too far. For a while I were too frit to even move.

He folded his arms and opened them again, then he stood up slowly and left the room.

If the initial contact didn't surprise me, the attachment Lukáš and Aleysha formed did. Two weeks passed of more guesswork, more riddles, but a lot less talking. Lukáš withdrew, and Claudio avoided me.

But Aleysha were suddenly back in the house, and Lukáš with her almost constantly, with increasing intimacy. It was a surprise to find them in the living room, with the baby on Lukáš's lap, and Aleysha beaming at me so full of glee: they looked like a right family.

She smiled, she radiated, she glowed, as if she were sure she had found a *real* father for her child. I didn't quite see it then, but Lukáš played his role well. And I hoped for one thing more than anything: that he would in the process get out of Claudio's hair.

Never mind they didn't talk to me now—ne'er mind I may have pushed them too far—I'd quite decided by then that it were

Lukáš who kept Claudio from finding love and happiness in the arms of another man. I went over all the conversations we had had since their arrival, while we waited for the father of the baby to come and take them out to the park.

It had always been Lukáš who asserted their straightness, and always Claudio who threw a spanner in the works—who was playful, coquettish even, with other men, and sexually ambiguous. And then Lukáš's confession that he found us promiscuous and dirty. That he hated queens.

After they were gone, leaving behind the smell of urine and talcum powder, I was just about to open the windows, when Jamie came down with Maurizio on his arm, the royal couple, waving to the crowds, ready to receive their adulation, then stopping at the last step, and kissing. Truly, it is like a stage play, my life: I move from scene to scene and people come to find me. Enter Jamie and new lover, stage right. They kiss, they fuck, *et exeunt*. That's what being in a wheelchair feels like: everything comes to you. You only have to sit tight and hold on to your knickers.

I like my wheelchair on those days, when I feel so inclined. Even if I can't reach to open the bloody window.

—Jamie, help me! I can't get the latch.

—What's that smell? Oh god, what's that awful smell?

—Did she change the baby in here? On our sofa table? Did she do it here?

Of course, by then everybody in the house knew about Lukáš and Aleysha and now the baby was back with a vengeance.

—They did. Lukáš and Aleysha.

—He's a right daddy then, is he? Doesn't even have to make his own!

—Jamie!

—What?

Windows ajar, we fled the scene.

Jamie and Maurizio had one of their cutesy breakfasts: Jamie gathering fruit and muesli, Maurizio sitting on his lap, the two of them preparing everything in an elaborate dance of four hands, and then feeding each other morsels. A bit of fruit, a spoonful of cereal, a long, wet kiss. Fruit, cereal, kiss, repeat. They looked so in love! It hurt me to think anybody could conceive of our Jamie as *dirty*.

—How's the mix-raced breeder couple doing then?

—They've gone out for a picnic with the father of the baby.

—Oh, straight people! Their relationships are so complicated, serenaded Maurizio, being fed a strawberry. Jamie poured me a cup of tea.

—The two of you seem very comfortable together.

They looked at each other, then said in unison,

—We are!

More hugging, more kissing, more petting. Maurizio were wearing a wide sweater which was now riding up over his tanned abs. He had a tattoo there too and clocked me noticing.

—It's new. He's got the same, he said, hugging Jamie.

Barely a fortnight and they had matching tats!

It looked like a penguin in the top corner of his crotch, but now that he pulled down his tracksuit bottoms—low enough so I could see that his pubic hair were trimmed to a small and neat triangle—I recognized it as the blossom of a rose, whose stem originated where his . . . other stem did.

I gave each a long smile. I felt maternal, caring—and a little sick when they touched each other again. I will always remember them that day, in that light, in that kitchen. They were like teenagers, like children almost. I felt as if my nurturing of Jamie had finally yielded something real. As if I had looked after him the right way. Now he graduated from one-night stands to true love. I wished it so much. And with such a handsome man too—such a swarthy, Mediterranean beauty. What daft nonsense Lukáš had spouted. All that tosh about friendship and putting down love. Love is what it's all about! Friendship is nothing without love!

—What are your plans then, boys?

—Today? We thought we . . .

—No, the two of you! What . . .

I realized when I said it that the question had been asked too soon. They had just begun to love each other! They weren't concerned with the future yet. It is a mistake you make easily as you get older: you always see the consequences, the future, the end of the affair, long before it has begun. Young love doesn't; it doesn't see further than the next caress. Even the tattoos aren't for life; they were only for the moment! Oh to be young again and love like that, wild and uncontrolled, like I were, Mr Dedalus. To get another chance, to love heedlessly and mindlessly, only in a blur of emotion—where every touch of the flesh carries so much meaning!

Lost in thought, I missed Claudio's arrival. He stood in the door frame, hands in his pockets. He was wearing a checked shirt, wide open, and with the sleeves rolled up. It made him look infinitely masculine, like a lumberjack in a porn movie, the muscles of his neck and chest gleaming in the soft morning light. He was—I briefly held my breath—like an apparition.

—Your husband, said Jamie cocking his chin in Claudio's direction, has gone out with his black wife, child, and the child's father! I know! It's disgraceful!

Maurizio and I giggled, but Claudio didn't react. He squinted when he took a step forward and the sun hit his eyes. It were the type of deliberate non-reaction that says more than any words. Except each of us read something else into it. Whatever there was between them, Claudio were keeping his own, eloquent silence.

—They make a nice couple, said Maurizio, climbing off Jamie's lap.

He walked over to Claudio and embraced him like a child, lowering himself so that his head would come to rest on Claudio's chest. Of course, that might have been the whole purpose of the exercise: to feel that flesh and make it appear like an innocent gesture.

—Poor Claudio! said Maurizio.

Claudio looked quizzically, but he didn't push Maurizio away. His hands remained hanging motionlessly by his side.

—Your boyfriend's going with *another woman*.

Claudio gave a quick and shy laugh, then said without much emotion behind it,

—He's not my boyfriend. He can do what he want.

It seemed curious to me that they would use the same phrase, with the same error in it. They seemed to give each other the same flawed breathing space, and insisted desperately on it.

Maurizio led his victim by the hand to the table. Claudio let it all be done. He didn't smile. The ménage were complete when Javier walked in. He was wearing long pyjama trousers and a faded sweater. He was unusually cheerful.

—*¡Hola gente!* What crowd! Who's shagging who?

Claudio sat down next to Jamie at the table, who pushed a yoghurt towards him. He opened it carefully, licking the backside aluminium cover. We all watched him do it. The mundane, practical gesture took on an erotic dimension when he closed his eyes to the sun—which reappeared from behind a cloud—and kept licking. We just stared.

Javier took a bite of something—I couldn't see what—then kicked the door shut and asked for more substantial fare.

—Is everybody hungry?

There were nods all round.

—Does anybody want to cook?

No reactions.

—I will then, *si puedo,* if you'll allow me!

Maurizio kissed him on the cheek and applauded, his hands held high over his chest.

—Make your *huevos rancheros*!

—I make *huevos* with whatever I'll find.

—There are onions, peppers, and some feta cheese in the green plastic thingy, I offered, rolling back into the corner to get out of his way.

Javier cooking is a marvellous thing. Not just because he is a great cook, but because he looks good working. I love watching men doing what they are good at—a job they love. It doesn't matter what it is, as long as there is dedication. It makes them shine with pride.

—They shall make it into the *huevos*.

Claudio asked,

—What are *huevos*?

—Eggs, darling. Javier will make his famous eggs with half the fridge in them.

—Like scrambled eggs?

—Whichever way they come out, said Javier. We just call them that. They aren't the real Mexican thing—Tim hates beans.

—Which Tim?

—The other one.

—One can never be quite sure how they come out, said Jamie playing with his fork, but they are always fanfuckingtastic!

Maurizio pushed his body between Jamie and Claudio, and then squeezed himself onto Claudio's lap.

—You poor straight boy. Abandoned by your straight lover-boy.

—He's not aban . . . adoned me. He seems to like her, Aleysha.

—Like, my ass! said Jamie. He's only doing this to spite you!

—To spite me? What means?

—He is doing it on purpose! He is doing it to show you who's boss. He's got you pussy-whipped, straight boy!

—Why does he do this?

—Because you were naughty. Because you made out with the gay boys! Don't you realize he doesn't want you to be gay?

—But I am not . . .

—You must admit, sang Javier, manipulating the cast-iron pan as if it were weightless, that you are a little bit gay. That you could be, if you wanted.

—A little bit poofy! Jamie trilled. Just a wee bit!

—What does it mean, if I wanted? If I am not . . . What I don't understand . . .

—What does it mean to be? And how do you know when you are? *Preguntas, preguntas!* warbled Javier. He continued:

—Straight men are always so confused! Coming out straight in a gay house is just—*issa hell!*

I could have killed him! I wanted to hear what Claudio didn't understand. We weren't seeing the signs, reading them correctly. But it were fun observing the young 'uns at their game. It occurred to me too, as Javier juggled a pile of ingredients past me, how perfectly Claudio fit into this household of gay men and how little he chafed. It were always in the presence of Lukáš that he became more awkward, more restrained. There you go, Mr Dedalus: more corroboration of my theory. Which theory exactly?

—I will put it that way, said Javier, cutting a huge slice of butter, his secret to anything tasty. If you meet a good girl, will you pack up your things and leave him?

Claudio didn't answer.

—I will put it other way, said Maurizio, hugging the Slovak, kissing his neck, and speaking entreatingly, making himself sound more important as he clung to Claudio's chest,

—If he stays with the Ugandan lady, what will you do?

—They are only friends, said Claudio. I don't think they are sleeping together.

—Oh-oh! sang Jamie. Wake-up call!

—What it mean, wake-up call? What?

—Your boyfriend has been sleeping with Aleysha for two weeks now! He goes to her room around midnight and comes back to you around five.

Claudio looked genuinely surprised, but said nothing.

—Oh, he can do what he want.

There it was again! It was like a mantra that lived its own life between them, a mysterious pendulum swinging back and forth and measuring their increasing distance.

—So, if he goes off with Uganda momma, you will be alone. What will you do then . . . find a boyfriend or a girlfriend?

Claudio didn't seem to take in the words. He was staring blankly ahead.

We all watched Javier busy himself most expertly with the cutting of bell peppers, onions, and olives. The blade moved so fast in his hands, it was dizzying. The difference between and amateur and a professional chef is quite astonishing. I thought then that I should never call anything I did at that oven 'cooking.' He threw everything into a bowl, then cut in the eggs. We were all looking at him when Claudio said decidedly,

—If Lukáš left me I go back to Slovakia. I will marry nice girl with a big farm and raise chicken and have cow, I want milk cow.

Maurizio giggled and looked at Jamie. At first, it seemed like a definite statement, something believable and well thought out. But one by one we realized he had said, 'If Lukáš leaves me.' Not 'when,' not 'when he gets married,' not 'when he finds a girl.' And even semantics aside, Claudio's dream of straight marriage and a bovine idyll were clearly contingent on the actions of his friend. He would seek all that only once Lukáš dumped him.

We all took a while to process this, and watched the eggs turn into a giant, delicious-looking omelette.

—What if he doesn't leave you?

—Then we staying together.

—What if *you* meet a girl before that? What if you are the first to meet a girl, said Javier, just before the omelette somersaulted over the iron pan in perfect slow-motion.

—He will leave first, said Claudio categorically.

Maurizio kissed Claudio on the lips, and Claudio let it happen, even pressed against his mouth. He put his arm around Maurizio's waist. Jamie noticed and frowned.

For a while they sat like this. I think, but I can't be sure, that Maurizio was grinding his bum against Claudio's hard-on. Jamie looked away deliberately. Maurizio reached for his phone and gave it to Jamie.

—Take a picture of us. Me and the straight boy.

But Jamie did not get up. Maurizio turned back to his prey.

—You are such a sad boy. I don't think you are really happy. I think that's it. You aren't really happy, are you?

That's when Claudio escaped, pushed the model away and got up.

—I am happy. Don't worry all. Don't worry yourself so much with me. Lukáš and I—we are friends. We are okay.

Claudio sat down again. Everybody noticed the strange gesture, which made his statement sound like a rehearsed declaration. And everybody noticed the bulge!

Javier gave us a thumbs up, just before the big pan landed in the centre of the table, and suddenly everybody had a fork in hand.

They must have been telling each other this for twelve years, that they are just friends, and that they can do what they want. They must have been telling each other what they were, until they believed it, and became it. So they let each other be *straight*, and called each other *friend*, and assured each other of their mutual independence, when in truth . . .

Oh, for crying out loud.

It were enough to tear your hair out!

How could we help them? I thought. All the while I watched Maurizio and Jamie feeding each other, sealing each mouthful of omelette with a kiss, as Claudio blushed, and Javier stole bashful glances at him.

Around that time, after Javier asked me if I thought he had a chance with Claudio, and I told him he better not waste his time, I had to explain to Philip—already off his hinges when he arrived, because Jamie hadn't answered his calls—that he needn't bother coming back.

I heard the car long before he came in, the Jaguar with its distinctive roar. Philip is an impressive man, demanding in every move and gesture. Jamie and Maurizio had gone to London. I told him that when he appeared at the door in his pinstripe suit—and that they were a couple, and in love, and that he better back off.

I told him that Jamie was crazy about his new friend; that he wouldn't want to see Philip again. He tried to argue with me.

—It's just not on, go away!

You should have seen me, arms akimbo, furious, protective, like a concerned mother.

I hated myself for speaking the way I did. I was like a meddling relative, haughty and arrogant, dismissive, too. As in, 'You needn't come back young man, my daughter is engaged to be married to another!'

Not quite that way, but I stumbled mid-sentence and ended up chasing him down the hall, shouting, 'Get out please! Jamie doesn't want to see you!'

He'd never said so to me, I thought, while I said it—I was interfering again in other people's happiness.

Philip reacted in the most unexpected way. He doubled up laughing, croaking briefly, bellowing, then croaking again and finally cackling hysterically. Then he fell silent and, glowering for a moment, he took a threatening step towards me.

—Jamie? In a relationship? Ha!

—Yes, Jamie, and he's very, very happy.

I got angry meself at the well-dressed banker, and wanted him gone. I wanted him out. Nothing ought to interfere with Jamie's happiness. After all these years of fucking around, after all the searching.

—He's not that kind of fag!

Philip turned towards me, smug and arrogant. So shagging

a man were okay, but living with one, loving one—that was perverse? I'd come across that type too often. The self-despising, lust-driven, schizo queer.

—What kind of *fag* is he then? You tell me, laddie.

—Well he took my money!

—He never asked for it.

—How can you know?

—Because Jamie wouldn't. He's not that kind of man.

—He's not a man at all. He's a ta . . .

He swallowed his words, and tried slamming the door as he walked out, but I caught it with my chair. He turned round again.

—It won't last. He's not a fairy like you people. He won't live with a guy.

—Oh, and you know?

—I know his type—he ain't really queer. He's just too . . .

—Too what? He's not queer, he just likes gay sex? Listen to yourself!

—Ah, fuck you!

—No, fuck you, mister! And don't come back, sonny Jim!

He stared, but then he turned and walked away. I had been afraid he wouldn't leave!

I felt it my obligation to clean up Jamie's past now; to shield him from his erstwhile lovers, to let nothing and no one interfere. Some did come calling at odd hours, albeit not with the regularity of Philip. Some called the house phone still. You could tell the friends from the *friends* by the tone of their voices. I got angry again.

Philip stood by his Jag, inserting the key, then hesitating.

—You are treating him like a whore! I shouted after him.

Big mistake. Philip turned round.

—That's because he is one. Fucking slag.

—Jamie's not a slag. He's a canny lad. *He* is fucking *you*, remember? He's more of a man than you'll ever be, you fucking coward!

The banker turned and glared at me, then, just as I thought he was coming back, he picked something up from the street and hurled it towards me! I couldn't retreat fast enough, and it hit me on the upper arm, hurting like hell.

I sat there for a while breathing hard. It had been a stupid thing to say, and to get involved in their business at all, but I couldn't help it. Jamie was mine to look after. He was mine to protect!

I couldn't move. I was about to start crying when I noticed the blood on my arm. I made an effort to control my emotions, and turned back towards the kitchen. I could only move the left wheel, the right arm hurt too badly. Suddenly the door opened again behind me, and I froze, thinking that Philip had come back.

But it weren't him, thank goodness. It couldn't be him; he didn't have a key. It were Aleysha. She looked happy.

—What on earth happened to you! she cried when she saw me, but brimming with confidence for the first time in months. I noticed the change at once: life had returned to her face. I forgot my pain and looked at her with surprise, until I realized that it was indubitably Lukáš who had brought about the change.

She pushed me into the kitchen, and cleaned up my arm, speaking to me in her slow, drawn-out accent with the deep As, and a clear pause between each word.

—That arsehole. I have seen him before. I have recognized the car outside. And he parked where he cannot. I have not liked him, this man.

—He's a rich arsehole.

—He was with Jamie, no? He was Jamie's . . . lover?

—Well . . . no. More a . . . ouch!

—It is good that Jamie is settling down. It is good. Here, it's not too bad. You will have only a little bruise.

I tried to look at the spot, but my neck was stiff from the sudden movement at the door; I felt totally helpless, and more like crying even than before. Aleysha pulled up a chair.

—Is everything all right with all-you?

I nodded. She took a napkin and wiped the sweat from my forehead.

—Thank you.

I studied her face. It was still aglow.

—What about you? You look . . . happy?

—I am.

—Is it because of Lukáš?

She gave no reply. Instead she said,

—Will you need a doctor?

—Oh, no, I'll be fine. Can I ask you a question?

She turned her head slightly.

—I will put the kettle on first. I will make the tea. You sit here and rest.

She got up and filled our nicked old kettle. She lit the gas oven and put the kettle down on the flame. The flame turned blue and shot out at the sides so wide it gave me a start. Seconds later, it bristled with the familiar sound—the sound that always began our kitchen talk. The introduction to portentous things. A most British form of lubrication, I thought.

—Are you sure you do not need a doctor?

—I am fine.

She returned to her chair, and took my hand. But when I had put my question to her at last, she dropped my hand quickly again, and stood up. She placed herself before me, arms raised slightly, pleading, but also angry.

—Why you ask me this?

—It's a simple question. Do you think Lukáš might be gay?

—Why you ask *me* this? Have I not dealt enough with you— all-you gays? I have a baby from a gay man! You think I am a good judge? You think I can tell? I must laugh!

—I thought . . .

She became even angrier. She gave a shrill cry that sounded almost panicked.

—Lukáš, gay? He is sleeping with me . . . you think I sleep with gay men on purpose? You think I enjoy it? Why you ask me that? Why you ask me? And why is always everything in this house about gay? Not a day I have lived here, not a day goes by without the subject! It is always . . . it is all all-you talk about!

—It's because we *are* gay. It's what we *are*.

—Yes, but you are obsessed . . . You are not satisfied until everyone talk about it. You are gay, all-you, but it is *all* you are. You are nothing else *but* gay! And maybe you hate yourself for it, because all you have is self-pity! You are always sat here in this chair and all you talk about is people being gay.

—Aleysha, I can understand that you have . . . cultural

reservations . . .

—Cultural reservations? What you think I am African so I am homophobic?

—You might . . .

—Is that what you think?

—I think you confide in Lukáš more than any of the gay men here.

—Is that why you need to know whether he is gay? So you can prove I am a homophobic African?

—No, god, Aleysha, no. It's not that! It's . . .

—Then why you need to know—because all-you are? All you talk about, everything it is about being gay, and you don't see anything else in the world. Lukáš has told me.

I had no strength to talk back. Lukáš told her what? Lukáš complained to her about us . . . about guessing he and Claudio were a couple? She breathed in and out audibly, and sat down again. The kettle had gone a little quieter, and we listened to its labours.

—When I got pregnant, Aleysha continued much more tranquil, I told you all. Do you remember? We all sat in the living room—your *gracious drawing-room.*

I tried on a smile, but it fizzled.

—We sat on the sofa, Jamie and Javier, and Flavio and Peter, in a group of gay men, I told you, because you were my friends, I told you I was pregnant. And do you remember what happened?

I tried to, but couldn't. I recalled that evening, her announcement, but nothing particular about it.

—Jamie said it was great, he congratulated me, and maybe Flavio too, a little. But then, within minutes, you all talked about gay things, and gay sex, and about Richard, and you called him a 'breeder,' and you made fun of straight men finding themselves, and coming out. You said things like everyone is gay a little, and a man who has never—you know! What Jamie always say, a man who has not been—you know!—isn't a man, and . . .

—But that's just . . .

—No, it's not *just!* It's always like this here. That's why I wanted to move out. Not because I don't like gays, but because everything, everyday, every conversation in this house is about *fabulous* gay things and *dirty, bad* normal things.

—I can assure you . . .

206

—Let me finish now.

The boiling water's noise grew louder.

—I am not a homophobe. But the gay people in this house—they are obsessed with their own lives. I can understand. I understand it is difficult. I understand it is hard to be different. I know what it means to be different. I come from a place where people are killed and imprisoned for being just a little different. I come from a much, much less tolerant place. But in your house, Tim, your wonderful gay B&B, people who are different—different from all-you gays—don't stand a chance. I made . . .

—Aleysha, I . . .

—Let me finish please. I made the most momentous announcement a woman can make. I tell all my friends that I am pregnant with a child. It is the biggest, most wondrous thing my body can do. And in exchange I get a pat on the shoulder, a friendly 'well done!' and minutes later, I am called a breeder and Richard a closet-gay, and we are back to your subject, and then Flavio said how all straight people are a bit stupid—you remember that? You say it all the time. Jamie does too! What are you disparaging by calling us breeders? Two people creating something wonderful? Something that is bigger than they are? Something that lives on, that is its own master, its own . . . I don't know! Something greater and more wonderful than two men can ever have together: the creation of new life? Are you disparaging that? You are arrogant, and self-absorbed, and that's why I am leaving, not because you are gay. You think everyone has to conform to your idea of alternative, gay living. And that's why . . .

I turned towards her when I noticed she was crying.

— . . . that's why Lukáš is so nice! He lets me be. He does not play with labels either way. All-you gay folks always complain about being labelled, but all you do, Tim, is go around trying to sound out people and making them either for you or against you! Exciting gay, or boring straight! And the gays you call adorable, and the straight boys breeders! Lukáš thinks you are obsessed! You know what we did the first night? We did not have sex. We did not sleep together. We played with the baby. He talked about his cousin's child, and how he wanted children. And he played with the baby like a real father. All we talked about was my life, and my difficulties. I told him everything about Uganda, and what happened to me, what they did to me—and he held

207

me in his arms, rocked me to sleep, and watched over the baby. He is the most caring man I have ever met. He is soft and loving and giving, observant and watchful and kind, and . . . all *you* can do, all *you* worry about is whether he is INTERESTED IN COCKS!

The kettle boiled.

I reached for her hand, but she got up and walked out.

I heard the door slam and sat there, shamefaced. I listened to the whistle of the kettle growing louder, but I could not move. My whole arm hurt now—a throbbing, insulting, demeaning pain spread through my whole body.

Three days later, they carried me up to Arthur's Seat on my birthday, as they have done for three year's now. Quite a tradition and quite a feat: the blob in his wheelchair, pushed as far as the muddy paths in Holyrood would allow. For some reason we always park at *The Sheep Heid Inn.* We never drink there, and yet we always park the car there.

The point where they abandon the wheelchair and carry me up to the top seems to come down every year. Jamie delights in the exercise and pretends that I am some celebrity, some queen (which I am, I insist), some dignitary, who on her birthday *must* survey her dominions from the highest point, and he my slave, my carrier, my muscle man—and if he weren't, oh how I would object to this farce, I am sure.

I could tell they enjoyed it more than I did.

My embarrassment is great. I feel like the character in *Little Britain.* Andy, is it?—in the wheelchair. I am small and bold and white and fat, and if I wanted (I feel, but it is not true) I could really walk. I could hike with them, my hunky young lads, and this year there were four: Jamie and his Maurizio, Claudio and his Lukáš, and of course my old Tim walking a few paces behind us, probably hating the spectacle as much as I do, but not saying a word.

Only this year I were horribly depressed, and tried hard not to show it.

I'd been quiet since the talk with Aleysha, I'd been rattled. I'd much rather they'd left me alone. I did not feel like celebrating. An enormity had been revealed to me—the caring, loving, mother hen; the matron of our boarding house, with its suffering tenants,

208

with its disadvantaged occupants so in need of support. But I was, in fact, a diabolical queen—insensitive and ignorant and only interested in finding out whether people would suck cock.

The woman from Uganda had turned my life on its head even before we'd had tea. And then I saw it: not her. She would have never made such a scene, had such an outburst. That quiet, delicate girl would have never dared, if it hadn't been for Lukáš. I looked over to him; he had his arm around Claudio's shoulder.

Like Greek warriors they carried their queen up to Arthur's Seat, which they had renamed Tim's Seat for the day. Someone made fabulous sandwiches. I assume it were Javier, even though he couldn't be with us that day because he had found a new job quickly, in a better restaurant. Now he was at home even less—sometimes absent over night.

I wondered what Javier expected from life. When he wasn't working and at home, he was in his room watching porn or playing video games. One can't spend a lifetime in such self-imposed isolation. I was grateful for every talk we had, every single instance of shared communication. And now he'd fallen for Claudio, hook, line and sinker. He was very discreet about it, but I could tell. So yes, Mr Dedalus, there too I had one of my premonitions.

They carried me up, laughing and gesticulating, and Jamie imitating trumpets, their strong hairy arms on my legs. I could see them, and I wished so deeply that I could feel them there.

I don't miss those soft touches Tim sometimes effected. The visual confirmation of intimacy couldn't replace our physical closeness. It had always more annoyed me, that playing with the hairs, but of course I could never tell him that.

Yet with the boys—my men, my warriors—carrying me up in a spectacle, a procession, I don't mind.

How do they manage, with my shapeless body, my limpness? I wish that I could feel their hard limbs pressed against my skin, that what I see—the firm grip, the hard male flesh holding me high—were *sensible*. I even imagine it, I try hard, but only on the upper body can I. So I pretend I get tired after a while, and uncomfortable. I tell them that I much rather limp and stumble between them, and have them support me by the shoulders. It is much more strenuous and uncomfortable. It is much harder to hobble uphill—first Queen's Drive, then, as I insist, across the fields, so we are farther away from the crowds.

I do pray for rain on each birthday, and yet I don't. When I am between them, they support my shoulders, and I can feel them—unlike when they carry me by the legs, which on top of it all makes me sea-sick. But here is the reason why I want that, that uncomfortable posture: because they are not shy. Because they don't want anything from me, that limp, wobbly shapelessness, so they grip hard, like carrying a dead animal, a big white flesh, up to the altar of hilarity.   And then, when we finally reach it, we look together over the Firth, and eat Javier's sandwiches. Everybody wishes me a happy birthday, but all I can think of this year is what Aleysha said about me—about us, in fact. All of us.

The presence of Jamie and Maurizio, who are now a couple in all our minds, and so very much in love it seems impossible that there has been a time when they were not together, renders Claudio and Lukáš mellow, I imagine, and malleable. They dissolve into the grey afternoon.

Clouds have drawn over the city as they usually do: dark and ominous, but of course entirely meaningless and arbitrary. After an hour, wrapped in our fleece jackets, Tim already preparing for the descent, we take one last look about us. This is what I see:

To my right, Jamie wrapping his arm around Maurizio, pulling him closer, and then kissing him. There are women nearby, and I notice two of them look over with obscene curiosity.

To my left, Claudio and Lukáš. There is more space between them. I can see the water between their shoulders, but now, in that instant, I am not dreaming. Claudio is raising his arm and laying it over Lukáš's shoulder. He pulls him closer. It is not the pull of a lover, not the pull that says 'you are mine,' but it is clear and decisive, and warm and *real*—and Lukáš lets himself be pulled closer. Then their heads turn and they look at each other, and Lukáš takes both his hands and ruffles Claudio's hair. It is the intimacy of equals; of two men who are entirely comfortable with each other, in a way; and an intimacy that doesn't need—I regret to say in that moment—all the preposterous second-guessing, and the desperate attempts at explanation and categorization.

They are just there. They are just fine the way they are. I feel terribly ashamed.

And then the ritual is incomplete, for somebody always starts the last torment. Somebody asks, as if I needed to pay for being carried up the hill by baring my soul, how it happened. My accident. Why am I in a wheelchair, and why is it that they had to labour so hard to carry me up; why were we all here on that grey day, looking over the city, each pair lost for the afternoon in its own welter of emotions:

Jamie and Maurizio, young and horny; Claudio and Lukáš, far from all that obsequious worship to the gods of hormones; and Tim and I, long past any form of needs. Except the one overarching, mind-numbing sensation that we never had in our lives what these couples have; never had the courage or the opportunity to be out and loud and wild, and to kiss, man-to-man, on Arthur's Seat in broad daylight, no matter what; nor the silent intimacy of Claudio and Lukáš, whose secret we still haven't discovered. Tim and I have something grand: friendship, and love, and complete trust. I think about what Lukáš said about friendship, and how it was so much greater than love. I didn't know that day if I agreed. I couldn't yet see past my own limitations.

It hurts to be old and see all that one has missed. It hurts more than the wheelchair, even.

If I could trade one or the other—the wheels for walking, jumping, stomping feet, or my youth for courage and being out and loud and proud and young and beautiful and gay—I would always want to be out and proud in a wheelchair, rather than walking and the man that I was in my youth. That shy, fearful creature. Handsome, yes—oh so much more handsome than all of my lodgers together!—but nothing like these boys I had surrounded myself with.

Is it at all believable that once I was the object of desire of two men? One left his family for me. The other took me on a cruise around the world, twice, and said to me in the Raffles Hotel in Singapore that if I would only stay with him, I could have all his money—and for some reason I got angry and threw a drink in his face and called him a swine. Why on earth did I do that? What possessed me, aged nineteen, to be so arrogant, and think that

211

the simple deal of money for youth, of meaningless wealth for a bit of fleeting beauty was so objectionable?

I look at them now, and I want to cry. Why is it that youth and beauty never see what they are worth, and how quickly they will be gone? Ten years from now, where will we be? Tim may be dead, so may I, and these youngsters in my care—what will have happened to them?

Aleysha's boy would live on, would grow up, would be the wonder of life we gays so often choose to denigrate. And my boys? Will they be the glorious couples they are now?

Is that rain coming? I can feel the first drops already.

We pack our picnic basket and run. I am pushed in the wheelchair downhill. It frightens me so, but I put my life in their hands: Jamie and Claudio will catch me. My head spins, the wheel catches on a root sticking out, and we fall. I roll down the ravine for an eternity, between heaven and earth, Tim screaming, Jamie laughing, Claudio shouting, and in the end, it is Lukáš who holds me. Fast runner that he is, with his long legs, he has sprinted down the slope and caught me a long way before the canal in which I would have landed. My hands are bleeding from the tyre-burns. Later I find that my knees too are wounded, and for the briefest of moments I feel Lukáš's breath on my face, as he says,

—I catch you.

Suddenly a strength creeps over him. He is strong and present, and untameable, and I know exactly what Aleysha sees in him, and why she took him, and confided in him and never in me. His presence is breathtaking. He is quiet and soft, and yet he holds me with a certainty that I know could last forever. He makes a wonderful father, a man one can trust with one's life. And in the instant I know too what it is that binds him to Claudio. I cannot say it. It is ineffable, an unutterable truth, but I know now what it is: the vision of truth as one is caught, seconds from disaster, in the arms of a man one can trust, infinitely and completely. He holds me, and I don't want this moment to end.

That's what he is, a man you never want to leave. A mystical certainty Claudio can never abandon. And why should he? He's not stupid like I were, Mr Dedalus. He's not a wanked-out, wobbly loser like me. He is old enough to see what counts in life: to bind

212

yourself to one other human being, regardless of gender, and then give all you can, no matter how badly you are hurt.

Aleysha said it: he is all *giving*. That's his secret. Most men only take.

I realize too, that in my silly old days—and despite Claudio being so much more attentive to me, and so much more handsome—I have fallen in love with Lukáš.

Tim approached as we lay there, and Lukáš got up. They dragged me back to the chair, sat me down in it and pulled the blanket over my legs—how I hate that! It makes me feel ninety!—then pushed me down to the car.

It had started to rain, large and deafening drops. Tim and I landed on the back seat, and Jamie was driving (he does not have a license, but I didn't say anything). I was happy—deliriously happy then. Tim looked at me, at first I thought accusingly, but then he softened, and he whispered in my ear,

—I know that look on your face . . .

I understood what he meant: the look I had when Lukáš held me.

Decades ago, I lay like this in Tim's arms, so he knows. He knows what I look like when I surrender completely. Of course, there is no point surrendering to a straight twenty-seven year old, and so my feelings landed aborted in the lap of my lover, who will—I can count on him—save me from making a fool of myself.

Tim said,

—Happy birthday, darling.

And I leaned my head against him, the way I have seen Lukáš do it. I want to capture that, that sexless closeness, that non-physical oneness, that true and eternal friendship built on only trust.

Their friendship is so deep, so intimate; they are friends so naturally that they need to reaffirm it only occasionally with a touch, or a quarrel. They will always be more than a gay couple, Claudio and Lukáš, I realize, and Aleysha is right—we do focus too much on being *gay*, instead of being *human* and caring.

We are all disabled, unable to fathom deep male friendships, because our soddin' pricks always get in the way. We are too

213

defined by our sexuality, when we should be defined by our humanity.

I looked at Jamie driving, Maurizio beside him. Even now they were holding hands when Jamie was not operating the gear stick.

Claudio and Lukáš had squeezed into the boot again, crouching down and holding onto each other in the shaking car. I could hear them breathe. How do you reach such a friendship, I wondered. How do you become friends like that, without thinking about sex? Being able to say I love you, without second thoughts. Try it out! I guarantee, it usually doesn't work among straight men. Only produces awkward chuckles, or worse. I prayed a little on the back seat, my body aching badly where it could from the fall.

I said, please, Mr Dedalus; one request for my birthday. Let me find out what it is that binds them together, that makes them the friends they are. And let it be beautiful.

Well, I found out, and it weren't beautiful.

Javier was waiting for us when we got home. His hard-on was visible in his sweatpants. He'd had the house to himself and Jamie was teasing him. We all knew what he had been up to on his own—that game for one we all play from time to time.

Jamie ran after him, pulling down the sweatpants, Javier fell, turned to shield himself, and landed on the stairs. I could see everybody's reaction to the so-abruptly exposed penis. Tim looked away. Lukáš looked at Claudio, Claudio at the penis, and Maurizio at Jamie. You can observe all that so clearly from a wheelchair. I am the eternal theatre patron.

Jamie, for the first time (we have played these juvenile games too often) turned away, embraced Maurizio, and then apologized. He said he wouldn't do it again, but Javier wasn't the least offended.

—I wish you would. Finally! Now you have lover, you stop playing your *juegos*!

Everybody were laughing, more at Javier's exaggerated accent than anything else, and the fact that his cock had collapsed so quickly, and that he still hadn't pulled up his jogging bottoms. At last he did, and bolted.

Maurizio took Jamie's hand. The two of them ran up the stairs, and we all knew what would happen now. Five minutes later, the house was full of the sound of their fucking. They screamed and moaned intentionally loud, just to make sure Javier could hear them.

Only then it hit me: I hadn't told them why I am in the wheelchair. My fall on the heath had interrupted the ritual.

A strange anticipation settled over me, as I did some chores and helped Tim packing his leather briefcase for the next day, organizing books, sharpening his pencils. He must be one of the few people left on earth to use pencils.

There were an odd draught in the room, coming from nowhere, riffling papers on the desk eerily. I grew apprehensive. The air was suddenly thick and foul. He had a dinner to go to, if I remember correctly. I were alone in the living room, with a whisky, talking, as usual, to the window and Mr Dedalus—only I didn't quite know any more what to say to him.

I wanted to apologize to Aleysha. I wanted her to understand that I were really sorry, and that she were right, and how could I have been so blind? Suddenly I were cold—so cold I went looking for a second blanket. I caught the door falling shut, but still saw her through the glass pane with Lukáš, walking away, holding hands. I felt a horrible jealousy, a bitter, devastating emotion—and suppressed it, when the door opened, and Claudio came in.

I knew instinctively why he had come.

I offered him a whisky, and he pulled up a chair.

—Are you worried? I asked when I realized that he must have brought Lukáš and Aleysha to the door.

He said nothing. He looked past me out the window for a while, then said something I didn't catch. He cleared his throat, but instead of repeating it, he just said,

—No.

I wanted to say, 'Are you so sure he won't ever leave you?'—but I knew it would lead me down the same road, and end up at the same point I didn't want to visit. I didn't want to go now, after Aleysha's accusation. No more mucking about, no more raking up people's secrets.

Claudio was staring at my legs.

—You want to know how it happened?

215

He nodded.

—You did not say, this afternoon. And when I first ask you . . . I wanted to . . .

—You want to know how it really happened, exactly, because your sister would have ended up in a wheelchair like me, if she hadn't died?

He nodded again.

—You want to know what it feels like to be in a wheelchair? You want to know if it is better to die in an accident, or to spend your life on wheels?

He smiled a little, then looked up at me.

—Yes. I want to know.

—I understand.

I had regretted all along not telling him the first time round.

—I can answer your question: it is better to live, if you have friends like you have, if you have a *Lukáš*; or as I have my Tim, somebody you trust with your life. Or like Jamie and Maurizio are trying to become. I hope it'll work out for them. Maurizio seems such a nice lad.

—I think he is very nice, said Claudio. I also think he very sexy.

He smirked. I realized then that he positively enjoyed keeping his sexuality a secret, keeping us guessing, denying it one day, flirting with men the next. But again, I checked myself and said,

—If you have friends like that, or *a friend* like that, you can go on living. Without Tim . . . I would have killed myself a long time ago.

—When I ask you first time, you say it was an accident only. But you not said . . .

— . . . 'did not say', I corrected him. No, I didn't tell you exactly. It was . . . I was on my way to a date—with Tim, actually—when it happened. Our second date, or third. I had just left the house, and was crossing the street to catch the bus, when a car sped around the corner.

—Spade?

—Sped—speeded. It came round very fast. And I didn't see it, or the driver, or anything, and . . . I was in a coma, like your sister, for two weeks. And when I woke up Tim was there, and I knew he loved me and . . . as I said, it was just a stupid accident. At first,

216

I was even more paralysed, but the feeling here ... and here ... returned, and it was only my legs—although sometimes I think I *can* feel them.

—My sister never wake up, he said, pensively.

—'Woke' up. 'My sister never woke up.'

He nodded.

—You wanted to die?

—To kill myself? Many times.

We both drank from the whisky, and then he said,

—After my sister die, without Lukáš ... I would not want to live. I mean ... I could not have lived on.

I just nodded and looked at him silently, this mysterious boy. Mary had said it first: that there were a woman behind all this. Only she could hardly have meant *that*.

Well Mr Dedalus, that were all that lead up to the bombshell. All the bits and pieces we learned, until, as they say, the shit hit the fan.

It were the weekend after that, the first in September, or the second. It were the weekend Craig finally came to repair the awning. It were after Mary had announced she would quit smoking and sell her television (she never did either, the poor soul). It were after Flavio stopped by for a surprise visit to introduce us to his new boyfriend, a French professor of mathematics who spoke absolutely no English. The two of them together looked most unlikely.

Maurizio had gone to France for a modelling job, but to everybody's surprise, I think not least Jamie's, he came round the house to say goodbye and promised to be back. His flight turned out to be at two in the afternoon and he came at ten in the morning, so you can imagine what their goodbye looked— or rather sounded—like. The whole house reverberated with the screams of pleasure, only we weren't sure whose they were exactly.

When you sit quietly on the stairlift, about one third down from the third floor, you can hear everything that goes on in that room of Jamie's. Not that I would intentionally stop there and listen,

217

but sometimes that infernal contraption catches, and you have to let it rest a bit. So I heard everything: especially when Jamie got his legs apart and Maurizio started pounding him, yelling and sighing in Italian. And spitting. I could hear him clearly. And slapping Jamie. Oh they were rough at it! Some boys like it that way. And I know Jamie likes it every which way. I were just a bit surprised at how wild Maurizio turned out to be; he looked so innocent and suave. But then again, he had ravished Jamie by the wheelie bins. Anyroad, he almost missed his flight!

Then they were gone, on their way to the airport, and the house fell quiet.

These soft, well-cushioned afternoons, when time seems to move slower, and everything seems to acquire round edges and a velvet lining.

I let in the Polish girl who comes to clean. I remember being in the kitchen with her, talking about how so many Polish people were leaving, going back home in the economic downturn, noticing how she looked so much older than only weeks afore, and telling her to be careful with the tile in the hall, under the mirror, which had come loose. People were tripping over it, and I were waiting for Craig to get around to fix it. I remember the day like it were yesterday—at least that afternoon, that evening.

Claudio were still at school rehearsing a play, and Lukáš had gone with Aleysha to the doctor's. Then Jamie returned from the airport, announced that he was off to the gym, but didn't leave, saying that he were too depressed.

It were their first separation, and we spent some time in the kitchen talking. He wanted only to talk about his Maurizio, and I were anxious that Aleysha wouldn't catch us. Ridiculous I know, but every time we spoke of gay things now, I thought of her, and her objections, and expected her to come around the next corner and give me an ear bashing. Her words were festering inside me. I felt uneasy, and tried to talk about other things: the shopping, films, Lukáš and Aleysha even. There were a strange compulsion to talk about her and the baby, but Jamie ignored me completely.

He started telling me what Maurizio was like in private: what he did with his hands in the taxi; how he smelled after sex; where he had hair in odd places and where not, and how oddly

218

coarse it was under the arms; and how he found him smiling at the strangest moments. I were saved by Javier, who came home around eight from the gym, took a shower, then started playing music. I washed up, paid the Polish girl when she left, and said goodnight to Jamie when he went to his room.

I had just got onto the stairlift when it happened. My hand was on the start button, then I froze. The faint music from Javier's room stopped, then there were a loud scream. A door opened. I looked up into the stairwell and saw Javier stumbling down a flight, then heard him hammering on Jamie's door, screaming,

—You have to see this, you have to see this, Jamie, quick, quick, come, you have to see this. Fuck! Jamie!

The same moment the front door opened and Lukáš walked in, alone, asked me if I needed help. I said no, still paralytic, wondering what Javier was on about. Jamie had opened the door, and Javier shouted again,

—You have to see this, Jamie, come quickly!

They became aware of Lukáš going up the stairs, and suddenly Javier fell quiet.

—See what? said Lukáš.

—Nothing, it's a gay thing.

I finally pressed the button and the lift ascended. I saw Javier and Jamie disappearing into Jamie's room, and Javier trying to close the door on Lukáš.

Lukáš said something, so Javier came back to the door.

—Really, Lukáš, *es nada*, just some gay porn stuff. Nothing for you.

Lukáš smiled, nodded, a little annoyed maybe that the lads didn't include him in their joke, even if it were something that could not interest him. Or so they thought.

He walked on, but when he saw me coming, stopped again. The door to Jamie's room was still half open. I could see them at Jamie's laptop, Javier pressing buttons, operating the mouse.

—Close the door if you're watching porn, I said.

Jamie turned, walked up to the door, one hand on the handle. Lukáš stared at me. I had a strange feeling that he should not be here, so I said,

—You look tired. What did the doctor say?

219

—The doctor? Oh, Aleysha. Everything fine.

—You look tired, I said again, you should get some rest.

He said goodnight, just as Jamie shut the door, and walked up the top flight of stairs. I thought I had him out of harm's way—except that Javier had left the door to his own room open, and Lukáš walked past it, heard the screams and yelps and stopped to look inside: there was the big screen of Javier's PC, beaming a porno, and Lukáš saw it.

Time slows down. I can sense the danger. I wish I had legs. I wish I could run up and stop Lukáš from watching! He looks down, past me, checking if the lads are really distracted, then takes a step towards Javier's open room and the big screen.

That very same moment, Javier shouts 'Shit!' from Jamie's room, and the door flies open again.

Javier storms out, up the stairs, Jamie on his heels, and that very instant realizes that he is too late. Lukáš is standing in the door, eyes glued to the screen. It's one of those really big flat ones for computer games, bigger than an old TV set.

I roll forward a little so I can see the top landing. There is Lukáš, staring. Javier and Jamie, slowly taking the last steps, comprehending that very moment—just about taking in the fact that they are too late. Taking in that Lukáš must have seen what they did not want him to see, that he knows all. That he is right now watching a sweet, hunky blond man getting fucked by a handsome tall youth; and will, if he doesn't turn away soon, see the face be splattered and the tongue flick over the cum-covered lips.

Of course I didn't know it then, I hadn't seen the video clip. One of hundreds, we discovered later. I just looked at Lukáš, his face pale, mumbling something, before he turned to their shared room shouting,

—*Juraj! Kde si?* and tearing the door open. But Claudio wasn't there.

—*Juraj! Kde si?*

Seconds later he rushed past Jamie and Javier, down the stairs, past me, looking for his friend, shouting again and again, and ever louder,

220

—Juraj!

We can all hear the front door, the keys turning in the lock. I am holding my breath.

Jamie and Javier rush down, and I get back onto the lift, catch them a little too late. Claudio has already taken off his jacket and put down his satchel, and is standing there flummoxed: Lukáš before him, yelling in Slovak. Then Javier stands next to me, his hands trembling, and says to me, or to Lukáš, or to himself,

—Fucking hell, I am so sorry! I am so sorry!

And Jamie,

—Oh shit we didn't intend him to see! You should have closed the door to your . . . oh, fuck, man!

Lukáš is not paying attention. He is screaming in Slovak,

—Je to tak? Povedz mi! Je to tak?

And then in English at the top of his lungs,

—Is it true? Tell me! Is it true?—a short pause, glaring at each other—Is it you in the film?

And I, behind them, in my wheelchair, putting two and two together.

Claudio just stands there, like me slowly realizing what is going off, and that there is no point in lying; that everyone has seen him on his knees sucking cock, and on his back getting fucked by one, sometimes two guys. I was in fact the last to see that, much later. He were very convincing.

In the hall, Claudio's eyes are watering up.

—It was just for money. I made good money.

—That's your rich uncle in Bratislava, isn't it? says Jamie quietly, before Lukáš yells again in Slovak.

Claudio nods.

—We needed money!

—That's where all the money comes from? I hear Lukáš asking. The money we used to pay my debts? The money we travel with? You made it . . . with gay porn?

Claudio nods, almost imperceptibly. He looks like a child now, before an angry parent. I pity him. I want to reach out and protect him. His friend's eyes are gleaming with fury, and disappointment.

Jamie says,

—That's why you are so easy with guys! You've done this for

221

years!

Lukáš shouts something again, then,

—Oh gosh, this is . . . and I sleeping with you! I holding you, all the thing we do together, and you promise me it okay. I think we were cool. And . . . all the time you were . . . all this time! We talked about this! You said you not homo! You freak! Freak!

And grabbing his own jacket from the hook, he stormed out the door.

It fell shut with a bang. We stood there, watching Claudio fall apart.

—He never knew? asked Javier.

Claudio didn't react.

—Well obviously he didn't. Lukáš never knew a thing, said Jamie. Oh this is priceless. You must be bisexual, at least. Aye?

I wished he would stop being so flippant, and not talk about sex now. I was close to speaking, when Jamie put his arm around Claudio, and noticed himself that it were time to shut up.

That were the night I ended up with Claudio in tears. The night I sat watching over him. The night he spent on the chair, draped like a sick swan, sobbing, chewing tissues, being miserable—utterly destroyed.

222

PART VI

Will ye lollop with me, Mr Dedalus? Will ye dawdle, maybe now, maybe here, in the grey light of dawn? Will you take me on your lap and show me the world, drying my tears when I need you to? Wipe me arse when I shit meself again?

Oh, don't laugh! It's happening more and more often. You have a bloody Rover roll over you and wreck half your bowels! See if you can keep your shite in.

Will ye play with me when I am lonely, will ye read to me again when I am bored? Will ya? Will ya—manipulative bastard that ye were—take me back? Take me in. Tug me in. Read to me, like ye did afore? About that Greek-Irish tosser and his fornicatin' Jews?

I am not muckin' about. I am just tired. Spot on, Mr Dedalus: tired, soddin', ploddin' tired is what I am, of life, of rolling about in me wagon, of being fucking nice to people.

What has the world ever dunn far me? What? I been sat here for nigh on thirty years, waitin' far me own bloody funeral.

Have I been to yours? Have I seen you sank into the ground? Have I thrown a handful a eirth onto your coffin? A can't remember. A can't remember nowt. Half the time I don't remember wipin' me own arse!

The funeral: a team of horses pulling the cart—the creaking wagon. Mr Dedalus's body draped in piebald. Piebald for the bachelors, weren't he one? Dun for the nun—as it said in your bible. Heads bowed, saluting, the masses, in New York. And I weren't there. I weren't there for the bloody funeral.

I told you earlier I was, didn't I? Well I lied. I never came.

Others were: lean-jawed and thick-cocked men lining the streets. There are more gay men in this world than there are *homosexuals,* ya used to say. Coffin—black, on a draped bier, tall candles everywhere. Lilies, lots of lilies. Beckoning the boys to kneel too. Sacred, sacred. Sod it, I need to pee. Ha! Wouldn't you like that? I'll come pissing on your coffin.

What did you expect? Would you have taken a peek? Would you have liked to see my corpse, stiff and pale, and bloodless and livid? They say they buried you face down, rectum pointing

223

towards heaven. Did they? Are you comfortable? Would you like a pillow under your hips? The wankers are just jealous.

They should have buried you with a fucking dildo up your arse. Too many funerals in those days; too many today. Too many loved ones. Died of AIDS like the flies. Disfigured, deported, destroyed.

Oh, not you, Mr Dedalus. Your cause of death: asphyxiation. Don't ask—please, don't ask!

I don't know his name, nor the act. I cannot describe it. But at least—oh for the glory, for the glory!—you did not die a natural death. You died of sex, of debauch. You fucking choked on your money, Mr Dedalus. You fucking choked on a hustler's cock! Good riddance, you manipulative bastard!

How I envy you now the wetness of your musty grave! The worms, the bugs, the crawly critters; the quiet, the sombre calm. What a shame it's not one of those pompous, cavernous vaults: the grand sepulchre of Mr Dedalus, with a winged door and heavy iron chains, with a sarcophagus, so I could steal my way in at night, and lie prostraterated, prostrate, prostitute—before you, my young knight!

You were young for me, I swear, even when you were old; and I were old already when I were still so young; and you were always, always handsome.

You were a man of the world I hadn't even begun to discover. The man who rescued me from the Dales; from the boredom of Leeds and her crumbling surroundings; from the decadence and the folly. You saw me and swept me off my feet, and took me to see life itself—to live, live as only young handsome men can live. You did not shackle me. You did not pick my brains. You wanted more than to shag me, old sod—you wanted to educate me. I understood old Greece when I was with you; what an older man can do for a younger—and what a younger can do for . . . but then, you were always a gentleman, aye. You never forced yourself on me. You never took what I didn't give.

Did you follow it all? Did you see all the connections? Did you see what went on in our *auld hoose*?

Did you see the commotion, the utter turmoil that swept over Edinburgh that summer of the flying midgets? Did your heart bleed for our little refuge? Did you witness its disgrace, its descent into chaos? Did your cock stir for Claudio, or Maurizio, or Jamie, or Lukáš? Did you pity me—little old me?

Are you with me, old man, *old chum*—in your wetness, your earthy-muddy grave? Can you hear me? We've got a porn star—not just any porn star! The top rated bottom for four years in a row—one of Bel Ami's top three!—staying at our house!

Can you believe we didn't recognize him? With all the porn we watch, it should have been obvious! We should have . . .

Can ya heah me? Hullo? Are you there? Can ya heah me? Hie-arh me! CAHN YOU HIE-ARH ME OLD CHUM? Are you still there?

Wait, I need a refill.

Men came again to our door, young boys, horny lads, and old men too, asking: Is it true? Is it true? Is it him? Him from that website? I knew it! I knew it! I recognized him! Is he staying here? Can I come in?

No, you can't. Piss off.

I made Jamie sit by the door and chase them away. After all, it were he who couldn't keep his mouth shut, again! And then I realized that a month earlier, maybe immediately, he had been recognized by some, must have been! That's why he liked the outdoors, the seclusion, being alone with his friend!

The phone we disconnected for several days. We could have triple-booked each room with twenty people, all come to see the famous porn star. The funniest were the executives. People in suit-and-tie, local bankers and lawyers, asking politely if a room could be had, while their homes were being . . . redecorated.

—I'll redecorate your fucking face if you don't piss off, said Jamie.

I sat behind my window, not wanting to see anyone.

That queer book what you read to me on the ship, did it have any answers? I guess not. But I am finding none now; not in me, not in Macallan, not in Madam Tallisker, not in an Oban even.

You know, I used to abhor ice in whisky, but it ain't half bad if you need the drink to last for a night by the window.

It's raining cats and dogs again. And spiders and manatees. Oh, manatees! You remember afore the cruise, after our flight to

Miami? You went to show me the Glades—the Everglades. I made a joke that I'd gone from the Dales to the Glades in a spiffy.

You took me to Versace's party, remember? Oh, I felt like a munter in that crowd. How many handsome men! All models of course—state of the art, top of the world.

Gianni pinched my sides. 'Quite a bit of meat on that one,' he said, the arrogant bitch, but you—oh, how you defended me; how you sung my praises.

You phoned Gore, if he wouldn't come down and go dancing with us. Latinos, you said to him. There'll be Latinos, you had them flown in. How grand you seemed to me, being able to command forty Latino boys, one hotter than the next. They came on a bus like the circus.

You remember the Cuban boy with the enormous cock? Everybody had a go. Really, everybody. Oh gosh! It were debauch it were, and everybody high on drugs, and you and I sitting in the corner, on the white sofa, together with that actress who kept quoting somebody—some German feminist—saying,

—The cock of the male homosexual is less a weapon in itself, as it is a symbol of the weapon. It is a *meme*. The homosexual act is the idealization of the sex act, the act without consequence, and thus the act without remorse.

Oh, the silly bitch! She took pictures of young men fucking, and of Gianni, and you, and me, and when he came—*came* I mean—of The Prince.

Do you remember The Prince? Il Principe? He must have been the most handsome man on the planet that summer. More handsome than Malone even, but of the same stock: the collision of North and South, the languid passion of an Italian afternoon.

Aren't I quite the poet?

We all fell in love with him: his upper class accent and his soft, perfect abs.

And we snorted another round and declared,

—There ain't nothing worth living for more on this earth, than for the beauty of man. Give me a pair of hard buttocks any day!

Those were the seventies. Those were you and I on a fucking boat around the world. Or on a boat, fucking, around the world. As you please. Only I were such a virgin. Of course, this is all so passé now, so un-PC. Shouldn't that be PI?

Now—excuse me, bit of a . . . I am sorry; gas—nowadays, people have gender identities and get married. We wanted to abolish the slavery of marriage, this ridiculous institution of patriarchy. We wanted to crush that yoke, and what do we do now? We celebrate another country introducing gay marriage.

As if equality with the warped values of a numb middle class are indeed a victory!

We had ideals! What a charade; what a shambles. What a . . . oh, bugger. We had ideas on too much coke, of course, and too much cock. What do I care? Daft cripple. Who listens to me? The Slovak is right, gay marriage is one big joke: the people who should never belong, trying to play mum and dad.

Did ya see that picture of that actor with his boyfriend—husband, pardon me—and their babies, centre spread in some gossip magazine? Isn't it preposterous? And everybody fawning over them—oh, what a cute family! Family my arse! But . . . different world, different rules. All's a-changing, and a-coming apart. And I am adaptadaptable! I am learning. I am learning. I'll shut up.

So she insulted me, Uganda-bitch, and she were right, so right, living with me head up me arse all these years. And now we've got a Slovak fucking porn star, and his quasi-lover, but they aren't queer, and they done bad things, summat we haven't figured out yet. Summat about money, about paying back debts.

It's like back on Fire Island, afore all the political rubbish started, where all the boys sucked cock for drugs.

Aye, but it just don't follow. I don't see the point, not in anything or any one around me. I despair of my abi-lilly-ties, of my cock-nitive functions. Of my own abstruseness, my own debasicality—basically, debased, destroyed, of my licensed licentiousness.

My jaw hurts.

I sit by the window still and ask myself: what gives? Why can't I sleep? What is still waiting for me to discover?

Let's recapitaliate, recapitallitate, recopernicate . . . a rerun, let's have a rerun, afore I doze off, dozy sod that I am. Daft and hopeless, and—got to cut me nails too, where's the . . . for your benefit, old mucker, where we stand. Maybe you missed a few hints, lying, as it were, down in thy musty grave. Oh, and Mary's on the booze again too. She were here earlier with a stew that tasted of vodka. Let's recall where we sit, still, in our wheelchair, not wallowing once in self-pity, but the pity of others: what have we done—what *have* we done! What have we *done!*

Oh bugger! Outed Claudio as a pornstar, discovering in the process that his real name were Juraj. Claudio were just his porn name, and his childhood nickname, after some Italian football player.

—Everybody know how spelling 'Claudio', nobody know how writing 'Juraj', Claudio had said with his constant overuse of the ing form, and Tim had asked,

—Why not 'George', then? Everybody can spell 'George'. And he had to explain that Juraj was nowt else but George; the same name but in Slovak. My Tim knows those things. That's what I've got hubs for—to explain the facts of bloody life to the degenerate likes of me. So scholarly. So above things.

So he were in porn, Mr Dedalus. Isn't that fantastic? Innit just fanfuckingtastic? I didn't even stick with you, didn't even *please* you—one man with money, in your decent above-board (should I say 'above-deck') relationship—and this boy goes out and shags every hunk from Bratislava to Bel Air. Well, of course we made an inventory. What do you expect? We Googled him all over, we did. We are but men!

I had expected it to be indecent, to be awkward, but it were not. It were quite arousing, seeing him naked in so many pictures and clips. Javier said he had a boner now every time Claudio were in the room.

—His dick's not that big, but he is a fantastic bottom! Listen to him moan! Rock-hard all the way, while he gets pounded. They say if you are hard while you get fucked, you are really gay.

—Which of course is utter nonsense, interjected Tim, very annoyed with the conversation. Porn for him, all that Internet porn, was just a sign of the times: the lack of culture, the lack of intellectual pursuit.

—People used to *read* Bel Ami, now they only watch it! went his not-very-catchy catchphrase.

—And all that bare-backing, all that cum-eating. Teaching

228

youngsters unsafe sex! It's totally irresponsible! Everyone is obsessed with porn! It's preposterous, the way . . .

But he didn't go on.

Then he said a few days later in bed, scratching himself under the chin,

—I wonder when I will discover the first porn actor in my school. There are bound to be some. I know some of them could be . . . One's running a teen muscle worship website. He is just seventeen, you know! I know everybody's taking off their trousers now. It's no big deal any longer. Did you know there's a website for amateurs, where thousands and thousands of people broadcast their genitals to the world? You don't even have to be a pornstar, it's not even a dedicated profession any longer. It's just a thing people do—fuck and wank, for the world to see.

—Fascinating. What will they think of next? Should we go on camera? Should we invent a new genre? Wheelchair-bound . . . cripple porn!

—Don't be absurd—and besides, I am sure it already exists!

He chuckled. I chuckled. He hugged me, and then he turned his back to me.

I didn't sleep. I couldn't. With or without booze, I lay awake now each night. All my lodgers were like children to me, my children, and I their mother. I felt deeply for all of them—still do—and finding out that one of my precious boys was regularly, habitually, engaging in blissful anal penetration for the benefit of dirty old men.

Of course, not only dirty old men. Look at Javier! Growing up now with pornography they are. All over the Internet. No more bees and butterfly, they've seen it long before.

I saw my first *Bijou* by accident, in a gutter, after the rain. My first film: you showed me that, in your apartment, Mr Dedalus— and then summoned up the actors, so we could see them live, and touch them, and wonder how such bodies were constructed. What money can do! Everybody did it, and nobody talked about it. Like sex with the staff in good old England. It's just the way we are becoming, as a global tribe: freer and freer, less and less bound by promises, or in the monstrous bondage of religion and

229

false propriety. It's the age of reason dawned now, and of fun porn. So what's the big deal? Why did Claudio sucking dick for money irk me so?

I lay awake, staring holes into the darkness, and thought it through, and the big deal was, of course, that I knew him, this Juraj, and his friend, and that they mattered to me, and that I cared for them, and that I wanted to see them happy and healthy and whole.

I also wanted them gay—but at least, I wanted them sound, and well. Yes, gay—but not *gay*. Oh I'm making no sense again! Where are my pills? (Last week I had two dizzy spells.)

I wanted them lovers forever—and now they were not; they weren't even together. We—our house—had ripped them apart.

So I kept awake that night, and started a whole sequence of sleepless nights. Of accusations and reflections. I went to my therapy with Alan, and told him to massage me good, for I just could not sleep.

Then I told him about Claudio.

—Is he then, on the Internet? A real porn star? Oh he must be handsome?

I didn't expect answers from Alan, but at least I expected compassion.

—Has he got . . .

—What?

—Well you know . . .

—No, what?

—Well you know, the tools of the trade?

—You mean the *tool* of the trade.

—In a way.

—Apparently his main asset is his hard bum, and the way he moans when they fuck him.

—And he isn't gay? Are we sure?

—Let's not get started again, Alan. Just press a bit harder. Right there—a bit harder.

All that earful about friendship Lukáš had given me—all that had sounded so wise. So was this a test? Would he want to be friends with a man who did porn for a living? What really did offend him—the porn, or that it were Claudio, or that that were where the money had come from? A man who had lied to him for ten years? A friend—betrayed by a friend? Who'd made up an uncle in Bratislava—exactly! An uncle with a porn studio! Was it that Lukáš insisted so much on their special friendship, their intimate, compassionate non-physical friendship, and now . . .

—Ouch! You're hurting me. Not so hard, Alan!

. . . and now, all the physicality, all the body—the body pornographic, the body sexual, the full Monty up his arse, intruded so absurdly. Had it destroyed Lukáš's self-image, the image of their world—their relationship? Of course it would, wouldn't it? Well of course it would. The poor things. Oh, the poor boys. What have we done with our prying? We've destroyed them—completely!

Naturally, all my self-confidence was out the window. I couldn't now possibly be the same person who had stood up—figuratively speaking—to eight rugby players, could I? I am now the villain of the play. That couldn't have been me!

Look at me now, Mr Dedalus: crushed! Trampled—what had he called it, *trammelled?*—under the giant feet of fate, in the big meat grinder. My life is over, if I can't solve this, if I can't get them back together! That perfect non-gay couple! Oh, oh!

What the bloody hell am I going to do? I thought. What on earth is there to do! Crushed I were by all the responsibility, the guilt. Still the drama queen, in her wheelchair, apparently, but crushed!

I'd been told that I was insensitive all along, that I only saw and spoke *gay*, and ignored pregnant women—that we all did, that all of us in our lovely house, in our *auld hoose*, were ignorant, arrogant pricks, only concerned with cock-and-arse stories.

I don't know where Lukáš slept that night, the night of the discovery, when I watched over a sobbing Claudio draped like a swan. I must have dozed off a little later, because when I woke, Claudio were gone from the chair. The tea cup stood empty on the table, and a blanket lay on my lap that hadn't been there afore; it were almost light outside.

I did my chores, I prepared some documents for Tim to take to the council. I called his mother in Oban to tell her—to promise

231

her—we would soon visit again, and sort out the problem with the veranda; and then I sat by the kitchen sink, and I didn't know what to do with my day. For the first time in years, I were listless and clueless. Not depressed, not disillusioned, not feeling like a waste of space—which I do every day—but a complete lack of motivation. Every possible option seemed vain ... and pointless. I did not even start cleaning, which normally gets me over the worst. I didn't want to go into the lodgers' rooms at all—I were too frit what more I would find.

I wanted to see Claudio, wanted to talk to him more. I wanted to find out what Lukáš did that night. Did he stay with Aleysha? I thought of calling her, but didn't. I could not face her.

I have no particular recollection of that day, and the next, and the few days after. But I remember dusting the little table under the mirror where we put the letters, when they came home, Lukáš and Claudio. They went into the kitchen at first, and I followed them, asking them if they wanted tea, speaking much too fast, and giddily forcing them to react to me, then realizing that everything were wrong. They were behaving all wrongly. They weren't talking, certainly not to me. They hadn't come home together, they had just met by chance in the hall.

All the lightness and intimacy were gone. They took pains not to touch each other when they went to the fridge to get drinks. Each took his own; neither asked what the other wanted. Just like strangers.

My heart froze over while I observed them. They now chose opposite ends of the table, where afore they had sat close enough to touch thighs. Claudio had suddenly become a leper. A Judas. A fucking faggot. The air was thick with resentment and fear even. I were alarmed, helpless, I wanted to mend the rift, but didn't know how. I said a few silly things about the weather, I think, and offered tea again, but they only shook their heads politely.

For a while they sat drinking in silence, then Claudio said he had to do his homework. A minute later Lukáš got up and returned the half-full bottle to the fridge, then said he had to look after Aleysha's boy and went out again. I don't know if he slammed the door, or if it just sounded so loud because my head were so empty. The anger was palpable. I don't think they had talked at all since it happened.

When they were out of sight, I put my whole bald heavy head in my hands, and I sobbed a little. I didn't know what to do. I needed Tim—I wanted him. I wanted him to tell me what to do next.

A week ago they would have said, 'We have to do our homework.' They would have arrived, and rested and departed together—now they were at odds. Two months under my roof, and their relationship was in tatters. Everything was coming apart at the seams. My own life, theirs ... everything was changing! Everything was falling apart.

Oh, Mr Dedalus, how desperate I were that day, and the days that followed! How alone I felt in my misery. How guilty for all that had happened. Why couldn't I let them be!? I called Tim in the middle of the day again, just to hear his voice.

—Give them some time, was what he said. But I am far too impatient a man to give anybody time; I always were. That's how I got to where I am, 'cos I never take time to think things through.

But I couldn't live with meself. Sat in my wheelchair it felt like it were on fire. For real then, wheels on fire. I were dying to get up, to have the use of my legs, to run up and down—to mend what I had torn apart, to fix, to assuage my guilt, my hourly growing guilt.

In the end, I got upstairs to knock on Claudio's door; there was no reply at first. I turned away, but he must have heard the rubber wheels, so he peeked out.

He had been crying; his face were flushed.

—Can I come in?

He opened the door for me with reluctance, but he did open it. I took it for more than politeness: he did want to talk. He had cried his eyes out again.

I rolled up to the bed, and he sat down on it.

—You can't go on crying like this, I said, putting my hand on his back.

He leaned over immediately, fell into my arms like a stone. He was sobbing, but his eyes were dry after last night—they were just red.

—I never want him to find out, never. I am so shame!

233

I pressed him close, and waited patiently for his body to stop convulsing.

—Ashamed. 'I am so ashamed.'

For some reason, correcting his English was no longer an issue. I had hesitated before, because I am not a teacher and I hate it when people correct *me*—but he nodded, and even smiled a little; then he repeated,

—I am so ashame!

—That's better. Just one 'd' missing. There's nothing to be ashamed of. Porn . . .

—I am not *a shame* of porn. I don't . . . I am a shame Lukáš know! He know now!

Strange noises intruded just then: the sound of a big bird, women chatting, and somebody throwing bottles into the recycling bin. I was acutely aware of everything around me, but most of all, the muscles under his shirt, as the hard body writhed in my arms. I noticed he had an erection. Just like me, I thought—emotional stress brought them on with me too.

We sat quietly for a while, until he spoke again. Everything came out in a babble, in broken, but ever faster sentences, like a river's water approaching the falls: everything he had done, all the films—scenes, he called them—he had shot for which studio. All the positions, the scenarios.

There were no uncle in Bratislava: just a famous film studio. He'd done it for the money; 500 Euros for a solo, 1000 to fuck, and 2000 to get fucked. So, he said, because he was earning for two—because he'd been making money for himself and Lukáš—he'd been getting fucked two or more times a month. He'd done well over a hundred scenes, and that's how they had financed their travel around the world.

All the trips, the hotels, the plane tickets—he had even taken Lukáš to countries, like South Africa, where they had been shooting. His excuse had always been the uncle's business: import-export. He'd cunningly even alluded to trade in illegal goods, to make it more exciting and prevent his friend from asking too many questions. Things that the West wanted after Communism had collapsed. Not weapons, not drugs, no—other stuff, not really illegal—and Lukáš had believed him, always.

234

—Remember when we arrive, I go away for one weekend to visit friend in Blackpool?

—Yes.

—But I don't go to Blackpool, I go to London for filming.

—I see.

I looked at him, quietly. It seemed, for the moment, impossible to unite the handsome, civilized young man sitting afore me with the groaning stud getting fucked on the computer screen. I pictured him in a suit, groped by bearded hunks—but the lad speaking to me now couldn't be him. And I knew by the way he spoke, too, that it wasn't all about the money.

—So you have made possible your exciting life together. You made it happen—all the hiking trips, the nature adventure. You are the provider. What's to be ashamed of? Without you, where would Lukáš be? Still at home in your village. Still in debt, no doubt.

He glanced sheepishly up at me, then wiped his face.

—And Lukáš never questioned it? He never wondered about the money?

—Lukáš never know how much costing things! He never asking! I always buy ticket and hotel. I always pay.

—He just assumed the money came from your uncle?

Claudio nodded.

—I always going to Bratislava some time before a trip. I always say I get the tickets when I going there, because where we live, we don't have travel agent—not good one. Only can do bus tour to Romania and Hungary. So I always take long weekend to go Bratislava, I . . . I get 2000 Euro—he blushed—and coming back with ticket, and . . . and now, I can never . . .

But the sentence broke off, and he whimpered again like a kicked dog.

I didn't quite know what to say, how to comfort him. It all depended on Lukáš now, in the end, and whether he could . . . forgive.

—He will never talking me again, never! wailed Claudio suddenly, and then collapsed, and convulsed. And for at least half an hour I just sat there, stroking his hair, listening to his sobs, until my fingers were quite numb.

But Lukáš made himself scarce. He stayed over at Aleysha's with the father of the child, and went house-hunting with them. He came home one afternoon to collect some things from his room, but when he heard that Claudio was in, he left again without going up. He snarled at me when I called after him, and I began to think he was blaming me for everything.

I wanted Tim to help me, to sort them out—but he were busy those weeks.

I took to watching them quietly, in silent desperation. The brief moments when they met, unavoidably, they didn't speak to each other, and I don't know what they did at school. Maybe it were a blessing they were in separate levels now.

That or the following evening Aleysha telephoned to ask what was wrong with Lukáš. She said he was acting so strangely, and that . . .

— . . . he doesn't even want sex.

—He doesn't want sex? With you? Because your husband's there?

—He's not even here at night, no! It's just Lukáš and me. But he doesn't touch me! He just goes to sleep. What have all-you done to my Lukáš!

To hear her call him 'hers' gave me an unexpected jolt. But the accusation felt good: it fit right in with my own guilt. I wallowed in it, and answered only reluctantly.

—Something happened with his friend.

—Something what? His friend Claudio? What is . . . oh, no, don't tell me . . . is he gay after all? Did I . . . ?

—Who?

—Lukáš? Is he gay . . . does he love this . . . Claudio, oh no! Oh Lord, Great Lord, not again!

—No, Aleysha, no . . . no!

—No?

—No!

—What is it then?

—I really can't tell you. They had a quarrel—a quarrel, yes. But no . . . they are not lovers. Lukáš isn't gay. He is just . . .

I said it like this, even though I still didn't believe it.

—Why is it that he is not sleeping with me, then? If he only had a quarrel with his friend? What have all-you done to Lukáš? It is that house, I tell you! It is that house—it is a cursed house. All men turn to . . . in that house, and all-you warp them and spoil them! You make everybody miserable! Everybody! All men here turn to . . .

—Turn to what? I asked, wishing to draw the insult from her lips, wishing to make her admit that she hated us, still did, even with all her womanly insight and frankness. But she had hung up.

Claudio settled into his own private routine: avoiding everybody. Javier tried to get closer, to apologize to the lad, but all they did was exchange polite greetings, and a word here and there about the weather. A pat on the shoulder. Javier, now even more in love with the boy, looking more miserable each day. But Claudio kept to himself, and I think he would have left Scotland altogether but for the classes.

Once he said to me that he had never been in this situation, that he had never been in a place where everybody *knew*.

—That also why we go away much, and so . . . remote place. I like hiking with Lukáš, I like nature . . . but also, in nature, no people coming recognize you.

—When you were in the States, weren't you recognized *all the time?*

—It's not like this. It not easy! I always wear baseball, and . . .

—A baseball hat.

—Yes, baseball hat, I always wear baseball hat there. New York Yankees—you know, a blue one—and nobody knowing me. And in the scenes, for the films there is always make-up and different hairstyle. They do on purpose.

I asked him to sit down with me, but he wouldn't. I wanted to know more about life as a porn star. It intrigued me—aroused me, of course—the whole idea. But he wouldn't talk—not for any length of time.

He did tell me, though, how he got started. He told me one night, lifted me from my solitude, joined me by the window where I was holding silent court with regret and self-pity. I quickly opened up to him, and then, in the wee hours, with a whisky in hand, he told

237

the story: how it had all begun; how he had become what he was.

Just days after his eighteenth birthday, he had been to Bratislava to visit relatives. By the Presidential Palace, coming down from the hill by the old concrete footbridge, a man had passed him a flyer and said, 'You are good looking. Come to this boat ... free party, all you can eat and drink, on the Danube.'

The man hadn't lingered, and Claudio had walked through the city with the flyer in hand. There had been written on it a time and a date, and a tiny map, and the image of shirtless boys drinking beer and having fun, and the hint that money could be made, if one would 'relax.'

He had walked towards the city centre in a daze, he said, past St. Michael's Gate, towards the bar area to meet friends, and almost tossed the flyer into a bin when the same man crossed his path again in the warren of streets just behind St. Martin's Cathedral, where Claudio had been leaning against a wall smoking.

—I have ... play around with other guys, he confessed. But not, you know, real sex. Never.

The next day he had gone there, alone, curious, lured as much by the idea of a party on a boat as by the promise of free food and drinks. He had observed from the road for several minutes, but in the end he had *crossed over*, he said, and boarded the ship.

The party had already been in full swing when he got there. There were only boys on the boat and in the end, the poor kid, it took him a while to realize what kind of party it was. He didn't see it immediately, although it was happening before his eyes: the touching, kissing, groping, the dancing with bare chests to naked music—all without the presence of girls. Then came the drugs, and, after sunset, the fucking in the cabin, on deck even—a boy on his knees with a cock held in each hand, and then cum over his forehead, in his hair.

—And I was in middle of it. I was there. And it didn't seem weird. Not what I wanted, but—I get horny too. And I did too, I join!

—You did what?

—I did it. I made sex there.

—I see. But ... you *do* prefer girls.

—Yes, but ... you know. It was fun. Mentally, I think I prefer

238

girls, but sex . . . I don't know. It not matter much, the difference. It just fun. Just sex. I don't mind making love with boys. I do get . . . very excited.

He looked up, his face red like a tomato, eyes and mouth contorted in an embarrassed smirk.

He went on about the party. For several hours, he had joined the fun.

—Somebody always open a condom somewhere. They were lying about in bowls. Like you have fruit bowl there—we had condom bowl, ha ha. I got first time fucked there, afternoon, and then again and again. I really like it! It's good feeling, you know?

He gave me a soft and pleading look, begging me not to be angry. Why should I be, darling? Don't I know how it feels! It's a wonderful feeling, getting buggered! If you can feel it that is! If your body's not bloody useless from the waist down!

At some point during the nautical debauch, the man had given him a card, and told him,

—You see, it's not bad. Even if you don't like boys all the time, it's okay, don't you think? With your muscles—you have beautiful muscles!

—Why are you so muscular? I interrupted.

—I was gymnast in school. Always do gymnastics and wrestling. And everybody always tease me, because of . . . they teasing me, so I always running away, so I becoming fast runner. Because I am shorter you see. I always building muscle because I am not so tall . . . tall as . . . We both like running, Lukáš and I. Anyway, so that man, he tell me, come and see me, here is address, a bit of fun, isn't it? We pay 150 euros for jerk-off scene, and more for other.

Come and see us, at this address, he had said, and behind him, a boy had fallen to his knees and sucked a big cock on a blond stud from Brno.

150 euros he had said, or 200, Claudio weren't sure any more, and 500 for a short scene with another boy—you know, he explained, *analni!* That was a year's salary in his last job. His father would have to work two years for that kind of money. Later they paid him more, because he was popular.

—On American site, when I get fucked (he almost whispered the word), I get over 300 fan mail a week, in beginning. And always tell me smile, smile into camera, when somebody come on my face. That sells. For many year, I am one of most popular boy.

I swallowed hard.

—One of 'the' most popular, I corrected, inanely, not sure what else to say.

—You see, the truth is I liking it you know. It's not difficult work. I like fucking.

Again his gaze fell away, to the floor, and he held his marvellous body perfectly still for a long time while I listed to my own laboured breathing.

—Can I ask you a question?

He nodded.

—If you get fucked, I mean if you like to get fucked, like you say ... doesn't that mean you ... I mean you are still saying you are straight?

—Ah, ha ha. So many people ask me. But active-passive, is not about straight or gay, you know. First, getting fucked not means being passive you know. there are active bottoms too. But I am not. Many straight men are submissive. I guess I am. I like other man or woman to ...

—Is that why you are with Lukáš? Is he ...

He thought for a moment, then whispered,

—Is he dominant? Maybe. I don't know. Maybe I needing to be punish, ha ha!

He blushed quickly, but suddenly neither of us could take the intimacy any longer. I rolled back and he jumped up, announcing that he was off to the gym. By the door he turned around again, awkwardly clutching his bag.

—Yes, maybe I needing to be punish.

What a strange thing to say. I put it down to the language. But by the way he stood there in the door, holding it open with one foot, bag now slung over his shoulder, the T-shirt as always a size too small, the boyish smile ... I knew it were all true. I knew he had stumbled into all of this, not against his will, but not exactly out of his own volition.

The things that happen to us in life, when we are young! Oh my, Mr Dedalus. The choices we think we make, but which are really made for us! A bus stop across the street, a car approaching too fast, a wheelchair for life. A chance encounter with a flyer, a boat, a few horny young men and . . .

He came back from the gym two hours later and caught me in the aisle again. Still holding the key, he continued our conversation as if no time had passed at all.

—You see, he said, I don't believe people are straight and gay. Lukáš does. He says always it's either or. For me it is not. It not matter, really. It just sex. I like bottom. Even with woman, I would be . . . passive if . . . you know. For me it is . . .

He pointed to his head, and smiled.

—But Lukáš, for him—it is very serious! It is either this—or that.

His smile fell apart, and his face assumed again that sadness I had observed so often, that look of disappointment. I watched him solemnly ascend the stairs.

Another fragment of a conversation was this, that once, Lukáš had almost found him out.

—I was going Bratislava, and we having photo shoot. It was all afternoon, and then I left the building, and there he was.

—Lukáš?

—Yes.

—He followed you to Bratislava?

—I think he do, yes. But we never talking about it. We act like we meet there by accident. Like an accident. But he looking back at the door, and he ask me what I do in there. Only the door of the studio, it doesn't say about what it is. Only a four-letter ab . . . berration.

—Abbreviation.

—Yes. Only four letter, not name of studio, so nobody can guess. Even if you search on Internet you cannot find. So I tell him is where my uncle has his office, and then I show him 2000 Euro they just pay me, and we go out to eat, very good restaurant.

—That was close!

—Yes, it was very close, just by the corner. *U Zlatého Kapra.* It mean . . .

—No, I mean . . . 'that was close' means . . . he almost caught you. You had a close escape.

—Oh . . . ! Yes. Yes . . . he almost caught me. And after that, he never ask again, really. Then he believe I really have uncle with company.

—But why did he follow you in the first place?

—I don't know.

And there again we stalled, and he left me—I don't know, somewhere in the house. Our conversations hadn't been like this before: they always had a conclusion, but now they were mere fragments, aborted and inconclusive.

It wasn't just porn, I learned in the end, when one night his pain of having lost his friend were unbearable. With fame on screen came a few discreet phone calls and trips to hotel rooms. Not many, he said, just to *top up* the earnings, and without the knowledge at first of his studio. There was also the generous son of a Russian tycoon seen in Bratislava society always with two long-legged female models,

—Whose hair always fell in my face when he fuck me. So long hair, I hate!

—The models' hair?

—No, the Russian man. One time he let a girl watch him fuck me though.

Their trip to the US then was financed in part by a man who months later was vilified in the press for his role in the collapse of a bank, and another who had made his money in oil, and liked to wear a Stetson while he bent Claudio over the gilded fauteuil.

—And he tie me up. I don't like tie up!

He told me of other punters, of married men in various European cities, of a French politician and his castle; of a German industrialist who bought him clothes, clothes he often chose not in his own, but Lukáš's size; and I listened in awe at the agility, the ease with which Claudio managed his stealth 'career.'

Closer at home at last was the money used to pay for their trip here, and the language school. The generous man sat right under our noses, and was in the news every fortnight. A man of property who liked to own land and houses as much as boys. Claudio had been to see him several times since their trip through the Highlands. He had found him on a gay dating website.

242

—Some time I skip school. But altogether 2000 pound! It pays for the school for both of us, you see? How you think I can pay the school?

—So what was his thing then? You said he . . .

—Oh . . . he? Nothing. He cried after sex. He always cry. I don't know why. I going to see him one more time, then we have left 1000 and minus the flight . . . no, I already pay that.

Claudio was careful with money as it turned out, never planning an expense without having secured first an income.

—But now, maybe Lukáš's don't want my money any more?

Time passed unobserved, marked only by Claudio's tears. He was at home every evening, alone, moving about the house like a zombie. His shame seemed to ooze from every pore, come out of his ears. Was it that he would readily exchange all his porn experience for one night with Lukáš? Or was it that he wished he'd never started? He constantly had his head low, whenever I saw him, and lowered his eyes immediately when he met me or anyone else. Only late in the night did words find them. Brief, harrowed utterances, full of scars and regrets and hesitation.

Tim decided we couldn't go on like this. He grew really worried Claudio would do something stupid. I didn't think he would. I just wanted to see him happy again. Happy and gay, and in the arms of a man or woman who loved him.

But afore anything happened, however, Maurizio returned, and we had another shock. It was entirely unexpected. Maurizio and Jamie didn't even bother to bring up the suitcase. It were left standing in the hall while they ran up to their room and started shagging as if they hadn't seen each other in years. They began in the afternoon, and when Tim and I dossed down at eleven, they were still at it.

Now the next day were a Saturday, and Tim and I went to a garden party—one of those traditional affairs for people who live next to a city park that's still private. We had classic sandwiches, cider, and wine; and chatted with women in hats, and parents of Tim's pupils, and acquaintances of Mary's, who, by some odd coincidence having to do with the building she lived in, actually owned almost half the park.

For an afternoon, Mary were the centre of attention as people brought her finger-food and glass after glass of plonk, and commented on her outfit and her new hairstyle. I'd given her a tenner to get it cut just hours before.

Tittle-tattle and the latest royal gossip, until we had to use my wheelchair to get her home—so pissed she were, leaving me sat on a bench feeding the grimy pigeons.

When we finally returned the house, we thought at first, was deserted. It was about dinner time, which we would necessarily skip, stomachs full of cucumber and anchovy sarnies, noses high and accents posh from all the mingling with the fine society of garden owners. But then, just as I was about to switch on the stairlift, we heard that noise—that wet kissing noise, and low, growling voices. An ursine growl, and a giggle. Another deep moan, and then the sound of a flat palm meeting naked skin.

I thought at first it were Maurizio and our Jamie at it again, but there were a different voice too, lower, one I'd never heard through these walls, by the stairs, where I stole my glimpses of Jamie's sex life. One that sounded nonetheless terrifyingly familiar.

—They are having a threesome, said Tim, his ear pressed to the wall, the dirty bugger. No better than me, he is, our headmaster.

—Who?

—Maurizio and Jamie. There is somebody else in the room.

—Who?

—I don't know. But I should've guessed right away.

We listened further.

There was kissing, and there were Jamie saying,

—Let's get your pants off.

And more sucking and slurping noises, and then Maurizio saying,

—You are the man, we suck you both. Get up.

There was silence, then slurping, then another moment, and the squeaking of bed springs, and then Maurizio asking,

—Where are the condoms.

And Jamie,

—Here!

And then the noises of lips meeting each other—lips on chests

244

and stomach—and then again the bed complaining and Maurizio asking,

—Are you sure it's okay? Can I fuck you?

And then we had the shock, like a stab in the spine, the way my back feels sometimes when Alan uses his elbows too hard.

The third voice said something very softly, and then a little louder,

—You can do what you want.

With the right intonation exactly. Only this time, the grammar were right.

Tim didn't get it, but I did. The voice said again,

—Yeah, come on. Fuck me.

I held my hand over my mouth, and then I felt like retching and laughing and crying at the same time.

Tim gave me a quizzical look, then said,

—What?

—What! Don't you recognize his voice?

Tim shook his head.

—Well it's Claudio, innit? They are fucking Claudio!

Anyroad! Moving on! So the boys had fun, what's the big deal?

There is something I remember about the garden party I mentioned, a curious incident which shed light both on the Slovaks' and Jamie's past in an unexpected manner.

We were stood in a circle with a newcomer, a rather attractive man in his thirties, who had just moved into Mary's building. She had explained how the gardens work, and he was surprised to learn that he had exclusive rights.

—Do you really mean that they don't let in strangers? he asked surprised. He was from the South, had come north to work for RBS and he knew Philip too, but we learned that much later, how it were Philip who had, in fact, lured him here.

—But yes, that's the point you see . . . these are private gardens!

—In the centre of town?

The conversation went like a pleasant river all afternoon: a babbling brook dotted with bubbly and canapés. I can't really recall who said what, 'cos I were staring at the new man's—what were his name?—trousers. You see, the outline of his cock, his

245

rather large and erect cock, were right at the level of me beady eyes. One advantage of a wheelchair!

—Mary, Mary, the lady . . .

—What, what you all excited about Adam?

Oh, yes Adam, Adam were his name. And he touched his hard-on, and I just sat there. I'd only have to reach out and unzip him. Does he know that I am staring at his boner? So the chirpy talking continues . . .

—The lady over there, I was trying to take a sausage roll . . .

—These aren't sausage rolls, they are cheese crumblies . . .

—Well, I tried to take one of them!

—Just for you? Why haven't you brought the whole plate, we would have all . . .

—But that's the point, she wouldn't let me!

—Who?

—The lady with the red hip-short jacket there . . .

—Next to . . . that's not red, that's pink!

—That is not pink. That is, well, it's not purple either.

—Well anyway she said I ought to get a label before I was allowed to touch any of the food so I told her we'd been standing here for an hour eating and drinking unlabelled and . . .

—It just means you paid.

— . . . she got rather upset then.

—Where'd you get your label Emilia?

—What? Oh sorry I was . . . it was like at the AGM, I am having trouble hearing and sometimes I just you know, doze off!

—Standing?

—Yes, even standing, yes. What was your question then again?

—Labels, where did you get yours?

—Oh, Lady Harnsley gave it to me when I paid her the three quid . . . she's . . .

It was surreal, all that talk about labels, and how everybody needed one. My head started to swim, and all that happened with me gawking at Adam's boner. I'd say ten inches, in old money. And then Mary came and put her hands on my chair and she noticed it too. She hit me on the shoulder.

—Ouch! What you do that for?

—Because I know where you are looking! I can see where your

eyes are!

—So what? I said, looking up to Adam, who, I swear, only then noticed that I was . . . half an arm's length away from his turgid cock.

—She's just over there with Pellerman!

—Well, yes, it is his father is dead isn't he?

—Has been for quite a while.

—Well it's . . . Mary, Mary where are you going, said Tim, and followed her. She just ran off.

—To get the labels!

—But you haven't got any money you said.

—That's because I paid already, so they ought to give me labels . . .

—How will you prove you paid already?

—Just let me handle this will you!

And just then, as Mary dived off to get the stupid labels, Adam looked down, took my hand, and smiled at me and said,

—You are Tim, aren't you? You run the B&B on Manor Place?

I couldn't keep my eyes off his fucking cock.

—Do you like what you see?

I swallowed—I felt like a little boy who'd been caught . . .

A silence then came over the group at the annual general meeting of garden owners. I felt everyone's eyes on me. But they weren't. They were looking at the other groups of people who had formed around us.

And then Adam said,

—I know your B&B. I almost stayed there when I moved up here. You've got a famous porn star staying with you now, I hear.

He had a beautiful accent, I noticed, just as he put his hand on his cock again, and squeezed it—rearranged it really.

I wanted to ask how he knew and how he had found us, but I only got as far as,

—How did you . . . ?

—Oh, how did I hear of your little love hotel? Or the infamous Claudio?

Love hotel? Never heard it called that.

—We are just a normal . . . He is . . .

—Jamie. You've got a lodger called Jamie, haven't you? An

American?

So that's it.

Mary was back with a handful of plastic badges.

—Thank god they have no pins, just labels!

—No that would be too much, too expensive I mean, people would take them home as a souvenir . . . We never do pins!

—No I meant because Mary pinned them on me almost pushing me over, she . . . you are quite a strong woman.

—Mary used to wrestle at the Royal Glasgow Wrestling & Fencing Club.

—There is such a thing?

—You don't say! said Adam.

—Tim, will you shut up, I don't want that particular part of my . . .

—Oh that's perfectly all right, wrestling is a perfectly respectable sport.

—I didn't mean the wrestling part I thought you were . . .

—Oh, oh, that you mean . . . Mary . . .

—Don't . . .

—How did you know Jamie—how do you know Jamie? I asked Adam, and then he said, loud enough for everybody to hear, everybody in that group, who were all now sticking the labels to their chests.

—Oh, Jamie and I used to be lovers. I used to work over there you see. We went out—we lived together for a while. He's a real stunner—very good in bed.

Adam—this man with the posh London accent; the banker in the spick and span suit—had spoken rather loudly, almost deliberately so. And everybody went silent.

All of them, because some realized that we were talking about gay sex; some presumably, like Emilia, because of the phrase 'he was very good in bed;' Tim and I, I think, because that sort of comment is quite unusual when uttered to a stranger, and because this was the first we'd ever heard of Jamie and his life before he had come to us; and then of course, the stunning presence of Adam, and the nonchalance with which he said it into the mild summer afternoon.

—I've also met your Claudio. I've got some connections in the

248

industry.

Then the woman with the freesias on her head said, with a vapid stare, pretending not to have overheard,

—We'll so's this it then, is it? There's an awful lot of people with dogs living here, and no pooper-scooper vending machine in sight. Why don't they sell pooper-scoopers here?

Adam in turn ignored her and went on,

—But we've met you know. I've been to your house! I've hooked up with Jamie a few months back.

—Oh he's coming over!

—Who?

—The . . . Do you, Emilia . . . Emilia! Do you know who that is? He's very attractive!

—You know that in German they call pooper-scooper a gacky-sacky-something? It's almost the same word! Only Germanic.

—I don't remember you coming to the house.

—Who?

—The gentleman on his way over here, with the dark suit and the greying hair.

—I think he's got his eye on Adam. I absolutely love it when people are honest about their . . . proclivities.

—On me . . . ? Who . . . oh, I don't know him at all! Would you like to meet him? Seeing as you can't have me . . .

—Can't have you? Since you won't have me, you mean.

—Yes, quite. And by the way, I think a 'sack' is a bag, not a scooper! It's not quite the same.

—Oh, Adam, do you speak German?

And so on and so forth. And just like this Adam became the gay bachelor of the gardens. Everybody accepted it, but Tim and I were wondering if that was the man who had treated Jamie so badly. The bad experience, the reason why he came over to Scotland in the first place. Was that the man who had destroyed our Jamie? Then why was he here? A stalker? It was just too much of a coincidence.

—You don't think he . . . ?

—Oh yes. What do you think Adam, darling? By the way, I didn't know you were gay.

—Think about what? Well you know now.

He turned to me again.

—I've tried to persuade Jamie to do porn. With his body . . . !

—What a way to come out to people. At a garden party. How . . . sophisticated! So suave!

—The gentleman . . . said Emilia.

—Yes I know who you are referring to but I don't quite . . .

—We think he fancies you . . . he's been eyeing him for quite a while you see. It's like a . . . here, trying to bring people together, only gay! How modern! How very modern!

She shook with laughter so hard her hat slid sideways a little.

—I am afraid I don't follow . . .

—Never mind then. You're absolutely gay then?

—I think so. I should know. I am almost forty.

—Absolutely, you don't take women at all?

She made it sound like a type of wine, or medicine one was partial to—or not.

—Ah . . .

—What happened when you tried to get Jamie to do porn? I interjected.

—Excuse me? Oh, Jamie, yes. I tried, but he wouldn't hear of it. He says a body like his ought to be shared freely, and for free!

—Well if you do change your mind, I do have a daughter. A rather lovely daughter. And I have heard you make tons of money at the bank . . . you are simply rolling in it, they say! I feel like . . . it's like one of these novels. I am trying to interest the gay bachelor in my daughter, ha ha! Only the meaning of 'gay' isn't quite the same any more! Ha! It would be a good match . . . you have the money and she has the title. Do people still marry for titles? You are American?

—I am afraid it's . . . no, no, I am not. And you wouldn't want me as a son-in-law, Madam.

—Yes I know, I know. Why is it that the best looking, nicest men, are always gay! Can you tell me that?

—I don't know. I for one am thoroughly depraved. You wouldn't want me as a son-in-law!

—Oh, oh! You know she's had a boyfriend who turned out queer. Very handsome fellow. Oh . . . am I allowed to say 'queer?'

She was looking at me.

—Are you asking me?

—Yes, of course. You see a lot. You've seen a lot, I mean. Why are the best-looking men always queer?

Mary started to wobble a little, and held onto the lady's arm.

—Are you ill?

—No, just woozy.

—Are you related?

She pointed at me.

Whilst Adam, now redder than the roses behind him, trying to avoid the approaching assailant, scrambling for a desperate and life-saving question to ask,

—So pray, do tell Emilia what sort of things do you discuss at the AGM? What important garden owners' issues? I am new to all this. I ought to know these things if I own half the garden.

Emilia was looking after Tim and Mary disappearing behind the rose bushes. That was the first time she vomited that afternoon. She'd simply had too much to drink.

—Emilia!

—Emilia!

—Yes, oh! I didn't hear you there. What?

—Adam was asking you about the AGM? What sort of drinks—I mean things—you discussed at the AGM. Be careful though. He says he is utterly depraved.

—Oh dear, oh dear. You are asking the wrong person. I quite missed half of it, I am afraid . . . it was all about dogs and fences! Depraved? Whatever do you mean?

—Fences?

—Yes, apparently we also own these other gardens down the street from here, although I must say I have never been there, and it hasn't got a fence . . . yet . . . that's what . . . Well, part of the meeting . . . the part that I overheard, as I am not a very important person here I pretty much missed the rest. Ever since my husband Horace died, I am afraid I am a bit hard of . . . Well, so that's what they talked about whether to get a cheaper fence or a nicely iron-wrought fence—are you really gay, it is extraordinary!—and it turns out that the expensive fence is ninety-thousand pounds and the cheaper one which I don't know which material they use, really, but they say it will last forty years, and as I won't be around

251

in forty years anyway ... Now that everybody is coming out, there seem to be a lot of homosexuals around. As for me, I am rather indifferent to the choice of fences.

—So how much was the cheaper one?

—Oh, the one we are getting?

—You are getting the cheaper one?

—Yes, it's been decided, at least I think—yes, that's what's been decided. They said the cheaper ... fence.

Adam looked interested—but his cock was still there. I had him down as a sexual pervert now. The man who'd broken our Jamie, and ... the man who talked about his sex-life at a garden party. The man who knew Claudio and all about porn.

—Forty-thousand pounds, that's what they said, for the fence.

—Forty-thousand pounds for the fence! You know, in my firm, on our trading floor, half the men were queer. We used to jerk off together in the toilet after a good deal. Forty-thousand is a lot for a fence, though. And we are paying this?

—It's a private garden. In the toilet?

—Oh, oh!

—That's why we are so happy you moved in. A rich banker. You see ... we are quite destitute. Oh, won't you change your mind and marry my daughter!?

We laughed politely, very politely. I was only startled out of my stupor when Adam said,

—Claudio, that Claudio chap ... Is he still together with his friend? What was his name ... Luke?

—Lukáš.

—Yes. Lucas. Wonderful couple, the two. I met them in Barbados once. They were together on a friend's boat. Friend was banging Claudio for cash, kept the boyfriend at arm's length. Sent him diving when they did it. Dumb sod never caught on. You know Claudio does it all to pay off some debt? Fair amount of money. Not his debt—Lucas's. He had massive debts and the criminal element was after him, or still is. It's quite romantic if you think about it, one boy selling his bum for his mate. Head over heels in love, the two! Oh I say, are those with chicken? I detest cucumber. Perfectly ghastly!

Somehow Adam disappeared out of sight then, and I didn't

get a chance to ask him ... to find out who he was, really. It were just a glimpse into Jamie's and Claudio's past, just that ... a sliver of information, recklessly purported over sandwiches. They do occur in life, these chance revelations. In fact, we never saw this Adam fellow again. I expected him to stop by the house, but he never did.

At home, I asked Jamie, but he denied everything. He said he knew no Adam, had never lived with one—he denied it categorically! But it might have just been because Maurizio was there, who, just as I left them to get on with their fucking said,

—Was he hot, that Adam?

So he didn't believe him either.

Of course I didn't ask Claudio. I couldn't. I just filed it away under ... curious. And I had a new theory then, or rehashed the old one: that Claudio was thoroughly in love with his mate, and would do anything, anything to stay with him.

Light-footed I danced with Kylie and 'All the Lovers'. It were the song that year, and I couldn't get it out of my head, especially now with Jamie so fragile. All the lovers ... what about them. Would he forget them? All the hundreds who lived with a bit of him inside them! But it's a danger, another one, and how do I protect Jamie from that? At least now, it's out of my hands.

Oh, Mr Dedalus, you would have been so at home at that garden party. I don't go to many, but this one were priceless. And I remember it because of Adam, and his bulge of course—it were *in my face*, as they say, but also because of who he was: a threat from the past.

Why a threat, you ask, smelly old Mr Dedalus? Well, don't you see? Jamie was quasi-married now; he had a lover, a real lover, a wonderful mate at last. And yet here I was talking to an ex at the garden party, and with it the knowledge came that there would be lots and lots and lots of exes, people who had come to the house even, without me remembering, without me seeing them.

How long would it be before one of these exes came between Maurizio and Jamie, and ripped, raped, rapripped them apart? It's always thus with our lads; it's the gay curse. No, not gay—it's the curse of handsome men who can't control their ... Oh, what am

I saying? Shutting up, shutting up. Lights out! Putting away the bottle.

It were that same evening we heard Maurizio and Jamie and Claudio shagging again. I was just come home from somewhere ... with Mary, I think, to pay taxes, or help her with summat official or other. She left me at the door, and I wheeled through the hall—I remember my whole body hurting badly from all the exercise, my arms sore. I rolled past the living-room when I heard noises, and turned round and found Lukáš reclined on the sofa, with the baby on his chest, making funny noises, gawking at him with a foamy mouth. He was playing with the baby, holding its tiny hands, lifting it a little, listening to it giggle, laughing out loud—what a strong voice the little bugger had—and Aleysha was sitting across the table, observing them both; I think she was close to tears when she turned round and looked at me. She got up, came over, and kissed me on the cheek, and crouched down aside my wheelchair. Then she whispered in my ear,
—He is wonderful with the baby, simply wonderful.
And then we sat there, and she took my hand. We watched Lukáš play with the tiny little creature, twirl it on his chest, back and forth and up and down and sideways, somersaulting and blowing kisses and raspberries and talking to it in Slovak, and smiling at it—they smiled at each other ...
I don't think he noticed at all that we were present and keenly watching.
I saw a current of love, a magnificent aura. I'd never observed a man with a baby—and I felt a pang of guilt. How on earth had I ever thought of this man as gay? Everything gay seemed selfish at that moment, everything Aleysha had said so perfectly right.
I felt guilty, and dirty—my whole life appeared filthy and worthless as I watched this man play with that new life Aleysha had created in her miraculous womanhood. It were far greater a picture of love than I had ever seen—far larger, far more real.
In my mind flashed the hundreds of lodgers we had had over the years: *my children,* all the men who had come here for sex, all the couples who had found each other, all the lovers ... and they seemed insignificant.

Suddenly Lukáš clocked me just as he held up the baby by its arms, so it stood upright on his stomach. The very same moment we heard a farting noise and the baby gave a curious, stunned look; seconds later it started to cry. Aleysha didn't move. We watched Lukáš. He spoke in mellow, deep tones in his native language, and at length grabbed the bag that stood by his feet, picked up the baby and rose to his feet. He smiled at us. Aleysha rose and held her hands out to take the baby, but Lukáš said,

—No, I do. I can change napping!

Aleysha and I both chuckled. Baby let rip another, then cried even louder. Lukáš said to me, as if an explanation were necessary,

—He make poo-poo.

He walked past me, nappy and baby in hand, into the kitchen.

I was alone with Aleysha.

I thought of something to do. The scene I had just witnessed had been so overwhelming, so simple and beautiful.

It was she who spoke first.

—He is wonderful with the baby, I told you.

—Aleysha, I am so sorry.

—Sorry about what?

—You are so right, about everything you said. We are awful people. We are so selfish.

I had never actually had that thought, it were never an emotion of mine. I never thought that us queers were indeed guilty of something, or even selfish. Her accusations had hurt, but until now, I hadn't really taken them in—until I had seen Lukáš with the baby. It hurt. So it came out like this, so daft and dramatic.

—Don't be silly. You are not selfish. You are one of the most giving, caring people I know.

—Oh, Aleysha . . .

She put a finger on my lips.

—I am saying sorry. For my outburst. I am sorry I said all those things. What was I expecting of all-you? You are gay men, what did I expect, even from men . . . you don't *feel it* like women.

She kissed me again and helped me reach the sofa. There was a bottle of wine of the table, and she poured me a glass. We sat quietly for a moment while she drank. I just held mine.

—He is truly amazing, Lukáš, I said. I must have been blind.

—Blind to what?

We heard the baby cry in the kitchen, and Lukáš talking to it, and the rustling of the nappies and him shaking the powder, and blowing kisses. Baby was already laughing again.

—How could I have ever, I mean . . . clearly he's got all the right genes, the right instincts.

—You mean because of his friend? Claudio?

—Yes.

—Well, it was natural for you to assume . . . I am sure, I would have drawn similar conclusion. And they came to your bed and breakfast! Yes, it was logical.

I was tempted to tell her about the debts. Would she want to be involved with a man wanted by some Eastern European Mafia? But I could not speak. I looked at her quietly. We heard gurgling noises, and Lukáš talking his baby-talk.

—But you know, Aleysha said abruptly, you *were* completely wrong about them.

—About Claudio and Lukáš?

—Yes.

—All-you were wrong. It has nothing to do with gay, nothing. He told me.

I had just put the glass to my lips, but now I swallowed hard.

—He told you? He told you what?

—He told me everything! Why they are so close.

—That they are good friends, just good friends.

—Yes, but . . . I don't think I should tell you. He told me in bed, he was crying when he told me. It's awful. It's really awful.

—What happened? It's because of Claudio doing porn, isn't it?

—No. No, no. It has nothing, nothing to do with gay stuff.

—It's because of the gambling then, the debts?

—What? Oh you know that. That's . . . I do not think I should break his confidence. He has to tell you . . . oh, there he is.

Lukáš was walking over with the freshly changed baby. There were sweat on his brow, and his cheeks were flushed. I don't think he were ever more attractive than at that moment. The last of the day's light shone into the room as he passed the gurgling creature over to Aleysha. She took her child, and said,

—I have to be going. Will you stay here?

256

Lukáš wiped his face. He gasped with exhaustion.

I wanted him to stay, I wanted to sort out Claudio and him; I wanted to talk to him, urgently. Why had he confided in Aleysha but not me? I realized that I would have never got to the bottom of their relationship. Lukáš would never have told me, he just wasn't that sort of man. He'd never *trust* another male with his innermost feelings, but he had told Aleysha. I were insanely jealous!

—I'll go with you, he said.

They packed their things, and Aleysha whispered in my ear,

—No doubt he will tell you one day. You must understand! while Lukáš was already outside, opening the boot of her car. I waved and watched the door fall shut.

Just as I had returned to the kitchen again, I heard the key in the lock. Lukáš came running in, past me, grabbing the talcum power from the kitchen table, saying,

—I forgot take this, then walking past me. But he stopped and came back.

He looked at me for a moment too long; he had something on his mind. I was close to asking 'yes?' when he spoke.

—Did you know they were HIV positive? Aleysha *and* the baby? Did you know?

Of course I didn't know, Mr Dedalus—I had no fucking idea! How could I? Tim knew though. He knew because it were he who had brought Aleysha to the doctor when she learned she were in the family way. And she had been living with HIV for years; she'd already come infected from Uganda, and so had her boyfriend. They'd been killed almost, bludgeoned to death in the street, when they had been found out. A priest had hidden them in his house, and a UK charity had got them on a plane to London.

They had watched, the night before, from their window, how a mob had dragged a seventeen year old boy from a house, accused him of being gay, stripped him, beaten him, spat on him, cut off both his arms and his penis, then set him on fire. The screams, Aleysha had told Tim, were still ringing in her ears every night. It was an almost daily occurrence now, the extermination of gays (in league with the devil!) all over Africa.

There are countries, Tim said, that were flat in the middle ages, and not just the Muslim countries. The mob in Uganda had been Christian! Christians doing this! They kill, maim and torture, said Tim, in the name of their ridiculous god, as if Kant had never been born.

So I learned all about Aleysha's ordeal, about the suffering, about unspeakable cruelty towards gay men, about the mutilation of women all over Africa, and I cried, and couldn't speak. It came as such an unexpected shock. But in the end—are we not selfish beings?—what egged me most were that nobody had told me about Aleysha being positive. Nobody had told me!

I asked Tim about her boyfriend. My first thought was: had he slept with Jamie? Don't laugh, Mr Dedalus, don't laugh. It's a natural assumption; it's logical. He wasn't very attractive, but Jamie, in his days ... What a horrific idea, his life destroyed now that he had found Maurizio, by HIV!

But then Tim told me summat else: that he had already taken Maurizio and Jamie to the clinic four weeks ago; that he had already made them get the test before committing to each other. And that he told them that they still had to use condoms for six months, then get tested again; and then, only then, could they start with the bareback stuff. And I had known nothing about it!

Tim was having intimate conversations with my lodgers, and I weren't part of it! Hadn't been for years!

I spent a terrible night. It was such a big revelation to learn that things were going on behind my back, a whole web of intimacies spun invisibly around me. Tim said it was because I couldn't do it anyway—accompany them to the clinic, because it weren't wheelchair accessible. So I shouted at him, just before we went to sleep, I shouted,

—But you could have at least told me!

And then, as an afterthought,

—Bloody hell, what else have you not told me? Why are you people keeping things from me? Why? You don't trust me?

I remember his look just before he turned off the light: there was fear in his eyes, plain fear.

PART VII

One by one, the Slovaks affected everyone that summer. History flared up and trust was broken, and revelations made. The two handsome men, mysterious in their union, were a powerful force, changing more with their intransigence, their silence, then I ever could with all my prodding talk.

Finding Claudio alone one day, and looking sad, Tim and I took him to the pub. We made him come with us, even though he were at first reluctant to the utmost. We needed to bring him and Lukáš back together, we needed to mend what we had broken. And I needed to know what was behind it all—what Lukáš had told Aleysha, but would never tell us!

I had a déjà vu as Tim ordered the beer, and why does everything important in this life happen over alcohol?

My dad taught me the facts of life and took me to the pub for it. Tim and I have had every meaningful discussion in a pub (getting together, staying together, starting the B&B . . .). And every sort of conflict resolution seems to involve taking people down the pub. As if the absence of familiar walls, the noise of the other punters, the clattering of dishes and glasses, or the stacked waitress—which one of these most, I wonder?—could instil some greater openness, some increased willingness to let go of one's pretences and defences.

Or is it just the booze, period?

Claudio were apprehensive, because it were two grown men take him there, two white-haired (grey if you want, or rather, bald), older (not to say old) men, taking him to the pub for a talk. He was trembling as he sat down, his hulking frame (he'd been to the gym every day since the débâcle, and was really puffed up), slouched against the table. I wanted to say, 'You've done nothing wrong, lad, nowt to worry,' but Tim stopped me, reminding me that we needed to try not to sound accusing. Although I wondered then what we should have accused him of.

Just as Vivian brought three pints, and put them down with her usual *charming* smile, I couldn't remember what we had

259

come for in the first place.

Claudio reminded me, by lifting his glass and saying, before even drinking,

—It doesn't mean I am gay. I've told you. I like the . . . fun.

It wanted objecting, but Tim embraced him, verbally.

—Oh we know it doesn't. If it were any other boy, we'd still ask you. If it were just that—the porn. If it was just porn, and you say you do it for the money, we'd believe you, readily.

—But you don't.

—We have our doubts. It's the porn, and then there is your relationship with Lukáš, which is . . .

—It doesn't mean I am gay, he said again, speaking very precisely.

I wondered if Tim would bring up the debts.

—Yes, but are you though, I burst out. You are almost thirty. It's not like you are twenty-one and still searching! You like being a bottom. You look up to Lukáš. You love him. And you fucked Maurizio and Jamie!

It just came out, like this, and I regretted it immediately. For a moment he stared at me blankly. I thought he were getting angry—I thought he was about to hit me. But then he controlled it, the flames died down, he looked away, and then he just shook his head and didn't speak.

—You've spent ten years living with another man—intimately. You are doing everything together. Lukáš says you are just good friends—it seems unlikely. You are paying his debts for fuck's sake! Now he is angry at you doing gay porn. Face it: you are doing gay porn to support . . . to . . . for a living—a living for two. You live like a couple on one salary. He doesn't seem to work at all, Lukáš, does he?

Claudio looked a bit shocked at the question, as if he just now realized that he had been the source of their financial freedom, the guarantor of their far-flung travel, as if nobody had ever pointed it out to him. Traipsing all over the planet on his bum's earnings! That maybe the reason they were together were his money. He looked bowled over.

—Do you think it's possible Lukáš is only staying with you because you provide the money? Because you give him money?

Wouldn't that be spiffy? The rent-boy actually paying the straight boy's rent! Claudio gave us a vapid look, but I think he knew exactly what Tim had said. He just took time to process it.

Tim repeated,

—Is Lukáš with you because you have money? Because you *make* money? Is he using you?

—No! came the emphatic answer. We are friends! Good friends!

—And you aren't gay? I said, and again I regretted it. But in my world, in my life, things were still either/or, black and white. And I couldn't conceive of a man who slept freely with others, and did it for a living, to be at least slightly queer! Bloody hell, there had to be some label one could stick on the bugger! Everyone had labels!

—I am not gay. I don't prefer men. I enjoy sex with men. I like to be bottom, yes. I enjoy any kind of sex. I do have sex with girls, privately. I do like girls! Mentally, I am much more attracted to women. The sex with men is hot, but ... Maybe I am bisexual, so? I would like to be with a girl, one day. A woman, have children, but ...

There he stopped. It occurred to me, rather comically, that he hadn't made a single mistake. If not for himself, if not for his soul, our talks at least seemed to improve his English.

—But what? said Tim.

—But I have to stay with Lukáš.

—You *have* to?

—Yes. He needs me. I need him. He must ...

—But Lukáš isn't gay. Are you sure? Are you ...

—No. Yes! He's not gay. He is with Aleysha now, you see yourself! He has had many girlfriends, always. Now he has Aleysha.

—But he always comes back to you.

—Yes.

—Why do you think that is?

I wanted Claudio to give his own answer, find it inside him, but Tim ruined that.

—Do you think, Claudio, that Lukáš maybe is in the closet? That he is really gay, but cannot admit it? For some reason? Some evil in his past, some abusive ... I don't know. We think maybe

261

you both need help to ... face, whatever it is. We are only trying to help.

—Not again! You always say you want to help. You are not helping!

Claudio, his lips white from the foam, put the glass down louder than he intended to, and bent forward, rearranging the coaster, in an effort to take back the affront.

He mumbled 'sorry,' while the fingers of the left tapped nervously, and with the right hand he started drawing lines through the condensation drops on the beer glass.

—You have all wrong! All of you. Why do you think it must be? Why do you always have to talk about gay!

He looked at me, then at Tim.

—You don't want to help, I think. I think you don't want to *help*, you just want to *know!* I have—we have right to privacy, no?

Privacy! I wanted to be coarse. I wanted to take him by the shoulders, shake him and scream, 'I am not the one getting fucked in porn flicks! Stop denying who you are!' But this time I held my tongue.

—And Jamie too! You have it all wrong, and Javier. Lukáš and I—we have nothing to be with gay or straight. You only think so because of the porn, and because you are, I understand. You want everybody being gay! I meet many guys like you, when I do porn. Many want to be my boyfriend, and I tell them I am sorry, I cannot, I don't want boyfriend with a man—I am straight I tell them. Sometimes in other country, people recognize or like in bar, or one time at the beach, some guy fancy me. Sometimes, I ... go out with guys. Just because I like the company. I tell you, honestly!

—But then you go back to Lukáš ... every time, I said.

—Let him finish!

—Yes, please. Claudio swallowed.

I am more than a little ashamed, thinking back to that talk, how we cornered him, not for his good, but just for our own greedy, unkind curiosity—and yes, to squeeze him into a drawer, to stick some name on him like labels at a garden party. Despite Lukáš's explanations, despite Aleysha's rebuff, despite everything that had happened, I was still sure that there was a truth there that had to come out. A truth which would—at last!—satisfy me.

We, the mature, gay friends we thought ourselves to be, the nurturing kind, into whose loving, understanding laps these lads had been dropped, we had to help them shed their shells, and re-emerge as self-confessed, proud gays. That's what coming out was all about, and doing good, being a *good gay;* helping others find their place in society.

Tim nodded, as if he guessed at what I was thinking. He was the teacher. Who better to help the Slovak friends find themselves than an experienced educator, who knew about human psychology? We felt that we needed at last to draw them out, and we started with Claudio. He was more receptive, more submissive to our psychology. And I mean, bollocks, really: after half a decade in gay porn, how difficult was it to come out? How different could it be to admit it? All that nonsense about not minding, and really preferring girls, mentally—what does that mean? I get gang-banged by every hunk in sight, but mentally I prefer girls? Please! The lad had to admit it, that was all!

—It does not matter I do porn. It does not matter. It's just one way—one type of make love. And it's fun be with men, I like. Men always horny, always hot. What is big deal?

—You are passive, I said.

—I get fucked, yes, so what? he said, very softly, then suddenly laughed boisterously and startled us. Ha ha! So you think I really gay, eh? You think I must be gay—you just same as normal people, think because I have cock in my ass I must be gay! It is just stereo! Just a stereo . . . type.

I had a sudden impulse to applaud when the difficult word came out without our help.

—It is just stupid, stupid thinking, to say, because passive, so I am gay. I tell you already. I like . . . dominant men. I don't know why. I am submissive. So you think I *must* be gay.

—Claudio, we are not thinking that. It's not because you get fucked in porn. It's not even that you enjoy sex with men some times. It's not because you slept with Maurizio and Jamie. It's not about sex. It's because of the way you act with Lukáš. We have our doubts not because of the sex, but because of the . . . the love. The love you seem to share with Lukáš. You seem like a couple to us; from the beginning, we thought you were a couple.

263

—Like a gay couple that's not gay, so you say.

—Yes, at the castle. You remember?

—I remember.

—That, and clearly you like sex with men. So we are thinking, maybe you need some help to find yourself. Maybe you need . . . a push.

Suddenly he banged his fists on the table in an uncharacteristic display of dominance. He looked at Tim, then at me, then back at Tim, and raised his voice.

—Please, listen to me! I don't mind sex with men—I like. I like get fucked—I like a lot! But I like women, I do. I like girls. You must accept. And that is end of it. End. No more. That is what I am. You call me in closet, okay, but no more talk about it, okay? That is my business. But Lukáš and me, what he and I . . . are, that has nothing, NOTHING, NO-THING! to do with gay or straight, or . . . nothing! You hear?

Claudio said it, and stopped there forcefully, shaking his head briefly and then finally unclenching his fists. He drank from his glass, took a big mouthful, and seemed reluctant to swallow. Neither Tim nor I dared to say a word. Suddenly—I reckon it was the smile—we were completely under his spell.

—What is it between Lukáš and I—it is not about gay. It is much, much . . . more . . . It is . . . about my sister.

There was a long pause, during which I thought about Mary. Mary who had said that there were a woman at the bottom of this. Clever Mary!

—My sister, she died, I tell you, no?

I nodded.

—Your sister? said Tim, to confirm.

—Yes. I have sister. My sister, I love her very much. We have a very big connection. Very . . .

—Deep.

I threw Tim an evil look. I wanted Claudio to find his own words, I needed him to get it out now. He was on the brink. We were there. I cursed my broken legs for I would have liked to kick Tim in the shins.

— . . . deep, yes. We always together. We understand each

other without speaking. We have the same . . . movement, when we do things, we are alike. My father, he was a bit violent, so often I protecting her. She hide in my room.

He drank.

—We have the same face expression, too, my mother say. The family . . . always surprise how boy and girl so alike. When I dress up in her clothing, people think I am her.

—Have you done that a lot? said Tim, sounding like Dr Freud.

—Only little, when I was little. Only for fun. Not what you think.

He laughed, we all laughed, a forced outburst to bring the conversation along, to ease this sudden tension after his assertion.

The pub were quite empty, and nobody paid any attention to us. Vivian came round to see if we needed anything. I were about to say something, when Claudio continued,

—Lukáš, he was love her.

It was meant to be an earth-shaking statement, because he looked up at us, waiting for our faces to fall. But because of his strange intonation and the missing particles, it took us a few seconds to understand what he were saying.

—Lukáš and your sister . . .

—Elena. My sister was called Elena.

The tears came to Claudio's eyes the moment he said her name. Then he added portentously,

—I can still feel her, be next to me. I miss her, always. I miss her so much.

Tim and I looked at each other.

—You mean Lukáš and Elena were . . . lovers?

—Yes. For one year. Maybe a little longer. Maybe not lovers, is big word. She was so young, still. We were teenagers only.

—So he is grieving, said Tim, more to the ceiling than to any of us.

He had the uncanny ability, my headmaster, to sound perfectly clinical in the most emotional moments.

—I beg pardon? said Claudio.

—I mean Lukáš, he is sad too, that your sister . . .

—Yes. He miss her very much. They were like . . . like . . . *Romeo a Julie!*

—*Romeo and Juliet* in English. They were so much in love?

—Yes, also, but like the movie.

—Like in the movie? You mean the play.

Claudio did not react, and my disappointed teacher-husband shrugged resignedly.

—Yes, in the movie, like: my father hate Lukáš's parents. He hate because they are not real Slovak.

—No?

—Lukáš, he is Hungarian minuty.

—Minuty? Oh, minority. Hungarian minority? A gypsy? I said, realizing my error immediately as Tim gave be a punishing look. Claudio laughed.

—No, no, not gypsy. Gypsy is different. His family really from Hungary, and move to our area, but already many many year ago. He not even speak Hungarian any more, only little. Many Slovak don't like Hungarian.

—I see.

Suddenly Claudio's eyes were very wet. He wiped his face with the back of his hand.

—When my sister die, my father one day, about two week after funeral, he see my mother cry, very hard, very bad, and he say to her, 'Maybe is better so, maybe better she dead, otherwise she marry that Hungarian.'

Now I too had a frog in my throat. Such statements of categorical hatred, the death of a human being preferable to something perfectly harmless as the mingling of races, that is so painful to me. How much hate is there in the hearts of people that they want their children dead rather than married to the person they love? What is it in humanity that blinds people so? What is the font of this hate?

Suddenly Tim smiled, rather inappropriately I thought. But the scholar had had a breakthrough.

—It all makes sense now!

He almost shouted in his eureka moment.

—That's it! Lukáš stays with you, because you are *like* your sister. He cannot leave you, because he is in love with … the image of her, in you.

Claudio nodded, just a little, and then I saw it too, the possibility. But it was … surely … it was …

—But that can't be healthy, I said. For both of you. Why don't you leave ... find a boy—or girl? I corrected myself. You should be happy!

—I am.

—But you are not in love with Lukáš?

—I tell you, maybe I am. And what is love ... ? Explain me! What is love, why everybody is so crazy about love? We are friends. Friendship is much more important in life. I just want to be with him.

It sounded like it was snatched right of Lukáš's mouth, yet he said it so loud and with so much conviction that a few people turned to look at him.

—Trust someone, enjoy life together ... that is good, no? For sex we can going somewhere else, no problem, you see? Lukáš and I, we have something far greater than love. We have friendship!

He took up his beer glass, and like an exclamation mark at the end of his proclamation, finished it all in one draught. He put the glass down, this time carefully, with a measured, deliberate movement of the hand, looking Tim and then me in the eye.

—It's very very, simple, he said again. We are friends!

We are friends. How truly simple. It felt like the right time to leave, to put an end to this, and to accept their link: the dead sister. And their belief in friendship.

Tim and I hadn't half finished our drinks, and suddenly a full pint appeared in front of Claudio. Vivian bowed down and whispered,

—From the gentleman in the blue jacket, by the bar. He'd like to be your friend.

Claudio turned, found himself facing a black-haired, somewhat shy-looking young lad with deep dimples.

—What do I do? he said to Tim.

—If you accept it, he'll come over and pick you up.

I looked at Tim.

—Times are a-changing for real! A man picking up another in a straight pub on the Royal Mile!

I looked over to him. Such a brave effort—to reach out for love in the straightest of places, the high street pub, and be rejected

267

so cruelly.

Claudio stood up.

—What are you going to tell him?

He didn't answer. He walked over to the man. We heard nothing they said to each other. It were a brief exchange. And then Claudio shook the guy's hand, rather intimately, and gave him a kiss on the cheek.

He went to the toilet afore rejoining us, and I thought about all the secrets in his young life. Tim and I sat in silence, waiting. I was delighted then to have him. I was happy and overjoyed that Tim and I had such a simple and uncomplicated relationship. That for us, it were just a game: that we could delve into other people's lives without too much bother, without danger to our own. He and I had complete trust. I knew everything about him and he knew everything about me. Everything that mattered, at least.

—How was his sister killed? he asked.

I realized that nobody had ever told Tim the story.

—She was mowed down by a motorcycle. It were an accident.

And then Tim gave me the most surprised look I had ever seen on his face. It wasn't just surprise—it were pure fright, as if he'd seen a ghost, worse even than in bed when I had accused him of not telling me about Aleysha. I wanted to ask what the matter, but then Claudio were back. Tim cleared his throat and said,

—What did you say to him?

—I tell him thank you, and that I am very sorry, and that he is very nice and has . . . courageous!

—Courage. Courage—courageous, said Tim the teacher.

—And then he tell me he don't want to be my boyfriend. He only want to know if it's me . . .

—If it's you . . . oh I see!

Tim looked very serious.

—Does it bother you when people recognize you from your porn flicks?

Claudio shook his head and started the new pint.

—Not at all. Porn is . . . is like acting. And it's . . . it's not me. You know? It's just fun, that sex.

Tim and I watched him that night, like a clinical study, on the laptop between us in bed. It seemed impossible that this boy on screen were acting. It seemed like a lie, all of it. With a smile like that, with a gleam in his eyes, with such a hunger as he fell upon the massive cock offered to him—how could he feel nothing? How could he be faking it, that intimacy, that ... final proof of love? How could he not be wanting what we saw him want—what we wanted him to want! It was the opposite of what we believed in—intimacy as some kind of affirmation of love.

Neither Tim nor I got aroused. We both looked at it as if it were a documentary; then Tim turned off the computer.

We lay in the dark for a while. Several cars drove by, before he spoke again.

—You know, maybe it is just that. A bit of acting. Just fun. Maybe sex never was what we thought it was, a deep expression of love. Maybe that too is religious baggage, to keep men and women together, and devout, and god-fearing, and the men from running off after the next skirt. So that they could raise children together. Maybe *we* got it all wrong. Maybe sex is meant to be just fun. Apolitical. Noncommittal. Just plain ... fun.

I turned away from him, feeling the dead limbs of my lower body between us like a heap of stones.

A few days later, I were about to doss down when Jamie came home, dressed to the nines in his sexiest jeans and tightest T-shirt, straining to keep all that well-formed muscle in.

—You been out? I asked, stating the obvious.

—Yes. And you won't guess who we met.

I didn't clock at first that he were asking something. I only heard the 'we' and felt a bolt of joy. Then Maurizio appeared in the door. He'd smoked a cigarette. He looked gorgeous—the two of them did. I felt like the proud mother of two boys again. Their relationship was so much simpler than the Slovaks, I thought.

—He'll quit when we move in together, said Jamie when he noticed my blank stare.

—He'll quit what?

—He'll quit smoking. He promised. It's an Italian thing.

—Oh.

I was so overjoyed hearing them planning to move in together

269

that I didn't register what that would mean—that they could *move out* first—out of this house. That I would lose Jamie for good.

—So who did you meet? Lukáš?

—Yes! How did you guess?

—He left the house without a ta-ta, and dressed nicely. Not his usual lumberjack style. He were up to something.

—And do you know what?

—No. Where did you meet him?

—Exactly!

—What, exactly?

—That's the point isn't it. We met him in a gay bar! A leather bar! We met him at Choppy's! He was in a gay leather bar, and some dude with a beard was groping him, and licking his neck.

My face must have collapsed completely judging by the way they stared at me.

—Never!

—I swear on my first boyfriend's eleven-inch cock! It was him! He didn't see us, I don't think.

—Eleven-inch cock? cooed Maurizio, grabbing Jamie's arm. He looked small, a little girlish in this pose—almost vulnerable. I thought of the garden party, and the trouser, the pinstripe trouser with the outline of a massive penis, and it slipped out,

—Adam?

—Yes! How . . . ?

Jamie stared at me, realizing what he had admitted, and afore strictly denied. And at the same time, we tried to keep all that exchange from Maurizio, who luckily didn't catch on. His mind was somewhere else: on the eleven inches.

—I never seen such a big cock, ever, said the Italian.

Secrets everywhere! Jamie gave me a look of gratitude, and I did not follow up. Instead I said,

—What's he doing there?

—Proving to himself he can be queer? Maybe he is?

—No, no! He can't be. Do you know the guy he was with?

—Only from sight. Not bad looking fellow. A bit too much muscle for my taste.

Why was all this coming back now, after I'd seen him with the baby, after he had so clearly switched sides in my mind? It were infuriating.

—Oh my god, Jamie, what have we done?

—We ain't done nothin' old man!

—Oh yes, we have.

—No we haven't. Whatever is between them must come out sooner or later. It's not just the porn. There is something else they are not talking about. Can you imagine being together for twelve years, lying to each other all the time? There is some big secret we haven't even begun to unearth.

—Don't you want to know?

—What's there to know? It might just be as simple as that, that they like women in bed, but prefer to live with each other.

—Oh, wake up! Hallo? Anybody home? said Maurizio. There is no such thing as non-gay!

—Is that the new word for it?

—What I mean is, you either fancy boys or you don't. You don't choose to spend your life with a man just because you can't stand women around the house.

—I am not so sure. It used to be quite the thing to be 'a bachelor.' There are lots of straight men who can't abide the company of women.

—Lukáš isn't one of them. Lukáš prefers women. I have seen him with Aleysha and the baby. I know. The lad's perfectly normal.

—Ooooh! Oh! Is that what we call it now, normal? Have we lost all our self-esteem?

They suddenly seemed too gay, too extravagant. I couldn't believe what was happening. I, the old queen, being annoyed, was trying to protect Lukáš from their frivolity.

—But they don't fall in love with other men and live with them. Please! And more to the point, they don't do gay porn and get fucked by Jan and Neil and Danny and Chuck and Chris for all the world to see. And . . . and . . . Jamie went red in the face.

—They don't have threesomes with Jamie and me! And let me tell you, Claudio behaved perfectly normal in bed. Like a normal gay guy!

—That's Claudio. Not Lukáš. Maybe you are right . . .

It were exasperating! On the one hand, we should offer them all the help they need to come out; on the other, we had to accept

271

what they said and stop prying.

—They still don't seem to talk now. They aren't talking to each other. We have to ... do something. We have to get them back together again!

—Is Claudio in the room?

—I think so, why?

Jamie just smirked.

—We didn't score at the pub.

—Keep your hands off him!

—Why? His lover-mate is out shagging the locals. We must go and console the scorned bride ...

—Don't you have enough with each other?

—Not while we are young, honey. We'll be alone and old soon enough!

Afore I could object, Jamie were up the stairs, Maurizio behind him, and I heard the knock at the door, and Claudio answer.

It's the privilege of youth to be so wild—and so callous. 'We'll be alone and old soon enough!' Yes you will be, my dear Jamie! Too soon.

I tidied the kitchen a bit, then took the stairlift. As it glided past the second floor, I heard voices coming from the room. They were talking, the three of them. I heard the sound of a can being opened, and Jamie saying,

—Well, take it off then!

Deep down I felt that I had to do something to fix their relationship, screw things down, make them whole again; that I had again to meddle. And then I reproached myself for even thinking it, Mr Dedalus: what you taught me, that we must make other people happy, like Liz Taylor said, that we are who we are, and we can only forgive each other, and help each other become what we are meant to become.

I hatched a plan. A simple, traditional plan. I was anything but sure it would work. But I had to make amends. If I had broken something with my nosiness, my pushing and prodding, my bullying—yes, I had bullied them both, tried to make them conform to my world—I had to try and fix it. I had to fix it and

272

bring them back together.

And of course, we had to watch! Maurizio, Jamie and I got there half an hour earlier, one of the nice fish restaurants at Leith Docks. We knew the waiter, and arranged a table by the kitchen, away from the aisle and hidden from the rest of the room. Then we had clams in white wine, a perch, and the most outrageous Spanish dessert you can imagine: Dulce de Leche. Four billion calories in one spoon. And we watched and observed!

It had not taken a lot to convince Lukáš. He were almost glad when Jamie asked him, grateful for the push. They arrived fifteen minutes late. There were two other gay couples there that night. That sort of company, I thought, would put them at ease.

Nothing happened during the meal. In spite of the waiter telling them that everything was on the house they ordered very little. They shared a salad, and each had a fish, without dessert. When they didn't ask for wine, I sent over a bottle. A little booze goes a long way in these situations.

Aye, it were a wonderful evening, and the atmosphere by the harbour is extraordinarily romantic. Even I fell into a stupor, wishing I was young again, wishing I could do all the things I had missed out on in my life, all over again. Only Jamie was unaffected, flirting instead with Maurizio. They were so in love it were hard to watch them. Like daft teenagers! I envied them their freedom, their fine legs. I thought of my own youth, and how secretive we had had to be and how open the two of them were in comparison. They held hands in the street in broad daylight, and now they were flirting with the waiter!

—Will you let off! He's married with four children. Four! Think of the expense if he marries you.

—We don't want to marry him, said Maurizio, we only want to suck him.

—He is gorgeous. I love tall hairy Poles! said Jamie.

—You love poles, period. And keep quiet. I think we are getting somewhere!

—It's a shame we can't hear anything. Couldn't you get a table closer to theirs?

—I don't want them to see us!

Claudio had lifted his hand and shifted it forward, then put it flat on the table. Lukáš was looking about first, saw a gay couple kissing, then moved his hand towards the centre. Their fingertips touched. All that was said was in their gestures: which didn't mean what we thought they meant, but there you have it. Then Claudio put his hand on Lukáš's, and they looked at each other intently. We couldn't hear anything they were saying, but we observed them, like a silent film: Claudio making long explanations, no doubt about his porn career, and asking forgiveness, and Lukáš . . . Well, what could he do? If they were such great friends, it couldn't matter really.

—Maybe, Maurizio had said, maybe now they do gay porn together. Maybe Lukáš . . .

—Oh shut up!

I had cut him off—regretting of course being rude—but as I said, baby-cradling Lukáš had become my holy grail. He was my icon of a sensitive straight man. Now engaged in this lovely bromance with a quasi-gay porn actor. Isn't life queer? Oh, Mr Dedalus—is that all life is? A sequence of such iconic, self-deluding, reality-distorting images? But it were such a comfort to think of them now in this new light.

I thought of them climbing Mt. Kilimanjaro, as they had said they had done together, and rowing for three-hundred miles down the coast in Australia. They were rugged, manly adventurers and their friendship almost an anachronism. They were so much more really than the sum of them, especially now that we had fleshed out their personalities; now that we claimed to understand them. We knew their history together, knew about the link between them: the sister, mowed down by an irresponsible driver, just like I had been. Rural beauties, simple boys from Eastern Europe, who'd rejected every bad role model and became such sensible creatures, such . . . real, honest, men.

Anyroad, in the end there were no drama, not a bit of it. There was no hugging, no crying, no outbursts, no getting up from the table and falling into each other's arms.

—Anything happening? asked Jamie after another hour. He was bored.

—Nothing further.

—What, no kissing, no heavy petting?

274

Nothing had happened. They had touched hands, and Lukáš had once reached to his friend's face and stroked his cheek, as if to wipe away a tear; then nothing. At eleven they got up and left, and we saw them arms linked over shoulders, walking to the taxi stand.

The restaurant's owner came to our table.

—So, gentlemen—a success?

—I am not sure. What did you think?

He pinched Maurizio's cheek.

—*E tu, che pensi?*

And to Jamie he said,

—He is adorable!

Giovanni was my age, enormously fat and round, bald just like me, with a burgundy birthmark over his ear, twice married, seven children. But when he had first come to the UK, many, many years ago, he and I had had a quick fling. Oh, he were handsome then! In his early twenties, black hair, dark, seductive eyes, an Italian god! It was hard to believe the man standing before me, surreptitiously squeezing my hand as he unlocked the wheelchair, was the same man I had once fucked in the back of a VW wagon.

Time doesn't heal anything, it just turns everything into a farce. And Jamie and Maurizio standing aside him, these sigils of youth. I could not help feeling sad at the thought that one day, many years from now, they would end up like us. If there is one thing we gays all have in common, it's this inextinguishable belief in youth and beauty. It is our downfall, that shallowness. It's the source of all our troubles.

—Your little love-birds, eh? Not much happening. I think one is the ... woman, you know. He like to adore his friend. But the other ...

—The plain one, said Jamie, who was sitting on the right?

—Yes. He no like men. He is ... *solo un uomo.* He is very normal, very straight. Not acting. He is very straight. I think he is very good with women. Very sensitive.

Funny for him to say so. Maybe you become attuned to people if you run a restaurant where people go on dates. Maybe it's just age. Maybe he was thinking of himself.

—It amazes me, I said as Giovanni pushed me to the exit and

handed me back my credit card without having even swiped it, how after all these years, you still can't speak English.

He gave me a mock slap, then, making sure nobody was watching, leaned down to kiss me on the cheek.

—Cheeky bastard, you old mucker. Look at you! You are enjoying this, surround by gorgeous young boys.

He weren't looking at me though. We were both looking at Maurizio and Jamie walking ahead of us, holding hands, arms touching, then stopping, kissing.

And then Giovanni let out a sigh that could melt a heart of stone.

—Well, what did he say? I fell upon Claudio the next morning at breakfast. How did it go?

—He said he go out to a gay bar to find me, but not see me, he also try . . . he say he want to see if he could . . . You know, he want to pick up guy. He want to know if he can do gay, like I do in the porn.

—Lukáš? Lukáš tried to get laid?

—Yes. He want to know. He say you turn him crazy, always say he is, and we are, and he want to know, at last . . . he think maybe because you push so much, you make him doubt. You make him think he is wrong to be friend with me. You make him feeling confusing. So he want to know.

—Once and for all.

—Yes, once and for all. He want to know if he can be gay.

—But haven't you two ever . . .

—No!

—So Lukáš really never . . . he's really never touched a man?

—He do yesterday in the club.

—He did? And?

—He don't like. And he watch guys make out, and he say . . . it's okay. We seen it many time. It mean nothing to him. Nothing.

—And you? Do you want coffee?

—I already make tea.

—What about you?

—What about me?

—Do you want him . . . ? Does it bother you that he will never

276

be physical with you?

—Physic . . . ?

—That he will never sleep with you, after all.

—Oh, why you keep on and on . . . why you don't see? No, it don't bother me.

There was a long silence, and it was Claudio who resumed the conversation.

—He also said he loved me. And that he wanted to stay with me. But . . . like before. And that he forgave me. And that there was nothing to forgive. He say that it was okay I did what I did, and lied, and that he was ashamed.

—Ashamed?

—Yes, for take all the money without asking. And making me do. He say he feel like a pump!

—A pump?

—I think he means a pimp, said Jamie behind me. Good morning! So you boys—no bum fun? It's a shame. I'd love to fuck Lukáš.

—Jamie!

—What?

—Oh please! Enough! We've put them through enough! It's not on! Give it a rest!

—Put them through what? They didn't run. They have to make up their minds! If they are such great friends . . . none of this will matter!

—Yes. So nothing change! Nothing matter. We still friends.

—And you? What do you think . . . after Jamie.

—What? I don't care about Jamie. Oh you mean sex. Oh I tell you—you don't believe me. It just fun.

Jamie gave a mock sigh.

—Yes. It's all just a game for him. Just a sport! Men! Bastards!

—Men? Where? said Javier, appearing in sports gear. I'm off to play tennis! How did your reunion dinner go?

—They are reunioned!

—Reunited! Don't teach him bad English.

—Well, he won't learn no good English from me, mama Tim.

Jamie gave Javier a hug, then squeezed his groin playfully. We watched Javier laugh, and drink a glass of water, then he was off.

Jamie said something else about the night he had spotted Lukáš in the gay bar, then just stood there by the sink, dipping his teabag into the hot water and burning his fingers again.

—So, Claudio . . . all the sex with hot guys—like I and Maurizio.

—Maurizio and I! I interjected.

—Actually, I think it's Maurizio and me. But not in Italian! Italian men are assholes grammatically speaking. In Italian you always put I first. *Io e mio marito*—thass me an' me 'usband. You can never say . . .

—Enough! I said.

—Maurizio teach you Italian? said Claudio. That's nice. I always want learning Italian. I like. And because of my name.

—But . . . about sex. It's just . . . fun. We haven't . . . Maurizio and I haven't used you or anything?

—Use me? No. I mean . . . you use me pretty hard.

Claudio laughed, but Jamie didn't.

—I mean emotionally. We are cool? Are we cool?

—Yes, man, we are cool.

Claudio and Jamie high-fived each other. I'd never seen that done in my house and for an instant I felt I was watching an American sitcom. Television changes how young people act, all over the world. There's a worrying thought.

—Cool. We are cool. Nice.

Was Jamie apologizing?

—So . . . we can do it again? I still want to . . .

—Eh! Maybe we stop now, okay?

Claudio didn't look at him when he said it, but then repeated to me.

—Maybe it is enough.

—You mean you're going back to Lukáš and being friends.

—Maybe I don't have to do in front of him, you know. Maybe . . .

—He would be jealous?

—No . . . but maybe yes. Maybe it not good he seeing me with you two. Maybe . . .

Nonetheless, I noticed he had sprung a boner. Yet suddenly Claudio became very serious again and said,

—I just want him; I want to be with him. I cannot say why. But it doesn't matter what I want, you understand? Even if I would

278

gay.

—If I *were* gay! I corrected.

—If I *was* gay! said Jamie.

—It's definitely were. Or is it?

—Which one? Claudio looked lost for a moment. Then he drank from his tea and said, —Anyway. We will believe soon.

—Believe what?

—We will believe . . . back to Slovakia.

—Oh, you will be *leaving* soon.

—And you will stick to Lukáš? said Jamie.

—What choice do I have?

It were an odd thing to say, that rhetorical question. Until I realized it were simply a statement of how much he loved his friend. He would stay with him no matter what.

—We are still friends Nothing has changed. Nothing has changed. Good, no?

—Yes. Good friends. That's all.

Jamie took a step towards him, and in a gentle, loving gesture put his palm against his cheek and stroked it.

—And you are sure you aren't gay? You are really sure? You are such a . . . stud.

Claudio nodded, then shook his head.

—Maurizio and I would take you with us, you know. We could . . . live together, the three of us.

Claudio laughed briefly, and when he clocked that Jamie were perfectly serious, he shook his head again.

For a while, nobody spoke. In a flat nearby, a woman shouted, then coughed. It were such a funny noise that we all chuckled.

—There is one thing I want to ask you, Claudio, I said.

Both looked at me. I had an impulse not to continue, but it were nagging inside me, what Lukáš had said. Gentle plucking. Not offending.

—When I asked Lukáš, some time ago, if he were gay or not, I asked him when he looked in the mirror, did he see a gay man, or a straight man, he said . . .

I swallowed.

—What? asked Jamie, always impatient.

—He said 'a monster.' He said when he looked in the mirror, all he saw was a monster.

Claudio cringed for a moment, but then relaxed, and it was clear that he had no idea. He had a look of surprise on his face, and said,

—A monster? Why a monster? I don't know why he say!

I was the first to see the shadow in the door. Standing there quietly was Lukáš. He looked at once furious and heart-broken. He was in pain. He had been listening to us for a fair while. He must have heard Claudio's confession of love. What else could I believe but that he is a lover, a true, caring lover? He stood so firm and yet so vulnerable. Time seemed to slow down around him. The light turned a strange colour, very soft and mellow.

Lukáš rubs his forearms, first the left, then the right, then his face. He has tears in his eyes. His face is flushed. He reaches again for his arms, then stretches out his fingers in an awkward contortion.

—Tea? says Jamie, instinctively getting out of the way.

Lukáš ignores him, then takes a few steps towards Claudio, wraps his arms around him. They stand, hugging each other, Claudio puzzled, and Lukáš crying now, sobbing, then checking himself, wiping his face.

Nothing is said, until they fall into a rocking motion, swaying slowly from side to side, their arms still wrapped around each other's bodies. Jamie looks at me. I shrug. We are helpless. Everything in slow motion, one small movement at a time. We have no idea what is happening, but we all know it's important.

I am crying myself. I can't help it. I don't know what to do. I suddenly know that this is it: we will learn the truth now. Whatever he confessed to Aleysha, whatever was left unsaid last night in the restaurant. The very heart, the fulcrum of their strange relationship, for I know, I know in that second, that it's not just a friendship. It's not as simple as Tim and I. It's complicated.

There is motion. The rocking has stopped. Lukáš takes Claudio's head in his hands, holds it before him, looks deep into his lover's eyes. Then he plants a kiss on his lips.

One quick and tentative. A second, a little longer. A third, holding his lips immobile on Claudio's, like a still life. We all stare.

But these are no lover's kisses. These are . . . they are pleas. Pleas to be forgiven. It lasts forever, that moment, as they stand there, linked by shared pain. Jamie is holding his tea motionlessly, staring ahead, then scratching his groin, the way he often does when embarrassed. All the clocks in the house stop. A fairytale spell in kisses. I sit in my wheelchair, tears running down my wrinkled old face, watching the wonder take place.

At last, the kiss breaks. But Lukáš does not let go of his friend. They keep their arms on each other's shoulders, hands folded behind the other's neck. Claudio is stifling a sob. The kisses are over, and the spell too is broken.

It is Lukáš who speaks first.

—You have to give me some time.

Claudio nods and says,

—I don't want to be without you.

Of course, that's the point where I can't keep quiet any longer. I sob like a baby, and so loud it splinters their concentration and the romance. I ruin the whole affair with my whimpering—silly old fool! They look over to me, the two of them, and to Jamie. He puts down his tea and walks across the room, pats Claudio and Lukáš on the shoulders, then comes to me.

—You pathetic old man. Sitting here crying.

I want him to wheel me out of the room to give them privacy, but Lukáš turns towards us.

—Stay. Listen.

His face is dead serious now, but he has an imploring look.

—Thank you for yesterday. Thank you for dinner. Thank you for trying to . . .

He looks at Claudio. Claudio nods.

Lukáš swallows. In an embarrassed motion, he wipes his nose, then licks his lips.

—The truth.

—The truth? I ask.

—Yes, we need tell you truth, says Claudio.

—But, I say, it's you guys, it's personal . . .

—Bromance is cool, says Jamie, you don't have to fuck.

281

Although . . .

—Shut up! Jamie!

Tim appears in the door. He is wearing his morning gown, and yawning, but when he sees Lukáš's serious face, he steps over to me and puts his hands on my shoulders.

—What's going on?

—Just listen, baby.

We hear a toilet flush, and everybody waits for Maurizio to join us. He looks in, searching no doubt just for Jamie, but finding this sombre assembly. He's wearing nothing but a pair of fashionable undies with a nice bulge. His body is tanned, flawless—and his nakedness seems like an insult to our purpose. Jamie walks out into the hall to fetch a jacket, then wraps it around Maurizio. They stand there, Jamie's arms around his lover. Then we wait.

Lukáš hesitates. I think his resolve is almost gone. He takes heart, gathering all his courage—all his simple, manly, courage—and he speaks.

—This is not gay or no-gay, like you say, Jamie. This is not. It has nothing to do with what you think.

Claudio takes his hand, and they stand before us like two children confessing a misdeed. But then, unexpectedly, Lukáš shudders, frees himself, and runs off. It was too much . . . too many eyes on him, too much pressure.

Claudio looks after him with watery eyes.

—Oh fuck, what is it now? Jamie is clearly losing his patience.

Without Lukáš, I fear, we'll never get to the truth.

Curiously, it's the bottom, the submissive Claudio, who's got the courage to go on alone.

—Yesterday, at dinner, we decide to tell you truth. You are very nice to us.

I feel myself blushing. We've been all too nice I fear, we . . .

—You know he was in love with my sister. I tell you.

I nod. Tim nods. Maurizio takes Jamie's hand.

—And I told you that it's no reason to . . .

—But I tell you it was motorcycle accident, no? I lie. I tell you lie, because the truth is . . . I tell her to go get cigarette! She said she has to go out, to do something for Lukáš and I was busy with television watching, I only watch stupid television, so I tell her get me cigarette, and I let her go alone. I should go with her, but I let her go alone. It was I! I ask her to buy cigarette for me. I send her! I tell her to go outside, when she . . .

He is staring at me, then at Jamie, then at me again, his eyes begging forgiveness. Is that why he craves *punishment*?

—She went to pub, to where we buy cigarettes, only place in the village there, and somebody attack her, and . . . rape her. She was raped and batted.

—Battered, says Tim reflexively.

—Shut up! says Jamie, and I'm not sure if he means out of respect or so he can hear the rest of the story.

—Battered, yes. They beat and rape her, three or four men, and she was only girl. She does not coming home. Lukáš come me that night, and we waiting for her, long, and then go out to find her, and we find her not. We did not find her.

Jamie is tap-dancing now, impatiently switching from one leg to the other.

—And? What . . .

—Lukáš find her, in the—how you say where you keep hay and tractor? Is next to the pub.

—Barn?

—In the barn. A barn.

—She was in the barn. We find her in the barn the next morning. They rape her and beat her with . . . you know the back of big gun, the handle?

—That's like . . . oh my god! That's awful!

—They were gang, crime gang. They steal and sell girls, and . . .

—Was she alive?

—We find her, and she is not . . . dead. She breathing a little.

—Unconscious?

—Yes, and in coma then for days, and then . . . she die. She die sixteen years old, after rape. They hurt her, with a gun, down here.

He pointed to his crotch.

—Very bad. They playing with her . . . torture her for many hours.

—Did they catch the guys who did it?

—What?

—The men who raped her . . . did they catch them? Arrest

them?

—No, no, never find. I tell her to go out, and let her alone! I am fault. It is my fault. I—he sobs—take away his girlfriend. I make him unhappy. I am the fault for he miserable! It is all my fault! I do not protect my own sister, and I kill his girlfriend.

I want to understand, but something is missing. Claudio is blaming himself for sending his sister out for fags, instead of going himself, for not accompanying her. He is blaming himself for what happened to her. His own pain is big enough—why Lukáš . . . ? My mind is racing. Why does Lukáš think of himself as a monster then?

—I kill his love, my sister! They are like Romeo and Juliet together, before Elena was raped. Only a kid. She was raped—by men, not only one, the doctor say. Lukáš liked her, she liked him, they were together some time and . . . all my fault he is unhappy now. He is how you say? His heart break! So we must being together! We must stay. I am his friend, and until he find new love, I must do anything for him! If not he may . . . you know. I break his heart too. I . . . I should have gone with her.

All of a sudden, there is an exasperated howl coming from the hall behind us. I turn, Jamie runs out. We all follow.

Lukáš is crouching, grabbing the carpet with both hands, sobbing, pounding it with his fists, clutching his knees, then raising his hands. He is in complete despair, it seems: beside himself. He is wailing, crying; his face is one big wound as he looks up, his eyes blazing red. For a second I don't know if it is pain or fear or anger or all in one—a cauldron of desperation.

—Is that what you think? he wails. It is almost like an ululation, stifled, broken by the sobs. His voice is high pitched, vulnerable, a terrible cry for help.

Jamie looks at me, I at Tim; we all stare at each other. We have no idea what is coming next, but we can sense it is momentous. I have a sudden premonition, a terrible, terrible sense of foreboding—only this time, I have no clue what is about to happen. Tim clutches my arm. Maurizio is close to tears, I can see it. His arm is trembling; so are my legs.

At long last, Lukáš gets up.

He straightens his shirt—one of these impossible gestures; to have time in such agony, and to think of it, the crumpled fabric. He wipes his face.

He walks over to Claudio. He takes his face between his hands, and then he plants a kiss on the lips. Again, there is no doubt. It's not a lover's kiss: it is a betrayal.

—Is that what you think? You take away my girlfriend, you kill her . . . ? You stay with me to comforting me—to comfort me?

Claudio nods. His eyes are shimmering with tears; he wipes over his face.

—You think I cannot live without Elena; so you take her place? You think you are replacement for Elena? You think . . . ?

Claudio wants to nod; his head bobs, but he doesn't dare. He is ashamed that his self-sacrifice is now discovered: his weakness, his guilt laid bare.

That's why he's desperate for alpha-males to punish him. Why he enjoys bottoming in a sex-act that's not really him. Well, maybe. I look at Lukáš and imagine them naked together. Oh god, why now! I am becoming aroused! Why is he crying? It's not just the loss of the girl! Was Lukáš really in love with Claudio, but used his sister to be close to him? So Lukáš is the gay one . . . the doomed love? Oh god! Why is he the monster then? And why are they so bloody attractive, now, with all this emotion?

Lukáš lets out another howl, a brief, choked howl. Then he pulls himself together. His back straightens. He looks dead serious. All of a sudden, that mechanical voice is back. The one I heard in the kitchen, when he first told me about the monster. And the blood is again gone from his face.

—*Nechápeš?*—Don't you see?

I suddenly realize that Tim has taken my hand and is crouching down. Maurizio is clinging to Jamie like a frightened child.

The two Slovaks are oblivious to anything around them, anything but their own pain.

—Don't you see? *Nerozumieš?*—Don't you understand?

—See what?

—Oh god! Oh god, how do I tell you! Lukáš bawls.

It is a long wail, a howl, a cry for help from the deepest abyss. Tim wants to move. I hold him back by grabbing his hands. Mine are shaking uncontrollably.

Whatever it is, it has to come out now.

Everyone is staring at the couple. Tim squeezes my fingers until I can see the white on his knuckles.

We all feel that this is the solution: this is what binds them, this is the truth of their relationship! Waiting for Lukáš to make his confession: Don't you see? I didn't love her, I loved you! You! But after her death, you withdrew, and you aren't gay, and I love you so! The whole silly romance rolling off before my eyes. My heart goes out to Lukáš. I want to interrupt and hug him. I want to hug him and tell him it's all right. That's why he must have been so angry, when he found out about Claudio doing porn. He must have thought, there is Claudio doing gay for pay, but he wouldn't love me. Oh, the poor boy! What torment, all these years. It's all the other way round! And I am still oddly aroused by what is happening—and Jamie, visibly, is too. How bizarre!

Claudio looks at us. He too fails to understand, but we see the figure of Lukáš before us, perfectly stiff and still, but writhing with pain—guilt, there is guilt and then I see it, clearly, Mr Dedalus; you open my eyes; I sit there in a welter and suddenly I understand it all. I think of what you've done . . . and then I know. In a flash, I know exactly what it is, and also that I have been completely wrong.

I want to say it out loud, the truth of the monster, why there is a monster, why they are together, what absolute horror they are going through, and that veil of friendship, which we all, all of us guilty, have defiled by making it a question of sordid, irrelevant sex.

I swallow hard, and under my breath, I say,

—Oh, Jesus, god. The debts!

Lukáš has heard me. He looks over. His eyes are blood-red, but his skin is white, almost grey. His face looks like a grotesque mask, contorted by the knowledge and the guilt. I can see the truth under his skin—it wants to come out. There is all the pain, all the self-recrimination in the world in this face: a disfigurement that has lasted all these years, the truth they've both been running from, from country to country, from mountain to mountain, a terrible pain that has eaten him from the inside, and now it shows, now he cannot keep it in any longer.

—*Zabil som ju!*

Claudio turns towards him. He repeats in English,

—I killed her! She was not raped by stranger. I owe money, which I borrow from a ... a bad man. I owed many thousand koruna.

He wants to let go of Claudio, staggering, collapsing, it seems for a moment, but Claudio is holding him.

—I told Elena. She knew. I borrowing money because gambling, and to buy ... for motorcycle. I want to buy a motorcycle—a stupid motorcycle! A red motorcycle.

He looks over at Jamie. We all remember his Glaswegian fling at Portobello.

—And I owe so much from gambling—not I, my father. My father lost his job after Communism, and drinking a lot, and gambling. I borrow money from bad people. Everywhere in Slovakia at that time bad people. Like Mafia. Elena knows, I tell her. She went there, that night, to ...

I put my hands in front of my mouth. It's worse than I thought. Part of me doesn't want to go on listening.

—She go there to offer herself for sex, to the man. He asked for her. He tell me I let him have my girlfriend for one night, he can forget half my debt. I tell him no, never, I love her. She is my friend's sister. But I tell Elena. She was only sixteen! She went there to pay my debt ... with her body. Only ... she think it is only sex. But they were drunk all of them. And they were bad men, really bad. I see them that night. I was there. I bring them part of money. They ask again if they can have Elena. Ask where is she? I tell them if they touch her I will kill them. They grab me, they ... beat me with the gun barrels.

Claudio interrupts in Slovak, then says to us,

—I tell him now I know the bruises on his face and shoulder, where they come from. I always wonder. He always say ...

—I didn't want you to know! I couldn't ... but then when I going to see you ...

—I help you wash, and we find a bandage, you remember?

Suddenly they look at each other again with that enormous

tenderness. Maurizio, Jamie, Tim, and I, we are all bawling like girls.

—I cannot know they do this thing. I think maybe the one man, the gang leader, maybe he has sex with her, is not bad. Oh god! They rape her, three, or four! They killed her! Because I made them angry. Because I make them angry, they rape her, and she bleed to death. She die for me. To pay back my money! She . . . she was . . . sixteen!

The absolute silence which followed was filled with unbearable noise: the blood pounding in my veins, the tension in the room. Then Maurizio started sobbing uncontrollably. We all waited for Claudio to react, to blame his friend, to pound his fists against his chest and accuse him, or do a bunk.

I think Jamie were anticipating a fight, and he wanted to nip it in the bud. But there was nothing. Claudio looked at me, at Tim, then at Lukáš. Then he said a word in Slovak, just one word, again and again.

Lukáš raised his head in surprise. The blood was back in his blotched face. He was trying to breathe normally.

He was stunned. Claudio said to us, by way of explanation.

—I know! I always knowing. I always know.

There was laughter now from somewhere in the room. I was tempted to turn and see where it came from, but it was Claudio himself: he was laughing. A brilliant, clear laugh!

—Oh, I know all the time! I know she did it for you. But still . . .

The amalgam of laughter and tears was curiously elating. We all sniffed, wiped our faces, tried to regain our composure.

Lukáš stood there, all the wind taken out of his sails.

—What you mean, you know?

—I know. I always know she go for to pay your debt. She tell me about your owning money. She tell me they will do bad thing to you. She did not tell me that night where she going, but when she do not come home, I know for sure, and it is too late. But still, it was her decision to go. I know she will go. I did not stop her. Even worse. I tell her to bring me cigarettes when she come back. I did not think.

A banal thought occurred to me then: that's why he didn't

want to be seen smoking, and I remembered his timid expression when he had hid aside the skip.

I turned to my husband for support, for confirmation. Probably he thought this was priceless: we had solved the mystery. But there was another look on his face too—one I could not read.

But what had we solved? What is it they are then, I thought, these two, welded together by a terrible fate? Other men would have drifted apart, withdrawn, never set eyes on each other again. Other men would have killed each other over all the pain, would have drunk themselves senseless, would have spent a lifetime in mutual recrimination. But these two need each other as what? Friends? Is that friendship, sacrificing your life so the other's pain is less sharp? So you can exist?

—I know if I don't want you, I mean, watch you, you will kill yourself.

For a second I didn't know who said that. To my surprise, it was Lukáš.

—I watch you, so you don't do stupid … said Claudio. I think you want to kill yourself, many time.

Lukáš's right hand reached forward.

—And also—he wiped away the tears—also, you are like Elena. You remind me in everything, you are like … I love you. I love you, man.

Jamie turned towards me. There it is. The big word. Meaning nothing of course. What's love, compared to such impossible friendship—such a power to forgive.

Claudio took a step forward, and they hugged, they hugged and banged on each other's backs, all manly, like kettle drums, and all the rest were in that language we didn't understand, and could only watch: and there were our proof.

This is the deepest, strongest bond you can have—this is real friendship. Forgiving each other anything, even the worst failures. And it's got fuck-all to do with being queer.

I felt unbearably silly. Months of trying to mould them into the perfect gay couple, and all there was was guilt, and sacrifice, and friendship. A love between two men forged in the fires of hell; on the *battlefield*, after all, but two men with real hearts, two

289

friends with true souls, bound together by agony, and the power of forgiveness.

—You see now, said Lukáš, a little while later, when Claudio was in the toilet. You see why we can never separate? He even know, and he forgive me . . . how can I ever leave him?

After Claudio, Lukáš used the bathroom. I had put on the kettle, and Jamie was staring out the window. Claudio came up to me and said,

—You see now, why we cannot be apart? He was so in love with her and I am like her. I must stay with him, gay or not; he's in love with her image inside me, and without me, he *will* kill himself. It's fate; we are friends. We *must* stay together, to stay alive.

I was still digesting the enormity of this utterance, when Jamie turned and said,

—That's like the first long correct English sentence you've said since you came here.

He put an arm around Claudio, pulling him closer. I couldn't help smile, and Claudio burst out laughing. Even Tim now . . . suddenly we were all holding our sides.

—Well, said Claudio, at least coming here was good for something!

We spent a magnificent day together after this dramatic morning, all six of us; and in the afternoon took Aleysha and her baby out to Princes Street Gardens for a picnic. We watched the squirrels prepare for winter. Maurizio and Jamie almost started making love on a blanket. People were staring, but the two of them couldn't care less. Tim sat on the edge of the bench, and my wheelchair was beside him. We were holding hands, for the first time ever in public, in Edinburgh. I had the baby on my lap. He grinned at me, the little bugger, all the time—as if he well knew what a fool his uncle were.

Aleysha said she would move back in if it were all right; they hadn't been able to find a flat. I wondered what would happen to Lukáš and her, but when I turned and saw him with Claudio, cutting a sandwich in two, handing it and a beer to his friend, just like they had been at the beginning, in love, inseparable—I knew that she would have to deal with it on her own.

Oh, what an emotional day, Mr Dedalus. All the drama, the upheaval. But it did not end there. There was more!

Tim and I lay in bed together that night, like always, listening for a while to each other's breathing, trying not to move because the old bed creaked so.

But everything were different that night. We didn't talk; he didn't hug me. He was distant, even more than usual. The Slovaks had brought us together a little, made us speak more, touch each other more often. But now, they had somehow ripped us apart again, and I did not understand.

We spoke just a little about the events of the day. I said things like how horrible it was to find out, after so much time; how difficult it would be for Claudio to forgive, and then remembering that he had known all along, that he had spent ten years with the man who was responsible for his sister's death, in a matter of speaking, and had long ago forgiven him, but not himself; and how forgiveness, really, was at the heart of all friendship, of all relationships.

—It's also at the heart of most religions, being able to forgive. It's also the part that most religious people tend to ignore. Look at all the hatred, the persecution, the intolerance. It's all so much against their own teachings.

Although he spoke with his usual, school-masterly tone, he wasn't quite there—he wasn't quite himself. He was moving prissily around some other subject. Keenly I sensed that there was something else. He made out the light, and in the darkness, I could hear him breathe heavily for several minutes. When it finally came, it was a massive relief.

—I have something to tell you, he said.

He sounded peremptory, despite an overtone of shame. I turned towards him in the dark.

—It's enormous—it's very important. It may destroy us. You must . . .

—Then don't tell me.

—I have to. I must. I can't live with it any longer. Not after today!

—Any longer . . . ? What happened today?

He did not answer, so I said,

—Is it something that happened a long time ago? Like with Clau . . .

—Yes.

—Then why rake in the mud? Why not . . . I don't want to know!

—Tim, I have to. It's about us.

—If it is about us, and if it will destroy us, then I really don't want to hear. Anyroad—I know you. It can't be that bad. You are not . . . And if it's about the boy you slept with a few years back, that boy from Taiwan, the one . . .

—Tim, baby, please! Listen!

It sounded final, as if he would not condone any more interruptions. I pulled myself up when he turned over. He helped with the pillows.

—Go on. I am listening. Confession time!

—It's . . .

He swallowed hard. It was a curiously loud noise in that big room, reverberating in the corners. As if the air were suddenly thinner and colder. A car passing outside sounded strangely remote. Then he moved and the bed shook a little—for an instant I thought I was on a ship.

—The accident . . . that cost you your legs.

I was all ears.

—The accident . . . the hit and run . . .

—Oh baby, you are still worrying about that . . . Lukáš and Claudio brought that back into your mind. They'll never find the driver. It's over and done. You don't have to open old wounds, I am resigned to . . .

—The driver . . . it was me. It was I who . . . I was on my way to fetch you. To pick you up for our date! It was I who . . . crippled you. It was our second date. It was I who . . . It was me!

I literally saw stars, I can tell you. I saw blue and red and green and golden stars. The scene which had earlier played out downstairs rushed past me. The girl going out to sacrifice herself, to pay her boyfriend's gambling debts with her body; the idea of Lukáš and Claudio knowing what had happened to her, but for years not speaking. A girl in a coma, for weeks; the agony of her family; Claudio, so young. Only then, slowly, did it set in, and I remembered my own accident. Standing under the awning because it were raining, waiting to cross the street, waiting for the bus, thinking I could get ciggies from the shop, not looking,

292

just rushing out into the street, and then there were just a big bump, a screeching noise, and lights out.

What are the chances, I thought, of two such confessions on the same day? Tim and I trusted each other. We had *no* secrets.

—I drove away when I saw you were unconscious and in a bad way. I drove as far as the next phone box, and then stopped to telephone the ambulance. They came quickly, and I followed you to the hospital even, but somehow nobody ever asked me. I was there, I took care of you, and the police never even came to interview me. They never checked my car . . . so I never said anything. Police work back then wasn't as scientific as it is now, or maybe because I was a teacher. Maybe because there wasn't much damage on the car. Phil painted over it in the garage, a month later. I didn't even ask him to, he just saw it and removed all the evidence. Nobody came to ask me, nobody asked me had you seen who did it. Nobody ever suspected I had been there. It's because in those days, people didn't think of men having relationships.

—They knew what you told them, later, that you had crossed the street. They were always looking for a hit-and-run driver, never for an acquaintance. It was just—it just happened that way. I am so sorry. I wanted to tell you, when you woke up from your coma, but you were so grateful, and we were so in love, and . . . I thought the best thing I could do is look after you. Nurse you back to health, be there for you, always. Remember, you were all alone? It was only me! So I thought, if I confess, my career is over, they put me in gaol, but you—you'll have no one at all. I wanted to tell you so many times! And I loved you so, already then. You must understand, it wasn't a difficult decision even. I wanted to take care of you. I wanted to love you. I didn't want to be away from you. I didn't want to be the one who had hurt you!

He was sobbing like a child, in a rather annoying manner: drawing in air in between sentences, and blurting out some words whilst swallowing others.

After the initial shock, I felt curiously unaffected by the whole confession. It was impossible to take in.

He said a lot more, about how he felt, about how he had kept it a secret all these years. About how our entire relationship was built on this one lie, exactly like the Slovak boys'. About how he could never forgive himself, but hoped that I could. That it were natural for him, had been logical at the time, not to leave me, and then, he said, then it had been too late. After we moved in together, after he had bought the chair, the stairlift.

I waited until he was finished. I didn't feel sad or anything. I was waiting for my own mind to catch up, to tell me how to react. But there was nothing; no reaction at all. I could have just turned round and said to him, 'Aye, good night then.' I felt no anger, no rage, no disgust. But I knew I should feel something. Something was boiling inside me, bubbling slowly to the surface.

And then, suddenly, in the warm darkness, waiting so desperately for a sign, I knew why they had come into our lives— Claudio and Lukáš—why they had been sent my way. All that talk of friendship, of sacrifice: their experience, it were all meant for me! For this one moment! All these months. The prodding, the mystery, the insults; they had no other purpose. We had needed to draw it out, we had needed to make them confess, to tell each other the truth—but not for their sake; for mine! All this, I thought in that instant, had happened, so that I could do what I had to now. What I felt was the only thing I could do.

And so I told him that I forgave him, that there was nothing to forgive. That I was grateful he had stayed with me, and not deserted me, and that it really mattered little. You see my legs were gone, end of story! What did it matter whose fault it were?

After a while, when he was quite sure that I weren't having him on, he turned his back to me and nestled into my embrace, and we lay there in silence, until we fell asleep.

It was the only time we spoke of it. We've not mentioned it since, and I don't think we ever will. It's in the past; it matters little— guilt, after so much time. And I will no longer live in the past, you hear me, Mr Dedalus? I don't need you any longer. Tim is my friend. Not just my lover, not my husband, not a mate, he is a friend. He's not a lover—I couldn't forgive a lover. He's a friend. And really, there is nothing greater than friendship.

EPILOGUE

We went up Arthur's Seat again on the day after we had brought Lukáš and Claudio to the airport. The day was glorious: so much sunshine Edinburgh hadn't seen in months, so much warmth, and a wind, even, that wasn't cold as usually they are—freezing you to the bone even on a hot day.

Jamie stepped onto a boulder and threw out his arms theatrically.

—When shall we three . . . four, five, six, we six, meet againe? In thunder, lightning or in raine?

He pronounced it 'rhine.'

—There's only five of us, Jamie, dear. I did a quick headcount to make sure I was right: Tim and I, Maurizio and Jamie, Javier. Aleysha and the baby weren't here and neither were the Slovaks.

—What? Maurizio inquired, just as he decided on a spot. Here! Let's sit here!

—*Macbeth*! clamoured Tim. Jamie knows *Macbeth*! I am impressed. Not all is lost! There is hope yet!

—Is it a book? said Maurizio, causing everybody to burst out in laughter. Even I found it funny.

—What?

—And there I thought there was hope!

—Macbeth! said Javier coldly. Even I know that!

—Do you think it will all disappear?

Tim opened the blanket, spread it over a patch of dry grass, and sat down.

He opened the wicker picnic basket and unlatched the cups, plates, and cutlery from their leather straps.

—Oh my goodness! cooed Maurizio. I never seen such posh basket! Real plates! So English!

—Will what disappear?

—And we've got cucumber sandwiches! It don't get more English than that!

Maurizio tittered, shook his head briefly, then almost dropped the thermos he was playing with.

—Classical education. Nowadays more people are familiar

with *Romeo and Juliet* films than with the play.

—What play? I said, grinning broadly. And don't ye dare remind me of *Romeo and Juliet*.

—Why? Oh—I see. The Slovaks!

—Like *Romeo and Juliet,* my arse! Romeo and Romeo, that's the ticket!

Jamie was still balancing on the boulder, and now began shouting,

—When the hurley-burley is done? When the fucking is over, the battle lost, and won?

—Fucking? Shakespeare wrote that?

—No, he didn't. Jamie made that up.

—That will be ere the set of sun! Where the place? Now everybody! On three: one-two-three!

Only Tim knew the verse.

—Upon the heath! Everybody!

We all fell in,

—Upon the heath!

Jamie laughed out loud as Maurizio wrapped his arms around his waist and tore him down. The two landed on the grass, wrestling.

—There to meet with Maurizio! Fair is foul and foul is fair!

—Foul? Foul? Are you calling me ugly?

—Oh no, my fair Italian prince!

They kissed, just as Maurizio had pinned his lover down, arms stretched out, their muscular young bodies heaving with exhaustion. The wind had stopped; the sun were burning down. It was like a real hot summer's day in Italy and not at all Scottish weather.

—Something about filthy air then, said Tim, can't remember the rest myself. But I am impressed, Jamie. I am impressed you know so much!

Jamie was panting. Maurizio was licking his ear, but at last he released his grip, and they both got up and joined us on the blanket. Javier was opening Tupperware: there were many different types of sandwiches, but also tapas, and some *dolmades* and *tsatsiki*.

—*Cucina Europeana!* announced Maurizio. *Di tutti i paesi!*

Nobody asked what it meant—we watched him taking off his sweater instead. His toned body glistened in the warm light.

—I auditioned once, Jamie interrupted.

—Auditioned where? You? For the theatre? Really!

—Some time ago, when I was still young and beautiful.

—Oh baby, you still . . .

—Shu'up . . . ! When I was still young and beautiful, I wanted to be an actor!

—You could have made it, you could have . . .

—Because I thought . . . well, you don't have to be good, just good-looking these days.

—Well, you do need talent of sorts.

—Bullshit. Maybe here in Europe or in art films. But not in the mainstream. What you need to be is well-connected. And if there's one thing I am not, it's well-connected.

—But well-*endovered*, you are well-*endovered*, said Maurizio.

Jamie gave Tim and me an exasperated look.

—I think she means 'endowed.' I'll teach her English some day! Jamie chuckled, and back they were tussling, tumbling away from us over the grass, until Jamie screamed and in mock rage came to sit on top of his lover.

—You do like it rough! You have a fucking boner!

—*Un che?* said Maurizio playfully.

They were grinding their hips together, and we looked away bashfully. Rubbish—we stared!

—I guess it's the same here too with all these reality shows. You don't need any talent. You just need to be reasonably attractive, said Tim.

—But the difference is, said Jamie, having freed himself from Maurizio's assault; the difference is that here in Europe people have a realistic view of the world. They know that most will never be rich, never be famous, never be a star—in fact, never be much good at anything, and that's okay. But in the States, the leading top percent income group, our aristocracy, constantly tells the dumb masses that they can be famous and 'live the dream.' America is built on believing a childish, pseudo-religious salvation dream. It's built on lies . . . a whole nation built on lies. Whole lives, of thousands of people, built on lies!

297

Tim looked at me. I gave him a quiet, understanding smile.

—Is that why you are staying over here? asked Javier. Is that why you don't go back to *Los Estados*?

—Yes. That . . . and—he looked challengingly at his lover—that, and scones with clotted cream. We don't have scones in America, you see. Or we do have scones, but don't pronounce them right. Not sure if we have clotted cream. Maybe in New Hampshire.

Maurizio of course took his cue, and hit him hard, a little too hard it seemed, on the thigh. Jamie gave a scream. They just couldn't keep their hands off each other.

The sandwiches were all very special. There was a little extra in each. The cucumber had slices of papaya; the jam thinly cut mango. I realized Javier must have spent hours preparing the whole basket. He seemed to say something with them: the extra tomato, the anchovies, the aubergine paste in some of them, and the folded napkins. I expected him from the moment he opened the basket to make an announcement, and a little later it came, like an announcement should: out of the blue, important, inescapable, but only when the scene were set, and everybody listening. And everybody was listening except for Jamie and Maurizio, who were feeding each other morsels, with Maurizio teaching his lover Italian: *verdura, frutta; tramezzini—i segreti della cucina Italiana; trombare—inculare.*

—What's the last two?

—What you want to do to me every night!

Tim had just put a blanket around me I didn't need, when we heard Javier say,

—I have an announcement to make.

Everybody fell quickly silent. Jamie turned towards us; Maurizio took his hand. They sat like expectant parents. But what Javier had to say was another shock.

I put down the sandwich I had been about to eat.

—I am going to move out.

Jamie opened his mouth, probably complaining that that wasn't much of an announcement, when Javier said,

—I am getting married.

Maurizio clapped his hands.

298

—That's fantastic!

Maurizio looked at his lover, and took his hand again. They beamed with joy. I knew what were coming from them, later, but now, when Javier spoke again, my jaw too fell.

—To a woman!

—A woman! shouted Jamie, as if the Spaniard had announced his conversion to Satanism.

—A woman, said Javier calmly.

—*Ma, sei* ... began Maurizio, for only one's mother tongue could convey the shock and—sense of betrayal maybe. But you are gay!

—I know—and then after a while—I am.

—So what are you doing getting married to a woman? said I, rather idiotically.

—And what's more, where're you gonna find a woman?

—I already have. I haven't been working as much as you think. I have been seeing her.

—Seeing her? Jamie gave me a startled look, as if to say, 'You didn't know this?'

—What's her name? asked Tim.

I looked at him in astonishment. What a strange first question. What did her name matter?

—But why? rejoined Jamie. Aren't you ...

—I don't want to be gay any more. It's no fun.

—It's not fun? said Maurizio, shaking his head. What do you mean it's not fun?

—I am thirty-seven. I have been gay for thirty-seven years. And what did I get out of it? I am masturbating to Czech boys fucking on my computer.

—Slovak, I said, and bit my lip.

Javier hadn't heard me.

—It's maybe okay if you have found someone, like you, Tim and Tim. Or like love-birds, like you two—*los tortolitos allí.*

He looked lovingly at Maurizio and Jamie, but avoided me strenuously.

—But I haven't found anyone.

—Is that because of ... Claudio?

Javier shook his head.

—Well, maybe. I just—I haven't found love with a guy, and even if I did—it wouldn't be enough.

—What do you mean, enough?

—Not enough . . . I want more.

—What more?

—I don't have your brains, Tim, to leave a legacy of learning, and your children in your school.

He turned to Maurizio and Jamie.

—I don't have your looks, to leave the world a million pictures of my beauty. Or to live just for love—physical love. It's different when you are older and don't look like much. I've got my cooking, and people eat that, and when they are done—*mierda;* then the only thing left is shit. I leave nothing to the world and I want to leave something.

There was a pause. We watched him take a bite of a sandwich, but he didn't seem to chew it.

—Children, said Tim behind him. You want kids!

—*Sí,* said Javier.

—How long have you known this woman?

—Three years.

—Three years? I was genuinely surprised. And you never said a thing! More secrets kept from me!

—I wasn't sure.

—Does she know?

—That I am gay?

—Yes.

—No—yes and no. I told her I slept with men when I was young.

—But you still do, I said, realizing the instant how wrong I was.

—I haven't had a love affair in six years. Sex with strangers in a pub; a handful of one-night stands, not counting . . .

He wanted to look at Jamie, but checked himself.

—Don't look at me like I am a criminal. I just want more out of life. I want children. I want to leave something behind other than tissue paper full of cum!

Jamie grinned, but it died on his lips.

—It's that Slovak slut who put them ideas in your ugly head!

—Being gay, said Javier, ignoring him and assuming an air of

300

desperation, being gay is nothing but an excuse for hedonism.

I waited for Tim, wise teacher Tim to say the elucidating words. He didn't let me down.

—We all have these feelings sometimes, Javier. You know you can have children with a man, soon?

—I know. What do you mean, with a man?

—They've developed the technique to have two male or two female, or any, really, DNA inserted in artificial sperm and egg. You can have a baby with two same-sex parents.

—You serious?

—Yes. In a few years, it'll be normal for same-sex couples to have offspring. Perfectly natural.

—But it's not! It's not natural. Children are supposed to be the product of straight love.

—Says who? We are on this world to overcome nature, to evolve. Free ourselves of the burden of procreation . . .

Jamie beamed and continued,

—Behold! A child will be born of two men and one of two women, and god will croak at last. A great wailing shall be heard, but it shall be a glorious day. We shall at last be free.

Javier's lips trembled. He looked piqued. He turned away from Jamie and gazed into the distance. Then he said decidedly,

—In the future, for some people, but it's—*que locura!* A child with two fathers. It's not natural! Not for me.

—You are very stuck-up, for a gay man.

Maurizio nodded appreciatively, then put his arm under Jamie's and looked lovingly at him. Their love was ever more persistent, persuasive—more palpable by the minute. I could feel what he was thinking.

—The technology is there to make us free. All technological advance makes us freer, frees us from being animals. We aren't. We are better. Only the god-squad want to keep us in the state of three thousand year old agrarian societies. Anyway, Javier, don't rush it. These may be your views now, but . . .

—I've thought about it. A lot. I want a child, the normal way, with a woman. I don't want to get old and sad and lonely, looking at dirty pictures. *Yo no quiero* . . . I want more than that . . .

—But a child is no guarantee that . . .

301

Tim didn't finish. The mood was suddenly gloomy. Jamie had an expression of death on his face, the blood drained from it. Every word Javier said sounded like an accusation, an assault on all our lifestyles, our very being.

—I know it's no guarantee. But it's my only hope. I've got nothing else to give. Nothing else by my sperm.

—Of which, if I may say so, there is plentiful! Jamie had started valiantly, but the humorous comment died half-way ... from embarrassment.

Maurizio wrapped his arms around Jamie, and drew him in, in a gesture that said, at least we have each other—we don't have to be so desperate.

—Promise me you'll think about this, Javier? said Tim pensively after a while. You are denying who you are

I thought of what I would say. Javier just shrugged his shoulders.

—I know. But is it so grand, what I am? Is it so important?

We were all silent, each lost in thought for a while. A sadness sank over us that was entirely inappropriate on such a beautiful day. It was oppressive, stifling—and I tried desperately to dispel it with something witty.

Jamie smashed it—or was it Maurizio who first spoke? Maybe they spoke together, like so often.

—We too have an announcement to make.

Only then did I realize Tim had said it too, at the same time, the exact same sentence.

—You go first, nodded Jamie.

Tim spoke from behind me, a frog in his throat when he started, but as he continued, he became quite elated.

—We are going to sell the house!

—Sell the house?

—Yes, to the school. We agreed on it last night. We are going to sell Manor Place.

—And the B&B?

—It will become a boarding house for the school, I said. Tim's mother is old, we have to look after her. We are going to move to Oban and manage the hotel; we'll spend the rest of our days

302

amongst men in skirts, highland-dancing, whisky-swilling . . .

—There are worse things, said Javier, visibly glad that the burden of attention was off him.

— . . . and caber-tossing!

—When? Jamie inquired.

—Oh, next year probably. Not quite immediately. We need to sort out the details with the school. But next year, Tim and Tim's B&B will be no more.

—Oh, sang Maurizio, rather too pathetically. I think is so sad when things end. I like caber-tossing though.

Everybody laughed.

—Then here, said Jamie, is to a new beginning!

He raised his tea cup, spilling half its contents in the exuberant gesture and pulled his Maurizio closer, so close that the handsome boy almost toppled over.

—We should have brought some whisky! Javier called out.

—And here is another announcement, said Jamie.

He put down the cup, took Maurizio's hand, and pulled him up. The two men were standing before us, rather stiffly. By then I knew what was coming.

—We are going to get married. We are going to Italy. What I mean is, we are going to *move* to Italy, and get married. I mean— we'll get married here first. Or somewhere, in Amsterdam perhaps. Don't know yet, or in Spain. We'll figure it out. Anyway, we are going to be the poster boys of the Italian equality campaign. The face of gay marriage in Bella Italia. Oh fuck, and I am going to have to learn Italian for real!

—*Matrimonio gay!* said Maurizio, blushing a little.

—To Italy? said Tim, making it sound like an accusation. We all forgot to congratulate them; the news of them leaving, of Jamie leaving us was such a shock.

—Good luck being a gay icon in a country that doesn't even respect women.

—Saint or whore.

—Won't even allow a harmless Ikea ad with two men holding hands. And you are going there? The heartland of conservative Catholics!

—I know, I know, said Maurizio. But *atta* least, there is

something to fight for there in my country. Here being gay is already so ... normal. In Italia we still have to fight discrimination. And I'll be the poster boy.

—We, said Jamie, will be the poster couple.

—Yes of course baby, but I have more experience as a model. And you've got crows' feet!

Jamie lifted his arm, brought Maurizio's head down in a vice.

—Well ... there is a lot of support for gay marriage, everywhere. Do you know why? Not just from gay men ... from women! Straight women. It's because two men kissing, two men loving, that's the antithesis of violence and war. Two men busy fucking don't have time to rape and pillage, destroy and abuse. In a world where men cause all the problems—greed is male, didn't you know?— and start all the wars, two men kissing, two men in love, is like shouting 'no more war!' That's why conservatives hate the idea of gay love, by the way. They need war and fear to intimidate the masses, to enrich themselves, and to justify their unjustifiable, irrational values. A society with men openly loving and kissing each other is infinitely safer for women to live in. More tolerance; less violence, peace, etcetera. Civilization, the arts, is what turns cave men into humans, fighters into thinkers. Two men kissing is a grand symbol of peace, the highest form of civilization, the end of all wars. If we win the fight, violent, raping, pillaging men will be the exception. Their reign of terror will be over, they ...

I nudged Tim, and he got the message. He shut up and for a moment we watched the young lovers who had in any case not been paying attention, kissing instead and looking into each other's eyes, holding each other's heads and existing somewhere far, far away. With their physical strength, their beautiful, muscular bodies, they seemed indeed like a message of peace.

Now they were kissing again.

—Absolutely massive congratulations, you two. Come here! Come here you both.

I managed to pull them close, one on each side, and made them kiss me. I felt like a grandmother gathering her offspring, pinching both Jamie and Maurizio's bum when they turned away again.

They sat down, and once more were quite gone from us, retreated into their own love for a moment while we listened to the birds. I had a million questions, but they could all wait. It was then, as I watched them, that I realized that all I had known for the past years was disintegrating before my eyes. They were kissing passionately to reaffirm their presence.

The sound of an aeroplane brought them down to earth.

—I will go to university, announced Maurizio.

—And I will teach English. I already found a job.

—I will give you a letter of recommendation if you need one, said Tim. Say you taught at the school—nobody will check. And the museum . . .

—Oh, I'll get letters from the museum, any letter I want. I've got the boss in my pocket.

—In your pocket? Not your pants?

—No . . . no, I . . . oh, let's not get into that.

—We won't be poor, said Maurizio. We won't be poor. We will not have to worry about money.

Everybody looked at him, including Jamie.

—What? Why you look at me? Well don't you think a model can put a little aside? I have made a lot. I have money in the bank. I haven't spent it all on shoes or drugs!

—I am only marrying him for his money, Jamie joked.

With a jolt, Maurizio was all over him: they rolled over the grass again, and ended up once more in a tight embrace. I could almost feel the ground myself, the soft earth, as the weight of a lover pressed me into it.

Javier looked wistfully; but I—and Tim I think—for the first time, looked upon a young couple in love without any bad emotion. The envy was gone, and the jealousy, and the sense of hopelessness and even my lame legs. I didn't want them any other way.

As I watched them speak to each other—now out of earshot, and probably talking nonsense anyway—I wondered about my own life, and a curious sense of contentment came over me. A very beautiful feeling, calm and warm, and not at all threatening.

It puzzled me for a while, this feeling, until I realized what it was. It was a feeling of salvation. Claudio and Lukáš had taken it away with them—all the guilt of a lifetime. All the selfishness, the envy, the regrets; they had taken all of that on their shoulders and carried it off to ... wherever it was they were now. Back in Bratislava, I supposed, or some place in their beloved wilderness.

I was amazed that I felt no anger at Tim, that forgiveness had come so utterly naturally.

I thought of the voice at the Anchor—the man who had spoken behind me, and whose face I had never seen. Some people are sent your way for a reason. They have no other purpose.

For a while we lay quietly in the glorious sun, doing absolutely nothing. My thoughts seemed to radiate but the next thing I remember is Jamie suddenly stood before me, panting, and then sitting down, angling for another sandwich.

—We got them all wrong, the Slovaks, didn't we? It's strange, that we could have been so wrong.

Nobody said anything, but we were all thinking of them.

A layer of fog drew up under the bridge, far off in the distance.

Jamie had his arm around Maurizio's shoulders, looking very manly and protective, until some private joke between them caused them to touch each other again and fall back on the grass.

A woman walked past us with a dog on a leash. I think what she screamed when she saw them kiss—and Maurizio stick his hand in the American's crotch, and Jamie clutching the Italian's buttocks—was,

—Well I never!

But the dog barked and drowned out her complaint, and then our laughter was louder than the yapping mongrel, and longer, and higher, and it rose, over the glorious day, into the cerulean sky, and carried far, far above, higher and farther than sound had ever travelled in these latitudes. Maybe as far as Bratislava.

ND - #0071 - 270225 - C0 - 229/152/17 - PB - 9781907133503 - Gloss Lamination